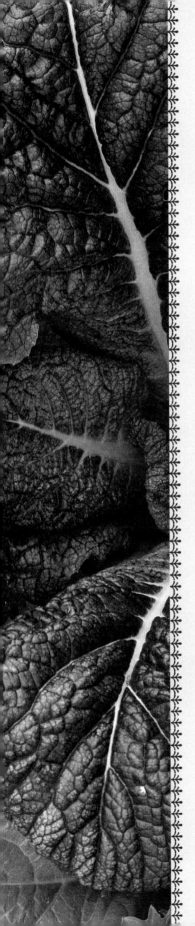

The
Heirloom Life
Gardener

Jere & Emilee Gettle

with
Meghan Sutherland

The Heirloom Life Gardener

The Baker Creek Way of Growing Your Own Food Easily and Naturally

HYPERION

NEW YORK

Library of Congress Cataloging-in-Publication Data

    Gettle, Jere.
        The heirloom life gardener : the Baker Creek way of growing your own
        food easily and naturally / Jere and Emilee Gettle. -- 1st ed.
                            p. cm.
      Includes index.
      ISBN 978-1-4013-2439-1
    1. Organic gardening. 2. Heirloom varieties (Plants) 3. Vegetable gardening. I.
    Gettle, Emilee. II. Title. III. Title: Baker Creek way of growing your own food
    easily and naturally.
      SB453.5.G48 2011
      635--dc22

                                    2011014347

SUSTAINABLE FORESTRY INITIATIVE
Certified Fiber Sourcing
www.sfiprogram.org

THIS LABEL APPLIES TO TEXT STOCK

We try to produce the most beautiful books possible, and we are also extremely concerned about the impact of our manufacturing process on the forests of the world and the environment as a whole. Accordingly, we've made sure that all of the paper we use has been certified as coming from forests that are managed, to ensure the protection of the people and wildlife dependent upon them.

To all who plant the soil:
past, present, and future.

To our parents and grandparents
who taught us to love the land.

And to our daughter, Sasha,
who teaches us the greatness
in small things.

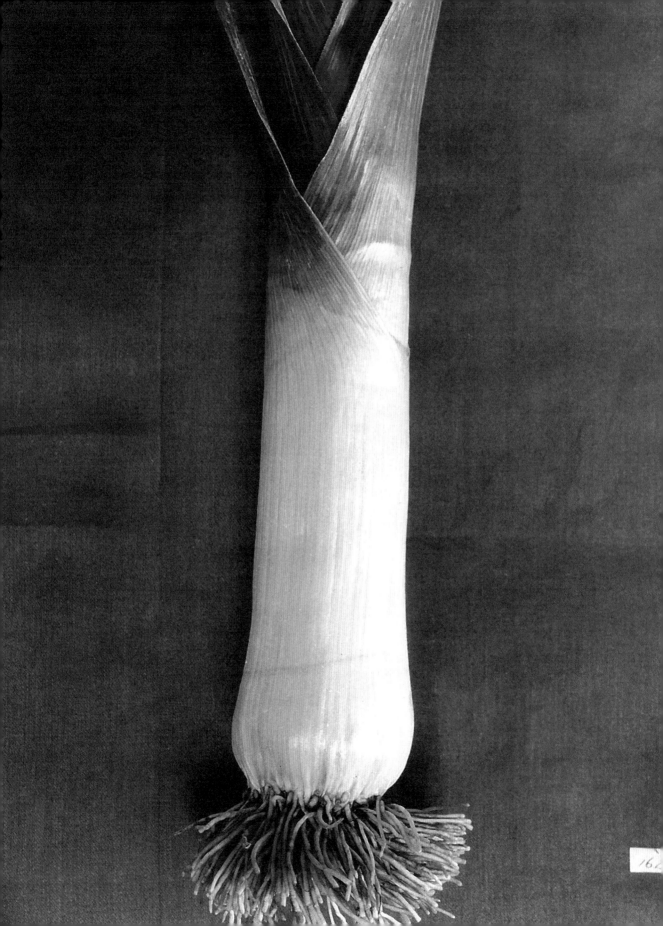

Contents

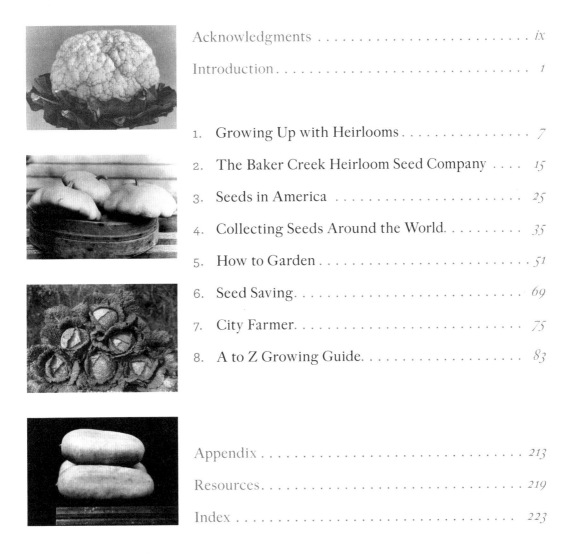

Acknowledgments

This book has been a monumental undertaking for us, and it took us on a trip down memory lane. I spent a lot of time thinking back to my earliest memories of gardening and everyday life growing up on a farm.

Many people were involved, and supported us throughout the process.

Thanks to Meghan Sutherland for helping us craft months and months' worth of phone, email, and manuscript ramblings into something worthy of reading. And thanks to Randel A. Agrella for sharing his vast knowledge of growing, and for his weeks of research and editing.

We would also like to thank Ellen Archer, Leslie Wells, and the rest of the staff at Hyperion, who have been incredible to work with and have helped bring our ideas into fruition in an unbelievable way. The following people also helped us in many ways: Marc Gerald, Bill Timmsen, Jerry Orton, Paul Wallace, Brian Dunne, Kathy McFarland, Hannah Shepherd, Wilma Freeman, and a big thank you to all our friends, as well as our great staff.

Finally, we also wish to thank our daughter, Sasha, who patiently played with her toys while we worked for hours on this manuscript.

The
Heirloom Life
Gardener

Introduction

There is a grow-your-own-food revolution happening in America right now, and vegetables have never been more exciting. Farmer's markets are popping up everywhere, seed sales to backyard gardeners are increasing, and more people are going out of their way to find out where their food comes from.

This book is a celebration of that movement, for people who are interested in starting a garden of their own for the first time, as well as for experienced gardeners who want to learn more about heirlooms.

Some people think you need special skills, a lot of land, or expensive equipment to cultivate a vegetable garden. But actually all you need is access to soil, water, sunshine, and seeds. More and more gardeners these days are choosing to plant heirlooms rather than the seeds that are on the shelves at "big box" stores around our country. Heirlooms are seeds that have been around for hundreds—and sometimes even thousands—of years, that have not been altered by scientists in a chemical-soaked lab, and they're the heart and soul of my business, the Baker Creek Heirloom Seed Company. Our mission is to promote pure, healthy food that is free from genetic modification and toxic chemicals, by educating people about natural gardening methods and historic seeds.

Food has become pretty generic these days. Anybody can pull into a fast-food place, grab a burger, and drive away without thinking where their "value meal" came from. This is such a change from how it used to be, when people had to work to grow most everything on their dinner plate. At Baker Creek, we like to remind people what life was like before fast-food chains became America's go-to "local food" sources.

By now, most people have noticed the unconventionally beautiful *jolie laide* spectacle of wrinkled yellow tomatoes at the farmer's market or seen them on menus at gourmet restaurants. You might think that tomatoes are the only kind of heirlooms out there. But actually, there are thousands of different kinds of heirloom vegetables on earth! *The Heirloom Life Gardener* is an introduction to that world, a celebration of the

The Gettle family with some heirloom tomatoes.

As far as gardening tools and equipment go, there seems to be a gadget for everything these days. But because I prefer to have as little as possible between me and the good earth, I use only a few tools when I'm out in the garden.

You may not agree with all of the suggestions and recommendations in this book. Working a plot of land is a very personal experience, and everyone who does it has opinions on the best way to do it. There are a ton of questions that come along with gardening: When should you sow your tomato seeds? What's the best way to deal with beetles or to trellis a pole bean? I'll answer some of those questions, but I'm not trying to be comprehensive. This book is a jumping-off point—not an encyclopedia that covers every planting scenario in every climate zone.

Rather than making you a master gardener in a couple hundred pages, I instead hope *The Heirloom Life Gardener* helps you discover how much joy a $2 packet of seeds can bring to you and your family, whether you grow on your back forty or on a four-foot plot in your backyard.

In 2011, because of the way that the world's food supply is structured, almost all of the seeds currently being developed in America are created by the giant chemical agribusiness companies for large-scale farm operations rather than for gardeners like you. This is because gardening took a backseat to "convenience" in the latter half of the twentieth century. The younger generations of Americans have been brought up thinking, Why should I dig in the dirt for my food, when I can buy what I need at the grocery store?

But the grow-your-own-food revolution happening in America is changing the way we approach food in significant ways. According to

joys of gardening and traditional growing methods, and a primer on the centuries-old practice of seed saving. It is our invitation to you to join us in living a sustainable, delicious, and healthy heirloom life.

At the Baker Creek headquarters, which is located on a farm in the Ozark Mountains in Missouri, we have 176 acres, 6 gardens, and 25 different kinds of animals. Our approach is always natural, which simply means that we use traditional farming methods such as mulching, nontoxic organic sprays, and crop rotation. We work the land in ways that are similar to how it was always worked until the 1950s, which is when poisonous chemical pesticides and fertilizers became popular.

Our friend Dave Kaiser enjoys summer's bounty with the neighbor children.

the National Gardening Association, the number of households growing food crops increased 10 percent between 2007 and 2008 and another 20 percent in 2009. In 2010, there were four times as many farmer's markets in America than there were in 1994. The momentum is astounding—and so inspiring to witness. More and more people are embracing a "locavore" or "growcavore" life-style—installing rooftop gardens or digging up corners of their lawns and putting in vegetables.

Not only is growing food and eating locally gratifying and delicious, it's also vital to the continued momentum of this movement. When you buy food from local farmers and organic grow-

ers, you're doing much more than just getting healthy, chemical-free food. You're also putting money back into your own community, instead of into the pockets of profit-hungry execs at multinational, government-subsidized corporations. Living a locavore life boosts the economy around you and helps sustain independent growers and food suppliers. The more you shop with organically minded organizations and small farmers, the stronger their businesses become. The stronger they are, the better off you and your local food supply will be in the long run. It will also help our nation develop real communities again—places where people can provide for one another and find local jobs, while living in a more caring, balanced, and earth-friendly way.

I just want people to stop and think about the dangers that are inherent within a corporatized food supply, and shed light on the fact that decisions about food and agriculture are made each day by our government and major corporations, with little input from the community. Growing food on your own land and supporting local growers takes power away from government bureaucrats and corporate executives and helps regular people maintain control over what they are putting into their bodies. Emilee and I are vegan, but that's not what this whole thing is about. Rather, I want to celebrate healthy, delicious food, and educate people about the magic that happens when you plant a seed and watch it grow.

First Things First:
What Is an Heirloom?

When many people think of heirlooms, they automatically think of tomatoes. And indeed, there are a lot of delicious, unusual heirloom tomato varieties—the pink-fleshed Brandywine, the dusky black Cherokee Purple, and the lime-colored Emerald Evergreen tomato—among hundreds of others.

But as more and more gardeners are discovering every year, the world of heirlooms goes way beyond tomatoes. There are more than one hundred thousand different kinds of heirlooms in the world. And most of them taste better than the frequently flavorless hybrid and genetically modified produce that is sold in most grocery stores these days. For me, my wife Emilee, and our staff at the Baker Creek Heirloom Seed Company, enjoying the world of heirlooms is a way of life.

Our daughter Sasha loves melons. Here she enjoys some on the porch of our mercantile shop in Bakersville, our old-time village.

In this book we'll tell you why, and how, to make them a part of your own life. But before we get started, it's important to answer a few questions.

The number one question we're asked when customers come into our stores is "What exactly is an heirloom?"

There isn't a universally accepted definition for the term "heirloom," but most people agree on a few basic points:

Heirlooms are nonhybrid and open-pollinated. If you plant an heirloom seed year after year, it will grow "true"—that is, it will grow to be the same kind of plant as its parent. This is in contrast to hybrid and genetically modified seeds, which typically revert to one or the other parent type.

Heirlooms taste great. Heirlooms taste better than genetically modified and hybrid varieties because they've been bred and selected for generations, and often thousands of years, by home gardeners and independent farmers, based on how they taste. The big chemical companies care more about thick skins, high yields, uniformity, and ease of shipping than they care about flavor. (We'll discuss hybrids and genetically modified seeds in more detail in Chapter 3.)

Heirlooms come with history. These seeds are usually more than fifty years old and have been passed down from generation to generation. This means that they come with fascinating stories and heritage from years past. For example, the Mortgage Lifter tomato, which was developed back in the 1940s by a guy named Radiator Charlie, who sold these tomatoes for a dollar per plant (his pitch was that one plant could feed a family of six) and was able to pay off his $6,000 house mortgage in four years. The Ananas d'Amerique a Chair Verte melon dates back to 1794 and was grown at Thomas Jefferson's Monticello garden in Virginia. One of the oldest seeds we sell is a splendid European heirloom radish called Black

Black Spanish radish.

Spanish, which traces its "roots" to around A.D. 200. In historic times, it was used to treat nearly every malady and sickness known to man and cherished as a tasty winter food staple for vegetable-starved Europeans.

We'll tell you about dozens of other fascinating varieties later on. But now that you know what an heirloom is, let's get started.

A Chocolate Stripes heirloom tomato—this lovely variety has a rich and earthy flavor.

1. Growing Up with Heirlooms

As you'll discover while reading this book, my passion in life is to inspire people to eat more produce, especially produce that is locally and naturally raised. I'm interested in heirlooms, which come from pure seeds that haven't been genetically modified. The most cost-effective and enjoyable way to eat heirlooms is to plant them yourself.

When I was growing up, there were gardens everywhere around my house, and that's where I spent most of my time. Even at a young age, I was a garden freak—enchanted by the possibilities of what could be created with seeds, sunshine, and soil. Exploring in the dirt and leaves, with all those different colors and shapes, made me feel like I was playing inside of a giant Crayola crayon box.

Many people think that growing your own food is complicated, expensive, or a hassle. But it's actually pretty easy. Planting, harvesting, and saving seeds is very convenient, and can save you a serious amount of money on groceries. It's definitely more delicious, and healthier for your peace of mind, when you know where your food is coming from.

I was born in 1980 and spent my early years in the Boise Valley of eastern Oregon, and Montana. That was the era of Ronald Reagan, fast food, and MTV. But at our house, it might as well have been 1880. My parents were homesteaders, which means that we lived off the land, almost entirely self-sufficiently, and raised most of our own food. We had cows, chickens, turkeys, and sheep, and grew vegetable gardens in the summer, along with fruit trees and flowers. Some years, we even made our own cheese. In the fall, there was always pressed apple cider, and in the winter, hundreds of jars of preserves and root vegetables lined the shelves of our damp, musty old root cellar.

Do-it-yourself homesteading and old-fashioned pastimes are quite popular these days, but in the 1980s, my family's independent ways were considered unorthodox. Our way of life was partly influenced by the "back-to-the-land" movement that had swept through America

CLOCKWISE FROM TOP LEFT: *Jere's mom, Debbie, with summer's harvest, 1980. ❧ Jere's grandmother, Opal, holds an infant Jere, while uncle John, grandmother Bertha and cousin Susan look on. ❧ A one-year-old Jere, in the pumpkin patch. ❧ Jere, his dad, Jim Gettle, and his great-grandmother, Hortense, with the hay harvest.*

in the 1960s and 1970s, and partly influenced by my ancestors, farmers who had worked the land in Siberia, Germany, and Mexico and who passed on a passion for growing things. Conspicuous consumption was the popular thing during my childhood. Americans were engaging in unprecedented levels of pollution and waste. (After President Reagan took the oath of office, he dismantled an array of solar panels that Jimmy Carter had installed in the White House.) Against the backdrop of that era, there were a lot of raised eyebrows at my family's lifestyle. But we kept going our own way and plowing our own row. People often asked my mom how she managed without a paycheck. She always replied with a friendly question back at them, "How do you manage without a woodpile and a cellar?"

The gardening bug got me early. When I was just three years old, I sowed my first seeds—yellow pear tomatoes and Scallop squash. By that time I'd been in the fields for years; when I was a baby, my mom used to bring me out to the garden and set me down in a bassinet, while she and my dad would pick beans and hoe as the summer sun rose above the hills.

When I describe my childhood, it reminds people of *Little House on the Prairie,* and that's kind of what it felt like. My sister and I were homeschooled, so if my mom wanted to whisk us into the forest to pick berries in the afternoon, that's what we did. If we felt like going on a camping trip, we hopped into my dad's 1975 Ford pickup and drove into the mountains, where we slept near a cliff looking out over the tree line and watched hawks and eagles fly past.

I was always outside during summertime, collecting bird's nests, dodging rattlesnakes, and picking meadow mushrooms in the fields.

LEFT: *Jere and his sister, Jessica, in the corn patch.* RIGHT: *Jere "helping" with the raspberry harvest, just before they ended up in the freezer and canned preserves.*

LEFT: *The root cellar at the Montana farm on a cold winter day. At least on this day, the sun was shining and it was above zero degrees.* RIGHT: *Our homestead in the Mission Valley, back in Montana.*

My grandparents were always nearby, and they played with me in the garden rows. I loved being at eye level with the grasshoppers and honeybees—I was only two feet tall, but I felt like a giant walking through a jungle.

As my gardens grew bigger, so did my knowledge of gardening and agriculture. By the time I was ten, I'd memorized the names, shapes, and colors of almost every crop, and I knew that I wanted to work at a seed company when I grew up.

Toward the end of each summer, a lot of canning and preserving took place. We often "put up" (in the country, that's what you call it) more than five hundred quarts of tomatoes, berries, apples, pears, tree-ripened cherries, and other wonderful goodies.

My mother and my grandmothers, Opal and Bertha, steamed, boiled, and carefully packed everything into jars, freezer bags, and boxes labeled in loop-de-loop cursive. This was our winter food supply, right from our own backyard.

We stored the bounty in our root cellar, an underground cave that kept turnips, potatoes, and other veggies cool and fresh throughout those bone-chilling winters. The pathway to the cellar was often covered with several feet of snow, and if my mom needed me to fetch something, I'd pull on my boots, clomp through snowdrifts, and shovel out a clearing so I could unlatch the enormous wooden door and climb down inside. Once I was down there, the earth warmed me—and then I'd remember the black widows that lurked in the dark corners, just as I was about to start hunting around for a jar of pink applesauce or a box of parsnips. Despite the snow and spiders, the taste of those veggies was always worth the search.

The Ozarks, in Missouri, where the Baker Creek Heirloom Seed Company is located.

I could have stayed out west forever. My grandparents, aunts, uncles, and cousins were all there, and we had total freedom. But my parents wanted more land and a longer growing season. After looking around for a while, they heard about a farm down south, in the Ozark Mountains, called Baker Creek—a 176-acre valley where I still live today.

When we started packing up to leave, I wondered if I'd ever see the Montana farm again. But at that same time, I was also daydreaming about the long, hot southern summers that would allow me to grow one of my dream crops: watermelons. I was only twelve years old and already thinking like a full-fledged farmer.

That road trip to Missouri, which we made in my dad's big pickup truck, was the longest journey I'd ever taken. Eighteen hundred miles, with a stop at Wall Drug, lots of camping by the rivers, and a few major firsts: I saw my first firefly in Wyoming, my first nutria in South Dakota, and my first glimpse of what a hundred miles of corn looks like while driving through Iowa. As we approached the Ozarks, large cropland fell away and pastures and woodland came into view. Down here, it felt as if time had stood still. Baker Creek looks a lot like it did when northern European pioneers settled it in the early nineteenth century: log cabins, red barns, and grain silos. I learned that people still made moonshine around these parts. This is where the term "hillbilly" became famous—and inspired the hit 1960s TV show *The Beverly Hillbillies.*

The farm that my parents bought was originally settled in the 1830s by a family of pioneers of German descent, on land near where Civil War battles were waged and the Osage Native American tribe traded and hunted.

Several structures on the property were still in use when we arrived. Right away, I started testing new seeds. The warm weather all summer would ripen as many tomatoes as we'd ever want to eat. It was heaven to a heat-starved little vegetable grower.

That summer tumbled into fall and, soon, winter arrived. Each night after dinner, my mom and dad sat around the wood stove reading magazines and catalogs, planning for spring. I was right there with them, perusing the new edition of the Gurney's, Gleckler's, or Tomato Growers catalog. I loved seed catalogs so much that I actually learned how to read from staring at their pages for hours, memorizing unique varieties with exotic names. Like my Crayola-colored gardens, the catalogs were full of possibility. But as I got older, things started changing. The big companies began to drop older varieties from their inventory, and in their place started to sell "perfect"-looking—but usually terrible tasting—hybrid varieties. Several of my favorite suppliers eventually went out of business. Suddenly, America's seed scenario was looking very bleak.

By the mid-nineties, a few big corporations, including Monsanto and DuPont, and the federal government started introducing genetically modified crops into the country's seed supply at unprecedented levels. We almost ended up losing some of the greats—the giant Banana melon, which had been offered in catalogs since 1885 and is one of the tastiest melons in the world, nearly went extinct. When you have a hobby that you're a little obsessed with, and you notice that 10–15 percent of the things that you really like about it are disappearing, it makes you want to do some-

Jere in his early teens with an Old-Time Tennessee Melon, shortly after moving to Missouri.

thing. I knew that I needed to fight to save these seeds. I started saving them when I was thirteen. Preserving historical varieties became my main mission in life.

In 1996, I joined Seed Savers Exchange—a nonprofit organization that is dedicated to the preservation of heirlooms—at an important time for the agricultural industry. My friends in the SSE and I discussed new agricultural technology and mulled over rumors of "terminator" plants that could kill off seeds so that they wouldn't grow the following year and stories of experiments in which human genes were being injected into plants. It was difficult to believe that could be happening, but it *was* happening. It is still happening today. And unless we work to maintain crop diversity, the number of colors in our crayon box will become even smaller.

With this weighing on my mind, I started my company—the Baker Creek Heirloom Seed Company—in 1998, when I was seventeen years old. By the time I was in my early twenties, I had saved a little money and trekked through Mexico,

Guatemala, and Southeast Asia to collect seeds. I wanted to see new cultures, taste new food, and talk to new people—but more than anything, I was searching for new heirloom seeds. I visited farmer's markets and little roadside stands to find unusual new veggies and fruits that I had never seen before. Once I found something, I'd pull out my knife and cut it open right there on the side of the road to have a taste and scoop out the seeds. Those moments at farm stands reminded me of being back in the garden as a little boy, eye level with all those colors and tastes.

Since 1998, Baker Creek has grown from a homespun operation with a photocopied price list to a company that sells more than 2 million seed packets per year, and my passion for pure, high-quality seeds is stronger than ever. I feel even more energized now that more people are beginning to understand the predicament we're in with the food supply and now that I have more opportunity to teach folks how easy it is to effect change.

Some rows in my garden, which I first planted back in the 1990s.

People often ask me how many seed varieties there are on earth. I wish I knew the answer, but it's impossible to say. Because nobody's been to every corner of land to catalog what's growing, countless undiscovered types are out there. But what we do know is that there are at least a hundred thousand varieties. At Baker Creek, we sell more than fourteen hundred of them, from seventy different countries.

When folks visit our stores for the first time, they're often just plain overwhelmed. This is because most Americans are accustomed to shopping in chain supermarkets, where tomatoes are red, eggplants are purple, and jack-o-lanterns are rarely anything but orange.

My customers' eyes light up when they discover the rainbow of diversity that exists. And it is literally a rainbow. In America alone, if you do a little digging, you can find up to ten thousand kinds of heirlooms. Pink, orange, yellow, green, white, and brown tomatoes; striped eggplant; blue pumpkins; horned cucumbers; purple carrots; white-fleshed watermelon; speckled lettuce . . . the list goes on and on. And as stunning as these open-pollinated varieties are to look at, they taste even better. This is because vintage varieties have been selected for magnificent flavor over the course of hundreds or even thousands of years.

But the argument for cultivating heirlooms goes way beyond just color and taste. The most important thing about pure seeds is that they are essential to our food safety. Within these little encasements lies the key to both the planet's food history as well as the health of future generations.

I love to imagine millions of tiny Baker Creek seeds going from our Ozarks farm into gardens across America and around the world, before growing into delicious vegetables and fruits that

Emilee and Sasha in the seed store.

get sautéed in woks, chopped into healthful salads, and eaten off the vine. Fourteen years after starting my company, I sell 2 million seed packets a year. It's hard to believe that it all started in my bedroom, on the farm at Baker Creek.

In 1998, biotechnology was all the rage in America's seed industry. Toxic chemicals and tasteless modern varieties had become part of business as usual on the majority of America's farms, and as more historic varieties disappeared with each new year, I realized I had to do something. I wanted to establish a company that sold the old, unique heirlooms that were being neglected, like white-fleshed watermelons,

yard-long beans, and yellow radishes. I sent out my first twelve-page catalog that year, offering seventy-five varieties of seeds that I had been growing on the farm. Soon after sending out that first list, my fledgling company suddenly had hundreds of customers. And within a year, my little operation was occupying all the free space in the farmhouse where I still lived with my parents and sister. Boxes of seeds, price lists, postage supplies, and drying racks were everywhere. When we ran out of room upstairs, we engulfed the stairwell (up to three people at a time can sit on those stairs to pack the envelopes, if you squeeze real tight). During the busy season, my bedroom was littered with seeds, scoops, and packets, so I'd often just crash on the kitchen floor in a sleeping bag after working until the wee hours of morning.

And then came Y2K. Many people don't remember, but in the year of 1999, millions of Americans were anxious and even a little fearful about the approach of the new millennium, due to what was being called the "Y2K problem." The concern was that a glitch might lead to a failure of computer clocks to switch over to a year that began with "20" instead of "19," causing a midnight New Year's Eve breakdown in the power grid and basically a shutdown of the country, and indeed the world. Folks in bigger towns and cities stocked up on supplies in case of power outages, and the gloom and doom was downright feverish in the mountainous regions of the South, not too far from Baker Creek, where folks have historically been mistrustful of technology and government. After hearing all the buzz, I gathered two- and five-gallon buckets from a hardware store, loaded them up with twenty-five bags of open-pollinated seeds, and labeled them, simply, the Baker Creek Homestead Seed Package.

From the first day the packages went on sale, they sold like hotcakes. Our phone line was inundated with calls, from hard-core mountain men who stacked shotguns in their basement, to conscientious suburban moms who wanted an emergency food supply, and every type of garden-minded person in between. Of course, the world didn't end, or even change all that much, on New Year's Day. And many people have actually forgotten that the fuss ever even happened. But a lot changed for Baker Creek, and for me, that year. Our sales increased from $1,000 in 1998 to $40,000 in 1999, and the boom in business taught me how important it is to listen to our customers and stay closely attuned to what is happening in the world around us. In 1999, that meant responding to concerns about Y2K. These days, social media and e-commerce are

TOP: *Heirlooms grow in a kaleidoscopic variety of tasty and nutritious colors.*
BOTTOM: *Vibrant illustrations are a hallmark of Baker Creek seed packets.*

important aspects of how businesses thrive, so my staff and I communicate with our customers on Facebook, Twitter, and via our website, rare-seeds.com. I write frequently about industry and gardening news, and enjoy receiving feedback from our customers via the different forums. It is a juggle to keep up with digital technology while clinging firmly to our roots, but the world is changing rapidly these days, and we need to stay connected in order to keep up.

After Y2K, sales were booming, and my parents' house was a zoo. My mom was a good sport about letting her home get taken over, but it was clear to everyone that we needed more space. Specifically, we needed a store, and we didn't have to look far for where it should be located. When my family first moved to Baker Creek in the early nineties, there wasn't much happening.

Just a lot of pastures, gardens, and the house. We had so much space that it made perfect sense to build the first seed store about forty yards from my front door.

To fund the project, I had about $10,000 from the Y2K business. I perhaps could've gotten more, through a loan from a bank—but I don't like borrowing money. So $10,000 was all we had, and that was our budget for the store. Construction began in 2000. My father and one of our Amish neighbors led the process, scouring local sawmills to salvage wood scraps and recycled tin for the roof. I wanted the store to feel historic—like the seeds themselves—and have an old-fashioned vibe, to remind customers of the old ways of the Ozarks, in the days before the Golden Arches dominated the "local food" scene. After two months of work, we had our first lit-

Our seed store during winter's chill.

*A "street" in the Bakersville pioneer
village on a winter's night.*

Dave Kaiser with a barrel of our ripe watermelons.

tle shop, with a "false front" and a wraparound porch. It looks like a building you'd see in an old John Wayne movie, and it still sits under an old oak tree, looking out over the rolling hills of the Gasconade River Valley.

For years, we kept the keys to that store above the front door. That way, if one of our neighbors really needed some turnip or rutabaga seed, they could come by, grab a few packets, and get back to us later with a couple of dollars or some fresh produce. It wasn't uncommon to find folks in the store after hours, which was fine with me, because they were always friends and fellow seed addicts.

After the seed store was up and running, we

kept building, creating a little pioneer village, which we call "Bakersville," around the property. There's an old-time mercantile, an apothecary, a brick oven, a grist mill, a bakery (with old Amish barn looms and a spinning wheel upstairs!), a blacksmith shop, a seed museum, an Opry barn, and an Asian-inspired vegan restaurant, where we serve curries, stir-fries, and my mother Debbie's zucchini bread, prepared with produce from the Baker Creek gardens and nearby Amish farms.

I love introducing folks to the beauty of the Ozarks, and in 2000 we began hosting a garden show, in a makeshift tent right in front of the seed store. About four hundred people showed up that first year, which is a lot more people than I ever imagined would drive the five miles down our dirt road to hang out with fellow gardeners. The success of that event inspired us to do a bigger festival in the spring, to celebrate all things heirloom, old-time, and non-GMO. Gardening gurus and natural food experts come from across America to what is now an annual event. Yodelers, fiddlers, and country singers perform, and there are local goodies, such as breads, cheeses, pickles, preserves, honey, and sorghum for sale by local vendors. Historic reenactors and campfire chefs offer samples of traditional food, prepared in our fire pits and stone oven.

We're surrounded by farms, so naturally a lot of farmers come by—from homesteaders in their overalls and plaid shirts, to younger hippie types in ponytails and tie-dye T-shirts, and many other types of folks, including retired couples; botanists; bonnet-clad Mennonite families with a dozen children in tow; city slickers from Chicago and St. Louis; and green-thumb seed collectors from all over. Families sometimes camp out on our farm through the weekend, in Native American–style teepees or nineteenth-century canvas tents. Ten years after they began, the festivals have become a major event for Americans who are enthusiastic about heirloom gardening and the simple life.

My passion for promoting sustainable, local food has long been intertwined in all aspects of my life, and in 2006, it led me to my wife. In May of that year, I did an interview about the seed company with a young writer named Emilee Freie over the phone, and we kept in touch via email after the story was published. After a couple of months I couldn't wait to meet this woman in person. When she walked into the seed store in March of that year, my heart stood still. She was beautiful and elegant, and I knew right away that I wanted to marry her. We have many shared interests and a similar background—Emilee was homeschooled, like me, and loves gardening, photography, writing, and trawling around antiques stores for old treasures. We were married in a little town called Mexico, Missouri, later

that year, and have lived happily ever after ever since—except when I'm grumpy!

Emilee and I soon moved into the old farmhouse, and my parents moved to a quieter spot down the road. Late the following year, our daughter Sasha was born. Now four years old, she already tries to help in the garden and loves looking after our animals (there are a lot of them): two cats; a yellow canary who lives in a windowed cupboard in the farmhouse; three dogs; two mini horses; a mini donkey; a flock of giant honking geese; black swans; Chinese goldfish; peacocks; sheep; a gaggle of ducks that guard the gardens from leaf-chomping pests; and twenty-five breeds of heirloom chickens and turkeys. (Similar to plants, the diversity of heritage animals has come under threat in recent years as a result of nontraditional breeding practices. I am now and have always been passionate about helping maintain a vast array of plants as well as animals.)

With a busy farm, there's never a shortage of excitement, and one of my favorite events of the year is the first melon harvest. Sometimes I even bring one of these sweet-smelling little orbs with me to bed at night to put under my pillow while I sleep, much to Emilee's puzzlement.

A few years ago, Emilee, Sasha, and I were driving through Petaluma, a beautiful little town in Sonoma County, California, when we noticed a FOR LEASE sign in front of a stately old bank building on the corner of the town's main drag. On a tour through the building a day later, we were dazzled by the sun-splashed windows and lofty ceilings. The streets nearby were lined with some of the world's best farm-to-table restaurants, as well as antiques shops, upscale galleries, and an artisanal chocolatier. Charmed and

CLOCKWISE FROM TOP LEFT: *Chad Wilt selling plants at our Spring Planting Festival. Jere and Emilee, at the Spring Planting Festival right before being married in 2006. The exterior of our Seed Bank store, in Petaluma, California. Sasha and a Silkie chicken at Bakersville.*

LEFT: *We spend our winters in Petaluma, working at the Seed Bank and getting to know the people in the local community.* RIGHT: *Comstock, Ferre & Co. in Wethersfield, Connecticut. Seed was sold here as early as 1811.*

inspired, we made a spontaneous decision to lease the building, which we called the Petaluma Seed Bank. We loved that it used to be a *bank* that held money securely, and now it would hold our seeds safely.

I've gotten to know many of our neighbors and customers around the North Bay since opening the Seed Bank. The gardeners are the most knowledgeable and organically minded I've ever come across, from the permaculture farmers who design plots of land to mimic the natural ecology of the earth, to freethinking city growers who harvest quinces, lemons, oranges, and apples on rooftops in Berkeley. Nowhere else in the world do Emilee and I feel as inspired about pure, local food as we do in Northern California. The famous plant breeder Luther Burbank, who developed the Russet Burbank potato and the Santa Rosa plum, said of the area, "From what

I have seen . . . it is the chosen spot of all this earth as far as Nature is concerned." I couldn't agree more.

Shortly after opening the Seed Bank in Petaluma, Emilee and I were driving back to Missouri and remembered a letter we'd received the previous year, regarding Comstock, Ferre & Co., an old seed company in Connecticut that had been put up for sale. I was very familiar with the company—Comstock is well known by seedaholics like me as the oldest continuously operating seed company in New England. The owners of the company had written us to inquire if we would be interested in purchasing the property, as it was on the verge of being taken over by developers.

Established in 1811, in the town of Wethersfield, Connecticut (a few minutes outside of Hartford), the company had operated in various capacities over the previous two hundred years.

Once we saw its magnificent old buildings (including a landmarked house that dates back to 1767), antique seed cabinets, and oak bins filled with vibrantly colored seed packages from the nineteenth century, we were intrigued. We moved quickly and soon signed the deed of ownership. Inside the old Comstock buildings, Sasha, Emilee, and I got lost in a maze of dusty rooms. From the basement to the attic, and on every floor in between, there were amazing pieces of agricultural history to explore: weird old tools, dozens of closets and abandoned offices with papers strewn around the floor, as if someone had just gotten up and gone to grab a cup of coffee. We were sifting through generations of history to start a new chapter for this American treasure.

And that's the story, so far. When people ask me what's next, I never know how to answer. I do hope that Emilee and I will celebrate more idyllic springs, blue-sky summers, and bountiful fall harvests. There will always be weekly trips to farmer's markets and a continued search for tasty heirlooms in foreign countries. We feel blessed to be able to work with seeds and spend so much time in the garden. Through it all, we will focus on educating and inspiring folks to embrace sustainable food by growing delicious heirlooms and supporting small local farms. After all, the more people we get growing and saving seeds, the sooner we can get the food supply back to its wholesome roots.

The Gettle family at Comstock, Ferre & Co.

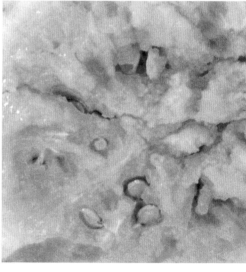

3. Seeds in America ✑

In the fall of 2010, an unusual event happened for the heirloom gardening world. In a showroom at Sotheby's, the prestigious New York auction house where billionaires routinely bid on $50 million Picassos and rare Fabergé eggs, heirloom vegetables were treated as art. Sitting in the audience of bankers, doctors, and glittery socialite types, Emilee and I watched while boxes of vintage heirlooms, such as Lady Godiva squash and Turkish Orange eggplant, were put on the block to raise money for charity. The asking price? $1,000 a crate.

It was thrilling to witness so much attention being paid to heirlooms. But I couldn't help wondering, how did we get to a point where a simple box of vegetables can command such fanfare? It wasn't always this way. Until recently, vegetables were just vegetables, planted year after year by humans in order to survive. Now we call them "heirlooms," as if they are a collectible item from our great-great-great-grandparents' younger days.

And actually, that's what they are. Traditionally, different cultures domesticated different crops to suit their needs: corn and beans in Central America; potatoes and quinoa in South America; rice and peaches in China; and wheat in Iraq. The seeds were then traded and transported from one environment to another—say, from a rural village to a seaside jungle—where the process would begin again, with that community developing a new version of some crops.

It was a golden age for the development of biodiversity. Unfortunately, modernized agriculture works in the opposite way. Instead of adding diversity, modern breeding and genetic engineering result in the loss of diversity, and sometimes varieties, of plants. As high-yielding hybrid and genetically modified seeds take up more real estate on farms, the older heirloom varieties fall out of favor, and out of the garden. Many varieties have vanished entirely, and more are teetering on the edge of extinction. With odds like this, it's no wonder people are starting to treat heirlooms like precious relics from a bygone era.

Paul Wallace of the Petaluma Seed Bank admiring a produce display at Sotheby's Auction House in New York City.

In the fifteenth and sixteenth centuries, Spanish and Portuguese explorers shuttled potatoes, corn, beans, peppers, chocolate, coffee, and other commodities from one corner of the world to another, where they were assimilated into new cultures. As a result, many national cuisines are based on vegetables that didn't originally exist in that country. Consider Italian food without the tomatoes, or Thai dishes without spicy peppers—but neither of these crops existed in those countries before the discovery of the New World. It boggles the mind, the diffusion of crops.

America has one of the richest agricultural histories of any country on the planet. The founding of our nation in the eighteenth century was, in many ways, predicated on the land and the way that we worked it. When European settlers arrived in the Northeast, the first thing they had to figure out was how to get food. In Massachusetts, the Pilgrims might have never survived that first winter without corn, squash, and beans from their Native American neighbors—and lessons in how to work the land.

From that point on, America grew up as a nation of farmers. As our population increased, agricultural centers sprouted up to feed their nearby communities. One of the most important hubs of the seed industry was in Wethersfield, Connecticut, which was settled in 1634 and home to seven early seed companies. Located in the fertile Connecticut River Valley, it was a natural home for startup seedsmen and onion farmers. One of the town's notable exports was the Wethersfield Red onion, a delicious variety that got shipped out to every sort of destination, from New York City all the way down to the Caribbean.

Our founding fathers, like Thomas Jefferson and George Washington, had huge vegetable gardens on their own estates. They encouraged agriculture, believed it to be one of the most important occupations of man, and knew it was necessary to feed our growing population. Between 1830 and the start of World War I, 30 million Europeans migrated to this country. In 1819, the newly established Treasury Department issued a directive to servicemen abroad to "collect plant materials" and bring them home to be grown in America's fertile soil. The United States Depart-

A field of Wethersfield Red onions in the Connecticut River Valley.

This seed packet is typical of early twentieth-century seed packaging in America.

ment of Agriculture was eventually founded in 1862, and to promote growing and food production on a local level, they once gave away 40 million free seed packets. By the 1890s, most towns had a seed store, and big cities had major seed "empires" competing against each other.

As the companies grew, so, too, did the marketing of seeds. The turn of the century was a golden era for seed catalogs—and entrepreneurially minded capitalists!—both here and in Europe and Japan. Brimming with spirited American salesmanship, the catalogs landed in mailboxes each January, illustrated with colorful, tempting drawings designed to entice farmers and gardeners who were eagerly awaiting spring. Each company had its own way of convincing customers that *theirs* were the biggest,

best, and brightest varieties, such as Prizetaker onions, King of Mammoth pumpkins, and Giant Ponderosa tomatoes. Some companies, like the ones in New England, came up with faraway-sounding names, like Black Mexican corn and Japanese Pie pumpkin, to evoke a feeling of exoticism.

By the 1960s, seed catalogs were much less popular, as people left the garden behind in exchange for the conveniences of supermarket produce aisles. Now we have "fresh vegetables" twelve months out of the year in most places. Americans can get whatever they want at all times.

Most people don't realize how unusual this is. They don't realize that prior to the 1960s, most fresh fruit and vegetables were only available from April through November, roughly. When

Jere in front of the Historic Belden House, which was built in 1767, and is located adjacent to Comstock, Ferre & Co., our seed store in Wethersfield, Connecticut.

grapes were ripe, people ate grapes. Asparagus came in April and melons in August. If your climate had very cold winters, that meant potatoes, turnips, and other root vegetables from the root cellar. Canned and preserved jellies and jams had to last until the soil had warmed up enough to start planting again. Even the hardiest of vegeta-

bles weren't looking so hot in the old root cellar by the time March rolled around.

Up until the 1950s and beyond, most American families—even non-farming families—maintained a small kitchen garden plot to grow vegetables and fruit for family meals. Traditional farms were much smaller than they are today (instead of five thousand acres; they were fifty acres, or five) and much more diverse, with cows, pigs, sheep, and horses, as well as a variety of different crops, instead of just growing one thing. And crops were typically rotated each year—instead of planting the same huge batch of the same one or two crops year in and year out, farmers changed the crops and their locations each season to keep the soil healthy and to avoid depleting nutrients from overfarming. Farmers and gardeners worked to select and save seeds that had better taste and higher nutritional value, just as their ancestors had done for thousands of years.

Throughout the first part of the twentieth century and long before that, gardeners and farmers had experimented with sprays, herbicides, and other tricks to help prevent or destroy pests and deter garden-loving animals. Most of these remedies were fairly harmless, and many of the old methods are used by organic farmers today to control pests.

In the middle of the twentieth century, seed companies started to develop hybrids for the mass market. This involved intentional crossing of two different types of a crop, which is also known as "hybridization," and happened with increasing frequency following World War II. This was also a major period of growth for the burgeoning chemical and industrial agricultural industry. At the same time, a new highway system was being built, and produce could suddenly be packed into refrigerated railcars and shipped thousands of miles, before getting dropped into the fluorescent-lit produce aisles of chain supermarkets. Once this full-blown industrialization of agriculture got under way, our food supply began to change dramatically.

Though Monsanto's Roundup weed controller is one of the most popular herbicides in the world, it wasn't the first of its kind. Heavy-duty insecticides were becoming very popular with backyard gardeners and farmers throughout the 1950s, actually. That is when the major chemical corporations, which had been developing chemicals for military use throughout the 1940s, started developing insecticides and nitrogen-based fertilizers on a grand scale. These companies had spent millions of dollars perfecting compounds such as DDT and Agent Orange to kill pests, disrupt a military enemy's agricultural food production, or destroy plants that provided cover during battle. Following World War II, the companies began to believe that the same chemicals could be put to use in America's agricultural industry. They set out to develop treatments that would maximize crop yields and food production. Indeed, their mission was accomplished: Pesticide use has increased fiftyfold since the 1950s. According to statistics by the Environmental Protection Agency, more than 1 billion tons of pesticide products are used each year in the United States.

In scientific and governmental circles, this movement toward mass industrialization was referred to as the "Green Revolution." However, the word "green" meant something very different in 1957. When we "think green" now, we mean we're concerned with things like sustainability, local origin, and purity. The Green Revolution of the fifties and sixties celebrated agricultural development based around chemicals and fertilizers that made things get bigger at any cost. Larger farms, bigger crop yields, and new, tougher, higher-yielding types of produce

Delicious Scallop squash are popular among small farmers.

that could be shipped around the world were the priority. Huge farms were taking over from small farms as the heart of the agricultural industry, in order to feed huge amounts of people not just in America, but in Asia and Africa as well. As "Big Agro" grew, the number of small farms dwindled, as they were either abandoned by their owners or bought by the bigger farms.

The pitch from chemical companies to farmers was based on the concept of more money for less work. Sounds pretty great, right? Nobody then realized that the pesticides and chemicals would contaminate well water, cause birth defects, erode our soil, and lead to the disappearance of wildlife. But in the 1960s, it was discovered that widespread agricultural use of DDT was rendering fish-eating birds sterile, which threatened biodiversity and almost led to the extinction of the California condor. Its agricultural use was banned in the United States in 1972. Many other modern agricultural practices have proven to be similarly harmful. The monocultures that now dominate the nation's rural landscape are linked to a reliance on cheap fossil fuels and an unprecedented obesity epidemic in America.

By the 1980s, big farms had become fully mechanized, and garden plots had disappeared from backyards. Americans had fallen in love with convenience, which was everywhere, as a result of developments in packaging, shipping, technology, and agribusiness. As a result, Americans turned away from gardens and land that their parents and grandparents had grown up working. The prevailing logic was "Why should I grow it, when I can just buy it?"

The floodgates of change were effectively opened up by *Diamond v. Chakrabarty,* a United States Supreme Court case that centered around the question of whether or not a plant could be patented. Prior to that time, Americans could legally claim "ownership" of an animal, but not an actual plant or life form. But in 1980, everything changed. In *Diamond v. Chakrabarty,* Supreme Court justices held five to four that living, man-made microorganisms are patentable, thus favoring commerce and inserting the concept of intellectual property law into the industrial-agricultural complex for the first time in history. This meant that in 1982, Monsanto was legally allowed for the first time to patent the plants it genetically modified. Today, more than 80 percent of the soybeans and cotton that are harvested in this country have at least one patented Monsanto gene in them, as does 70 percent of field corn.

Most small farmers choose to sidestep corporate agriculture by selling to independent grocery stores and restaurants, at farmer's markets, and at their own roadside stands. But most of the big farmers are linked with Monsanto, DuPont, and other corporate seed and chemical suppliers, because many like the convenience of being able to spray large amounts of weed killer on crops that have been genetically altered to withstand, and even thrive in, a toxic chemical shower that kills nearly everything else. This spraying of chemicals means that farmers need to spend less time in their fields. Unfortunately, higher yields and convenient farming methods are coming at a price. Traditionally, farmers improved varieties by saving their seeds and carefully breeding. But many modern farmers don't even know how to save seeds—the practice itself has nearly gone extinct, because farmers who buy patented varieties are not allowed to save seeds. Specifically, they sign contracts promising that they won't save or sell their seeds, or even exchange them.

To ensure that the stakes don't become much higher, it's important to acknowledge that certain conveniences of modern agriculture are actually mixed blessings, which have the potential to jeopardize the health and well-being of future generations.

A hundred years ago, children spent time in a garden while they were growing up. If you wanted to eat lunch, you often needed to work in the garden. Hundreds of schoolchildren visit Baker Creek each year to take tours of our Bakersville pioneer village. Many of them have never planted seeds or even seen a garden up close. I love watching them giggle when they see our big old turkeys wobbling around—because although these kids may have eaten a fair share of turkey sandwiches in their life, this is the first time they're getting to see where the turkey comes from. When they see our gardens, they are excited. *Wow,* they say, *I can actually grow my own food? I can plant a garden all by myself?* The idea of getting something to eat anywhere outside of a supermarket, convenience store, or fast-food restaurant is fascinating to them. Their eyes nearly pop out of their heads when they see what we're growing and realize what it is possible to do on a farm.

As thousands of varieties of vegetables are lost each year due to the increase of hybrid and GMO seeds, it's easy to see how a crate of squash or tomatoes is now viewed as worthy of celebration at Sotheby's.

4. Collecting Seeds Around the World ❧

My First Trip: Mexico, 2002   As a kid, one of my biggest dreams was to travel through Mexico. Just hearing the name of this vast country conjured up images of sweeping ranchlands, strolling mariachis, and fresh corn tortillas being cooked over an open fire by a pretty señorita. The country is in my blood—my father's mother was born there—and I was curious to see with my own eyes the land that gave her and me our olive complexion and jet-black hair.

I'd heard for years about Mexican farmers. They're widely respected as some of the best growers in the world, which makes sense, since people in this region have been working the land and cultivating corn for thousands of years. Upon discovering the tall, wild grass called *teosinte* growing in their arid plains, Mayans selected and bred it over generations into one of the most popular commodities on earth. Corn now comes in nearly every color of the rainbow: red, yellow, orange, pink, black, blue, purple, white, brown. In the southern city of Oaxaca, they even grow an antioxidant-rich emerald-green variety that is made into hearty tamales (the original "fast food").

A land with rainbow-colored corn and four thousand years of agricultural history under its belt would be the perfect place to find old seeds and new adventures, I thought. And it's easy to get to—all you have to do is drive south, right?

I made a spur-of-the-moment decision to do just that one day when I was traveling out in Oregon, fishing with some friends. I tried to convince someone to come along with me, with no luck. They were ready to head back home to Missouri. But I knew this was my chance to finally get south of the border. I was twenty-two years old, and I'd never set foot outside of America; I didn't speak Spanish, and I'd be traveling alone. Looking back now, it seems kind of crazy. But that day, as the clouds were gathering to dump a rainstorm on the Cascade Mountains, my friends packed up their gear and started heading home to Missouri and I hopped into my Saturn and drove south.

A cornfield in the autumn in Mexico.

Jere traveling in Mexico, age 22.

These days I travel with a cell phone, GPS, and a laptop computer. But in 2002, I had basically nothing to help me along the way, aside from a tattered Rand McNally road atlas, bottles of water, fruit and nuts for sustenance, a few plaid shirts, a straw hat, a pair of cowboy boots, some country-western CDs, and a map of Mexico I'd picked up at an insurance office.

On my way down the Pacific Coast, I got out to stretch my legs in the Redwood forests that I'd seen in *Sunset* magazine and made a few stops at seed farms and farmer's markets. It was nice to see the beautiful country, but at the end of the day, I fell asleep dreaming about reaching the border.

Within four days, I arrived in Mexicali, a border town located at the very top of the Baja Peninsula. It took me a while to explain to the border agents where I was going, since I didn't even know myself, but once I'd answered a thousand questions and convinced them I was just a harmless hillbilly looking to enjoy the land, they let me through. As far as the legality of transporting seeds between countries, it really depends on what you're transporting and where you're taking them to and from. Some plants, cuttings, and seeds are allowed into America from foreign lands with a phytosanitary permit. Some are prohibited entirely, and threatened or endangered plant species need a special form. (For more information about how to import plant products, visit the Plant, Organic, and Soil Permits Page on the Department of Homeland Security's website, www.dhs.gov.)

I drove, rather nervously, I'll admit, through chaotic downtown Mexicali and the shantytowns on its periphery, and my heart was racing. But I soon found the road out of town, and before me stretched a vast, pretty desert blooming with cactus and vibrant ocotillo plants.

For hundreds of miles, I drove through little

towns that looked straight out of the 1930s and along roads flanked with cattle fields owned by wealthy rancheros. I had only a vague idea of where I was going most of the time, which turned out to be the theme of that trip. My navigation was pretty slapdash. Often I just picked out an interesting-sounding place and drove in that general direction.

After barreling through the desert for twenty-four hours, my quest brought me to Durango, a historic city filled with opulent cathedrals and regal, Spanish-style buildings. It was late evening when I rolled into town; the sun was setting against a backdrop of palm trees and mountains, and I was dog-tired. One of my self-

imposed rules for the trip was that if I couldn't find a room that cost less than $20 for a night, I'd drive along a back road or around the corner from a gas station and find a place to park, lock my doors, and sleep until dawn, for free. I wasn't quite brave enough to camp outside in the middle of nowhere and the car was cozy, if a little cramped for my six-foot-three-inch frame. But I was so excited that I didn't get much sleep anyway. There was a lot of land to cover, and I hadn't found my seeds yet.

Soon, the ranchlands gave way to lush valleys and twisted jungle paths that were inhabited by poor, indigenous families whose ancestors had lived on that same land and medicine men

Northern Mexico is mostly a desert.

who used feathers, smoke, and chanting to wash away evil spirits. I'd find myself passing through yet another dusty old cowboy town, with tough-looking old señores who looked as if they'd been around since the days of Pancho Villa. As these men stared me down suspiciously, señoras in long, colorful skirts served tamales from roadside stands. There were many fascinating things to see, but there wasn't much farming in that arid dirt. Since seeds were what I was here for, I kept driving, my eyes peeled for produce *mercaditos,* or markets, which I knew I'd come across sooner or later.

After three days on the road I approached Guadalajara and the climate changed abruptly—the dry desert air gave way to humid, balmy breezes. My heart raced when I felt the cool, refreshing air, and I was dazzled by the vivid blue, purple, and crimson wildflowers that dotted the highway. They signaled to me that a host of botanical variety was growing nearby. And then farms and gardens came into view, with their sprawling squash, pumpkin, and cornfields.

Just west of Guadalajara, in the village of Te-quila—where they make a lot of, yep, tequila—rows of enormous, spiky agave plants stretched for thousands of acres. The air was so fresh. It didn't surprise me when I found several varieties of gourds, squash, and flowers that I'd never encountered before. I wanted to load up my Saturn with samples of every variety and take them home to show my family, but the border agents would have been too curious on my way back across, and anyway there wasn't room enough in the car.

I did have room for seeds, though. The only challenge was how to explain to a crusty old farmer or his shy daughter that that's all I wanted. But eventually they'd realize what I was looking for, and then I'd select the vegetables I wanted. They'd watch me patiently as I placed my bounty on the ground, chopped it open with a machete, which I'd picked up along the way, and scraped seeds out of each gourd or squash with my hands. Then I'd place the pulp into a paper bag and label it in English—Pipian Tuxpan squash, Cassabanana melon, Cobán Red Pimiento pepper—before wiping off my machete blade

LEFT: *A scene from a typical market in Mexico.*
RIGHT: *Squash from a roadside stand.*

and folding myself back into the Saturn. I'd head off down the road while the farmer stared after me in puzzlement.

That evening, I'd spread the seeds out to dry on newspapers and sleep until sunrise, and then wake up and do it all over again. I felt a great rush from finding these new varieties of vegetables, and the surreal beauty of the landscape energized me. Every so often while driving in the countryside, I had to pull over to gape at the wildflowers, or at a massive field of corn or amaranth, or to sit in a grove of deliciously fragrant citrus trees. The hardworking Mexican farmers planting, weeding, and gathering crops with their bare hands were inspiring to watch.

I was twenty-two years old, alone in a foreign country, enjoying the local people, even though I could barely understand a word they spoke. I felt as if I was on a modern-day Lewis and Clark expedition, documenting and discovering new forms of life as I traversed the land.

I quickly became an expert at spotting roadside markets, which were not so much markets as they were, say, a lone guy sitting in a chair on the side of a dirt path with twenty-five pumpkins and a few jars of hand-labeled honey. Or a bunch of garlic and a little pile of peppers and tomatoes. Or bushels of coconuts, bananas, and other tropical fruit that I couldn't even guess the names of. No matter how many times I stopped, it didn't get old.

A field of amaranth.

I collected squash seeds from this gentleman at a roadside stand near Mexico City.

Thai Green eggplant is a staple at sidewalk markets in Thailand.

Corn is everywhere in Mexico, and I ate it every chance I got. The nutty-flavored white-and-pink variety is popular served inside husks at local festivals and on the street. Unfortunately, many of the old Mexican varieties are now being lost, due to contamination from genetically engineered varieties. Like many countries in Europe, Mexico has long banned the planting of GMO varieties, and Mexican farmers have been vocal about their right to grow pure seeds. But the chemical corporations have been relentless in spreading their varieties, and now many seeds in Mexico are contaminated with unapproved, and untested, genetically modified strains. In recent years, farmers have gone to the streets to protest what is happening to their traditional way of life, and the contamination of the food that feeds them.

Nearly a month had passed by the time I was on my way back home, and a crisis hit in Monterrey, a hundred miles from the border. My cash supply was basically gone, my gas tank was far from full, and my ATM card had stopped working. I held my breath and drove carefully for almost twenty-four hours, back through the desert, up to Texas, and to the Oklahoma border, before finally reaching Missouri. Once I reached Baker Creek, I said hello to my guard donkey, the ducks, the chickens, my garden, my family, and showed my friends my haul. It didn't turn out to be as much as I had hoped to bring back, but I had weeks of adventure under my belt and a passion to do it again soon.

Thailand

After Mexico, my life began to revolve around finding and growing new varieties of heirlooms. Searching for "new" old varieties became my main reason to travel abroad. I also wanted to experience different cultures, see how they gardened, and taste new cuisines.

A fruit stand in central Bangkok.

The idea of Asia had always fascinated me, with the food and ancient cultures that abound there. After my Mexico trip, I kept hearing about what a great place Thailand is, and how much of the country continues to farm—about 70 percent of the Thai population still works in agriculture. It was only a matter of time before I booked a ticket to go there, along with my two friends, Jon and Tim. They were two brothers who were up for a trip and wanted to go fishing and exploring. My business was humming along well enough that I could afford to take a few weeks away from the store, so we bought tickets and packed our bags.

I spent most of the time on our twenty-five-hour flight from Kansas City to Bangkok just waiting to land. I loathe flying, so I distracted myself with the in-flight magazines and counted down the hours. Once we finally arrived, I was tired and quite stiff, but relieved to be back on the ground and pleasantly surprised by how efficient and friendly Bangkok's airport was. In no time, we were off to our hotel.

The bumper-to-bumper drive to the hotel was amazing. Zooming past produce and flower stands and fragrant outdoor food stalls made me wish I wasn't so tired. It was amazing for three country guys from a town of fifteen hundred people to be dropped into a 10-million-strong city like Bangkok. Asian spices from street vendors blended with diesel fumes in a heady aroma, and the hot, humid air reminded me of summer nights in Missouri. It was both chaotic and relaxing. We threw our backpacks in a corner of the hotel room and spent the next few days wandering through the streets. Everywhere you turn in Bangkok, you can't help but notice that this is a city that loves food. It's available anytime, day or night, at one of the hundreds of great restaurants or cooked in the open air, on the sidewalk.

One of the first things we did was find a local guide to take us on a fishing trip to the lakes around the city. Jon was excited to try catching some of the massive fish that live in the murky Thai waters, and he managed to land a sixty-five-pound Mekong catfish and a forty-five-pound Siamese Giant carp, which is rarely caught. I caught some large fish, too, but none as large as the ones Jon got. Fishing was fun, but I was ready to head out in the countryside and start searching for seeds.

From Bangkok, we hopped on a ten-hour bus ride north to Chiang Mai, which is one of the most culturally significant cities in the country.

Jere with a catfish in Thailand.

We passed massive rice fields, small villages, and temples (or *wats*). The roads were better than I'd expected, and we found a hotel in the old city for $2 a night when we arrived on a drizzly evening. The city was founded in 1296 and is surrounded by a towering mountainscape. The first evening, we visited the famous Night Bazaar, which is an open market filled with antiques, crafts, tribal people, Europeans, Israelis, and, of course, backpackers on their personal journeys. Hmong villagers sell handwoven silk textiles and ancient axe heads alongside opium scales and gardening tools.

The food, the native garb, and the soothing melody of bamboo flutes—all was as I'd envisioned. Imperfections recede at night in any town. In the dark, you can't see the litter, or a building that needs painting, or a window that has a crack in it. In the dark, things look perfect, and the night market in Chiang Mai is no different. The shapes of the buildings, pagodas, wats, spires, and triangular rooflines are juxtaposed against the mountains to dazzling effect.

Tables were piled high with roasted silkworms and spiders, which I found interesting,

A Thai man selling vegetables in Bangkok.

though I would never be able to actually eat such "delicacies." Turtles floated in buckets at my feet. We stocked up on fruits and vegetables, the flavors of which were incredible. I met a Filipino man who worked as a minister and teacher, and he translated for us and helped me find a seed store to visit so I could look for Thai seeds. We found dozens of varieties of eggplant, thirty kinds of leafy greens, unique squash, spicy peppers, brilliant orange melons, giant radishes, bitter gourds, baby watermelon, fiery Thai garlic, winged beans, and much more.

Many Americans think that farmer's markets are something new, but they've actually been a central part of most cultures for thousands of years. Anywhere you don't have corpo-

Organic farming is a popular way of life for hill tribes.

✿✿✿✿✿✿✿✿✿✿✿✿✿✿✿✿✿✿✿✿✿✿✿✿✿✿

When you're traveling in a foreign country, don't be afraid to talk to the locals. They're a great source of information about agriculture, plants, and veggies—and you'll be greeted with a smile. People are usually very excited to meet visitors to their country and are interested in hearing about your adventures. They also love to practice their English. Most farmers are interested in what other farmers do—how they grow and what's going on in their food supply.

✿✿✿✿✿✿✿✿✿✿✿✿✿✿✿✿✿✿✿✿✿✿✿✿✿✿

ratized big-box stores, they are an integral part of people's daily lives. Markets are where people meet up and see friends, listen to music, obtain food for their families, talk to their butcher or local farmer, or just meander around and think about the week ahead.

The markets of Bangkok alone could keep me busy for weeks, but the markets of the Hmong people are also very special. These tribal people live in Thailand's mountainous north and farm intricate terraced gardens that spread across the rolling hillsides. When we traveled through their countryside, we found many new varieties, including a cowpea from a local grandmother's garden and giant, bright yellow cucumbers on a bamboo market table.

The people in these mountainous regions grow much of what they eat, living off the land like their forefathers did. They always have fresh food and therefore don't need a lot of currency or outside commerce. Elephants and water buffalo are still used for transportation and heavy labor: pulling trees, moving large stones, and plowing

fields. Everything was fresh and healthy at the little markets: bunches of fennel, herbs, peppers, pumpkins, kefir limes, "Phrik" bird's-eye pepper, angled loofahs, nubby little bitter melons, enormous daikon radishes up to two feet long, and bok choy, alongside a variety of crafts and poultry. I collected unique cowpeas and hyacinth bean seeds from the Lisu people and tasted half a dozen of the most succulent mangos that I've ever had.

I've been back to Thailand and Southeast Asia twice since my first visit, and I look forward to returning periodically for the rest of my life. The Land of Smiles, as they call it, has a rich history of farming and so many varieties of vegetables, it's a never-ending source of fascination for me. Until my next trip, I whip up Thai food in our kitchens and plant the seeds from that area with fond memories, remembering each adventure with a smile.

Guatemala

A lot of people travel to Central America to tour lush cloud forests and see the colorful birds flying through the treetops. The forests here yield an incredible variety of fruits and flowers, and the farms are rich in history, so it was a natural spot to find more heirloom varieties to bring back to Baker Creek and grow in our gardens.

To get there, my sister, our friend Andrew, and I drove through Mexico and Belize, stopping along the way at open-air markets, temples, and ancient ruins with produce fields sprawling around them. In Central America, biological diversity is everywhere. Exotic flowers—eight-foot-tall dahlias, castor beans, cosmos, and more—grow wild along the roadside. It's as if the countryside is one giant garden.

Wild dahlias grow all over the place in the jungles of Guatemala.

COLLECTOR'S CHOICE

Since 9/11, the transportation of seeds between countries has become much more regulated. To avoid awkward encounters at Customs, apply for what is called a phytosanitary certificate if you are going to travel with seeds from one country to another. To obtain a permit, visit the department of agriculture office where you are staying. Submit your paperwork immediately upon entering a country, as it can take ten to fourteen days to process.

Cassabanana fruit collected for seed at a roadside market.

My ultimate goal was Guatemala, because it is a developing country and I'd heard they still used traditional farming methods—much more than they did in Mexico. The country had recently been involved in a civil war, but my seed fever allowed me to risk a bit of danger in order to find some rare varieties to add to my collection. As we entered the country through Belize, we thought the highway would continue—as it does when you travel between states in America and countries in Europe—and that generally the landscape would look similar, despite our having entered a different country.

Were we ever mistaken! Immediately upon passing through the Guatemala checkpoint, the road abruptly became a dirt path. For thirty miles, swaths of it were washed out and pigs waded in puddles in the roads. Turkeys, chickens, and sheep moved in and out of the jungle, along with a few half-naked children who looked after us curiously as they played in the dirt.

We traveled through this impoverished area for hours before finally reaching a highway. The rest of the drive was on paved road. After crossing several rivers, we reached the mountain city of Cobán, where we happened upon an old hotel from the nineteenth century, with magnificent columns and lovely courtyards. The rate worked for us—it cost about $50 U.S. for a room—and we crashed happily until the next morning, when things got even better.

The city's central produce market was just steps away from the front door of our hotel, in a tall building downtown. It was as if we'd traveled through a tunnel and landed in a vegetable paradise. Native people there sold every kind of tropical fruit imaginable and many vegetables, some of which were harvested wild in the jungle and much of which was picked from the lovely farms that filled the area. Instead of stands, the vendors sat on the ground in circles, so people could walk through them and look at the goods.

That day, I found one of my favorite tomatillos, the Purple from Cobán, as well as corn smut, a fungus that is thought of as a delicacy in Central America. There was also a dizzying array of mushrooms that had been harvested from the

The central produce market in Cobán, a historic mountain city located in central Guatemala.

nearby hillsides. I couldn't wait to cook them up with tortillas, avocado, and a wedge of lime.

At Baker Creek, customers often send us seeds from their travels, but it isn't the same as when you go to farms and markets yourself, to see how produce is grown in its native land. I like to experience the climate and the culture, and I relish the chance to document the history of where the exotic varieties came from and how they grow.

After Cobán, we drove up into the mountains, through a lush green jungle and virgin rain forests. Waterfalls and pools flanked the winding roads, and towering, dripping green vines covered everything, from ancient temples to hilltop lagoons. It was dreamlike—something you'd expect in a movie, rather than real life.

Then you drive over the tall mountains, up a very steep pass, to about nine or ten thousand feet, and back down on the other side. That's where most of the Guatemalan population is centered, near Antigua. That touristy city was our last stop in Central America before we started heading back north.

In addition to returning to these countries, there are many other places I have yet to visit. For me, the most alluring places are where English is not spoken and where they are still practicing traditional farming and gardening techniques. I want to go where people plant seeds that were passed down to them from their ancestors; places where you can't buy seeds online, and the seed supply isn't so thoroughly contaminated by huge, multinational chemical companies. I'd love to, say, go hang out with a grandmother in the Ural Mountains who's planting traditional melon varieties. An enormous swath of historic, uncontaminated farmland runs, roughly, from western China through the Far East and contains myriad cultures and historic varieties of vegetables and fruits. It is a dream of mine to travel there and help them save as many varieties as possible before these culinary treasures are lost.

At times when traveling in a foreign country, it's a test of will to persevere in an unfamiliar culture, but it is always worth the challenge. These trips also give me a chance to think about the company with a new perspective. And whenever I plant a seed that I collected from afar, it brings a flood of wonderful memories of past adventures, and anticipation of what's to come.

Children dressed up for a festival in Guatemala.

5. How to Garden ✒

I planted my first vegetables when I was three years old. By the time I turned eighteen, my garden consisted of two acres, and it's even bigger today. But big or small, my approach is always as simple and natural as possible. A vegetable garden should be the safest and healthiest place on your property. If chemicals are added to it, that harms the soil, the water supply, and the wildlife—and it also gives you lower-quality produce. Here is a guide to some of the time-tested methods that we use in our own heirloom gardens.

The Right Spot: Selecting Your Garden Plot

The first step to a successful harvest is selecting the right space. Most vegetables like a full day of sun, so pick a spot with **good light**. If you live in a cooler climate, your garden should face the warmest southern exposure available. For convenient harvesting, put your garden **as close to the kitchen** as possible. And get some **distance from trees**, if you can. Some trees put acids into the soil that aren't good for garden plants. Black walnut trees, for example, produce a chemical compound called juglone that can harm or even kill certain plants. Trees and large shrubs also have very long roots, and you don't want your veggies and fruit to have to compete for moisture, nutrients, and sunlight. Finally, check the **drainage**. Before you plant, look at your would-be garden plot after it rains. If there are puddles, switch to an area that's higher or on a slight slope.

Prepare the Soil

Your soil is the foundation upon which your whole garden is built, so it's important that it is good quality and rich with nutrients. In most parts of the country gardeners don't sow seeds until spring, in which case soil should start getting prepped as early as February or March. To do this, once the earth has thawed from winter, walk outside and take a look around. The goal here is to see how your soil is doing and begin the process of getting micronutrients moving underground. Start this process six to eight weeks before the last frost of spring.

1. Clean up from last year. If a garden was planted the previous year, till the leaves and roots from last year's crops back into the soil either by hand or, if you have a large space, using a rototiller. If you don't have one, borrow one or rent one, or hire someone to do it for you. I used to clean up our family garden

Dave Kaiser and Sasha check the soil at Baker Creek.

with my father when I was a kid. We'd bundle up in wool sweaters, pull on our boots, and till the soil all afternoon. It's hard work, but it feels invigorating to be back outdoors after the long winter.

2. Plant a cover crop to prime your soil. The process of planting a cover or "green manure" crop is one of the most important steps in sustainable gardening. There are many different crops that people use for this purpose, but I particularly like rye, barley, and vetch. Cover crops are planted in late fall or early winter, in advance of when the official planting season begins, to optimize productivity in the soil. Sow the seeds in the same space where your garden plot will be located. As the "green manure" crop grows, it will build organic matter and capture beneficial micronutrients, preparing your garden space for the veggies.

3. Four to six weeks before sowing your vegetable seeds, turn the cover crop into the soil by hand or using a rototiller. If the cover crop grew very tall, you can mow it with a lawnmower so that it is easier to till.

4. Once the soil is prepared, apply and till in a three- to four-inch layer of compost, aged manure, or other organic matter on top of the soil. We use **fresh poultry manure**, which is a rich source of the macronutrients (nitrogen, phosphorus, and potassium). This mixture will linger for up to eight months in the topsoil, acting like a sponge to hold on to water until hungry plant roots need the nutrients later on. For a typical backyard garden, purchase composted manure by the fifty-pound bag at nurseries or farm stores. After applying it, till it into the soil.

5. If you applied fresh manure, let the soil rest for six to eight weeks. This resting period allows nutrients to break down into soluble compounds that the plants can utilize. If you plant seeds in that soil any sooner, you run the risk of "burning" the plants, so be patient! Clomp back to the house, cozy up with some cocoa, and wait for the earth to wake back up.

If you don't have six to eight weeks, don't use fresh manure. Instead, you can use aged manure, cottonseed hull, or mushroom compost. The latter is a mixture of composted wheat or straw. Because this kind of organic matter isn't as "fresh" as "fresh compost," you don't need to let the soil rest after you apply it. Instead, you can go ahead and start planting immediately after you've tilled the material into your soil. Both fresh and aged organic mixtures are available in spring and summertime at nurseries and garden centers, and online year-round. Or better still, ask around

WORMS

In addition to manure, compost, and other organic matter, worms are an extremely beneficial tool in organic gardening. If you don't already have a worm population in your garden plot, you can easily add them (you can buy about a thousand "red wigglers" for $25 or so online or at hardware stores). You may notice that worms disappear once you start tilling in the spring. If you add more organic material, they'll eventually return.

to see if you can find a local farmer who is willing to sell you some—it is usually dirt-cheap if you buy it that way.

Plant Your Seeds

Once the eight weeks are over and weather is warmer, it's time to begin planting your seeds. For early crops, the instructions on many seed

Manure spreader with horses, borrowed from our Amish friends.

Planting lima beans.

Jere planting a tomato seedling.

packets say something like "sow as early in spring as soil can be worked." In the South, this usually happens in mid-March. For colder areas up north, it might be as late as mid-May.

Different plants need to be started at different times, depending on what kind of crop they are. **Cold-weather crops** go in first, four to six weeks before the last frost. A good bunch to start with is potatoes, spinach, lettuce, and corn salad, which is a green, leafy plant that grows all the way through winter. Two weeks later, put in brassicas, such as cabbage, broccoli, spring turnips, and radishes. In general, root vegetables and leafy crops should be planted before the weather heats up, because their flavor is enhanced by a little frost. Peas and fava beans are other good cold-hardy crops to consider around this time.

Once we are pretty sure that the last frost is behind us, the **warm-weather crops** go in. First up are corn and beans, which are followed by squash, cucumbers, melons, and peppers. Somewhere along the way, when temperatures are consistently above seventy-five degrees, we transplant our tomato seedlings into the ground,

followed by eggplant. Be careful not to put eggplant out too early—an unexpected cold snap can do damage to its growth cycle. If it's exposed to a couple of cool days in a row, it'll "sulk"—which makes it sound like plants think, and I don't know if they do or not, but they do respond in sophisticated ways to their environment.

HOW TO "HARDEN-OFF" TRANSPLANTS

Before a tender young seedling is transplanted outdoors in the garden, it needs to be acclimatized to prepare for the elements. This process is called "hardening off." To do this, set the seedlings outside for a few hours each day, letting them spend gradually more time outdoors over the course of a week or so.

While they're outdoors, especially in the beginning, take care to see that they are shielded from wind. Bring them indoors if extreme temperatures—either hot or cool—threaten. Once they are sturdy and the weather is mild enough, they will be ready to go into the garden.

Later on, when summer starts winding down, put in **fall crops** like Brussels sprouts and other leafy vegetables, as well as root crops, like turnips, rutabagas, and carrots. The timing here is, once again, a tricky balance. You can't wait too long or put them in too early, or the seeds won't germinate. Gardeners in the South sometimes wait until September, but people up north may want to put them in earlier.

Our hot, humid growing season lasts a long time, five to six months. If your climate has shorter summers, and not as much heat, orchestrate your actions to ensure maximum growing time, so that you have a good harvest before the temperatures drop.

Weed Control and Mulch

Weeds aren't a major problem for us at Baker Creek, and that isn't because they don't exist in the Ozarks—they certainly do! But we have bountiful weed-free harvests because of one thing: *mulch.* Mulch is one of the most important tools in your gardening arsenal, and helpful in many different ways. In addition to adding nutrients to your garden, it also helps retain moisture and is a superb weed control.

At Baker Creek, we use both plastic and straw hay mulch. I'd prefer to use *only* natural mulch, like alfalfa hay or straw, but the natural mulches are more than ten times as expensive as plastic. For a backyard gardener on a budget, or if you have a very large garden, plastic is a practical, affordable alternative to natural mulches.

A tomato seedling that was just planted, with red plastic mulch around it.

These days, some plastic mulches on the market are degradable, in an array of weights. But even if you use nondegradable mulch, there are still benefits to plastic. Plastic is highly effective at retaining moisture, which reduces the need for heavy irrigation. And as a weed control, it is virtually impenetrable (whereas weeds can actually still poke up through straw or hay mulches). It also warms or cools soil, depending on the climatic needs.

Plastic mulch is available in a variety of colors—including black, white, red, blue, and green. Black warms soil, and white plastic mulch reflects heat and keeps soil cooler. Some studies have shown that red plastic will give you higher-yielding tomato plants. I haven't tested this, but it seems to help in our gardens. And other folks think different colors repel different kinds of pests.

The main drawbacks to plastic are that it doesn't put any organic matter into the soil like natural mulches and that you need to dispose of it at the end of the season. Heavier plastics and reusable woven ground covers do exist. If you are flush enough to afford such materials, talk to someone at your local nursery and find out what suits your needs.

We use natural mulch as much as we can, and I think straw is the best all-round if you can

HOW TO PROTECT YOUR PLANTS FROM AN UNEXPECTED FROST

Every so often I dream that it's summer and it's either freezing or snowing on my garden, on top of my tomato plants. For me, this is akin to a nightmare, actually. If a frost is coming and your plants aren't covered, and you don't have mulch down, use whatever you have to protect them from the freeze. Temperatures that are even just a few degrees below freezing can wreak havoc and zap a plant. Put row covers (see sidebar, p. 60) or lay blankets or newspapers over your plants to keep them warm. You can also overturn a bucket or cardboard box.

CLEAN CULTIVATION

There are millions of weed seeds in the ground, and every one of them is waiting for a chance to grow. Nature, after all, uses every niche and opportunity to do its business. Once weeds get a foothold, they sap up moisture and nutrients, competing with the plants that you want to thrive. Then those plants get stressed, the weeds get stronger, and it's a disastrous domino effect.

Instead of putting weed-controlling mulch down, we used to try to keep our soil free from weeds by using a method called "clean cultivation," which is when you regularly hoe soil with a tool so that weeds don't have a chance to grow. If you think this method sounds like a lot of work, you're right. The bigger a plant is, the more difficult it is to hoe around it. And if you take a break from the hoeing for several days, the weeds will inevitably get the upper hand, after which time it is basically impossible to take back control. After decades of weeding and aching backs, we decided to stop battling nature and started mulching, and I'm so glad we did.

The moral of this story is that organic gardeners should wince when they see bare ground.

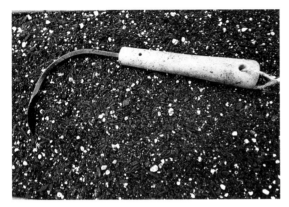

A CobraHead hoe—my favorite hand tool!

get it. In addition to alfalfa hay and straw, other natural mulches include **shredded bark, chopped leaves, pine needles,** and **grass clippings.** At the end of each season, you can till that mulch right back into the soil. By springtime, depending on what you use, the soil will be dark and fluffy, the result of decomposition.

Some people use **woodchips** and **sawdust** as mulch, but I don't recommend this, because wood products remove nitrogen from the soil, and sawdust usually has harsh tannins and acids in it. If you do have woodchips or sawdust around, stick to using them on bushes like roses, blueberries, and other hardy perennial plants.

Newspaper and **cardboard** are wonderful—and very inexpensive—ways to mulch. Break salvaged cardboard boxes down, cut them into strips, and lay the strips on top of your garden. Once the cardboard becomes damp, you'll have a fantastic, carpetlike layer of protection over the soil. Newspapers have soy in their ink and are a good source of nutrients, too. (If, like many folks, you don't like the way that newspaper looks when it's used as mulch in the garden, put some

straw on top of it.) The only drawback to paper mulches is that they don't heat the soil, so they are best for warmer climates.

Irrigation

A vegetable garden needs at least one inch of water per week to thrive. There are many ways to add water to your soil. If your garden is small or if you're using containers, a watering can or a hose will do the trick. **Sprinklers** also work, but be careful about using them in humid regions, because they leave moisture on leaves, which can lead to diseases and fungi.

For typical backyard gardeners, I highly recommend **soaker hoses,** which are porous tubes that water streams out of and into the soil.

FROSTS

Every region has average first and last frost dates, but they are just that—*averages.* Some people think there are ways you can tell when the last frost will happen by looking at spring leaves or the moon, or listening to the song of a bird or the call of a bullfrog. There are lots of old legends, indeed. But I don't put a lot of stock in them, as the weather always surprises me.

Deciding when to plant seeds and transplant seedlings into the garden is entirely up to you. And when you do it depends on whether you're adventurous or a bit more conservative.

Some conservative gardeners won't plant until they're really, fully, absolutely sure that the final frost has passed. Others will gamble in hopes of getting an early tomato or zucchini. In all my years of growing, I've found that nobody has the right answer all the time!

EQUIPMENT

People ask me all the time what my must-have gardening tools are. Here's a secret: A gardener doesn't need a lot of gizmos. All you really need are dirt, sunshine, water, and seeds. If you want to gear up, get a pair of gloves to protect your hands when you're digging in the dirt and a spray bottle or two from the hardware store to apply organic controls or fertilizer and to water delicate seedlings. My personal favorite tools are made by an American company called CobraHead. I don't garden without them. Many of my friends in the Ozarks do everything they need to do with a shovel, rake, hoe, and hand trowel. To find out what works best for you, test a few tools out by buying them secondhand at garage sales or borrowing from friends—you'll eventually find your go-to.

WATER WORKS: IRRIGATION 101

Don't overwater. The number one mistake that beginning gardeners make is when they love their plants to death via too much watering. Your intentions may be good, but be careful not to overdo it. A good test? Stick your finger into the soil. If it is dry past an inch, it needs water. If the soil feels like cake in your hand, it's too moist. Let it dry out, so the leaves even start wilting a little before watering again.

Don't spray the whole plant. Instead, apply water down into the soil. That's where it will make a difference.

Water in the morning. This gives time for extra moisture to evaporate from the leaves, which helps you avoid fungus or other bacterial infections.

They're easy to install and available everywhere. They usually cost between $10 and $15 for a fifty-foot hose. Soaker hoses emit water along their entire length, so you can fold them in a zigzag configuration if your plot is more square, rather than laying them out lengthwise.

While soaker hoses are great, **drip lines** are the most reliable method of irrigation and the preferred watering method for serious gardeners with large spaces, because they allow emitters to be placed exactly where you want water to be, so that it's not wasted. This method saves money and is healthy for the plants. The installation process for drip lines can seem a little daunting, but it's not that complicated if you follow instructions carefully. Some drip lines have a timer setting, which allows you to spend time away from the garden. Drip lines are available at garden centers, nursery supply stores, and online. We would not be without this system in our gardens!

Pest and Disease Control

Chemical companies spend billions of dollars on researching and developing so-called "miracle cures" to prevent diseases and to deter pests. But bugs, weeds, and diseases are age-old problems that have existed for centuries, since humans started working their land. We've always had to operate within the larger ecosystem that surrounds us. And there will always be critters and diseases. The trick to keeping them from wreaking havoc on your harvest is prevention.

Here are some basic defenses to keep insects and fungus at bay:

1. Rotate your crops. Planting a crop in the same place year after year is a surefire prescription for pest and disease problems. You gotta move things around! If you don't, you're basically handing bugs an invitation to a smorgasbord, and a home where they will settle in and feast for life. This is because pest populations build up, and over time, plants deplete specific nutrients in the soil. Future plants in that soil will be weaker and more susceptible to infestation and diseases. The way to avoid this is easy: Move your crops around every year. Put something totally unrelated in their place. Always rotate out of family, because veggies within the same family are likely to have the same pest problems. Rotation is tough in small gardens—but try switching things from one end to the other. You could also plant in containers, if necessary.

2. Use row covers. Row covers (see sidebar on p. 60) keep noxious insects at bay. Apply the covers, which you can buy from a garden store, after planting or transplanting seedlings into the garden, so that bugs can never reach plants in the first place. (Do a quick check to see if any bugs are inside the covers after you put them down, though; otherwise the bugs will get busy!)

3. Apply organic treatments. There are tons of chemical-laden sprays and insecticides that are "approved" by the FDA, but many are actually not safe for humans or the environment. Try organic treatments instead. It's good to have a combination of a few different kinds to experiment with. Keep in mind that organic stuff doesn't kill creatures on contact like chemicals do. This is more trial and error. Here are my favorites:

Spinosad. One of the most effective organic treatments for bugs. We spray it on chewing insects such as cucumber beetles, flea beetles, and potato beetles. It doesn't knock bugs down right away, but they quit feeding almost immediately.

Neem oil. Great for prevention of fungus problems. A light misting once a week will keep problems at bay.

Bt. This bacteria-based organic control is known for successfully eradicating caterpillars, moths, butterflies, and corn earworms.

Other organic remedies include pyrethrum preparations (which are derived from daisies), lecithin-based oil sprays, sesame oil, and fish oils. Some oils can cause leaf scalding, so follow instructions carefully and apply them at the proper time of day. Safer Soap is good on soft-body insects, such as small aphids, spider mites, white flies, and thrips.

THE BEAUTY OF BENEFICIALS

Not all bugs are bad! Do some research to find out what different insects look like. That way you can avoid harming the good guys, which include **ladybugs**, **praying mantises**, **lacewings**, **spined soldier bugs**, **wasps**, and **bumblebees**.

ELEMENTS OF NATURAL GARDENING: ROW COVERS

A row cover is a lightweight, semitransparent fabric that is used to cover plants and is one of the most important tools in an organic gardener's arsenal. They might not be the most attractive thing you ever put out in your garden, but they can be used for a variety of purposes, including:

- 🌱 Protecting plants from frost
- 🌱 Keeping pests away
- 🌱 Deterring small animals, such as squirrels and voles
- 🌱 Trapping heat to extend the growing season when temperatures start to drop

The two main manufacturers of row covers are Reemay and Agribon. Different grades of row covers exist, from very thin and lightweight (which is great in hot weather), to very thick (for frost protection—there are versions that can give up to eight degrees of protection). In most cases, the plants themselves will safely hold up the fabric, which has tiny pores to allow water to penetrate, thus precluding heavy rain from pooling on the material and crushing your plants.

To apply row covers, just throw the material over your plants and weigh down the edges of the fabric with stones or pieces of wood. It is best to put covers on either very early or very late in the growing season, so that you can retain heat and allow plants a few extra weeks of growth.

If you're saving seed, row covers prevent additional crossing on any species that are self-pollinating. (Though it won't work on plants that need insect pollinators, nor will it prevent wind-borne pollen from reaching wind-pollinated plants.)

Inside a row-cover tent—this protects plants from insects and light frost.

THE WEATHER

Wherever you live, know your climate. Refer to a United States Department of Agriculture zone map to find out the last average spring frost and first average frost in fall. And talk to other gardeners for insights. Some old-timers believe in certain weather-predicting "signs," but I don't listen to that chatter. Instead, I recommend thinking about what the weather's been like for the last few weeks and checking the forecast on Accuweather.com. The bottom line is, you won't be much of a gardener if you don't know what's happening with the weather. Where I live, weather is often the first thing we talk about when I see friends. And once you've planted a few seeds yourself, you'll find yourself saying things like "It's shaping up to be a hot one today," or "I can feel the winter coming on"—just as farmers before you have done for thousands of years.

GROWING TIPS

Most vegetables like full sun, but if you have a **shady garden**, you can still try working with sun-loving crops. Just keep in mind that your harvest won't be as robust. Carrots, beets, and radishes can get by with just four to six hours of sunlight and can tolerate more shade.

- If you're purchasing **seeds from catalogs, place your order in January**. That's when you'll usually have the best selection of exciting, new, and very popular varieties. Some crops are sold out by the time March or April roll around.
- Remember that you want your family to actually eat what you grow, so think about what they like to eat and plant that.
- **Raised beds** give you control over the type of soil you're working with—which is a bonus if your regular soil doesn't have the proper balance of nutrients. The soil in raised beds also warms up more quickly, which allows you to get an earlier start on planting (see sidebar below).
- Grow veggies that are expensive in the grocery store but grow easily in your region. Asparagus, for example, costs up to $4 per pound during high season, which means that it's cheaper and more fun to grow a patch in your own yard.

Sweet corn, on the other hand, is probably not a good idea for the average home gardener (especially if you have limited space), because you only get one or two ears per plant—so the return on time and energy is low. Ask your local extension service for recommendations.

- It's tempting to kill leaf-chomping caterpillars, but remember that they turn into butterflies. I think it's worth losing some leaves when you know you'll have a **stunning butterfly** floating around your garden a few weeks later.
- **Grow what works in your area**—which is to say, don't try and grow ultra-hot habanero peppers in the cool shady summers of Seattle. Likewise, cool-weather brassicas like broccoli will have a tougher time in Miami than they would in a cooler climate up north.
- **Starting a garden in your lawn** is easy: Mark out the area where your garden will go and cut the sod with a sod cutter. Turn the pieces grass-side-down and let them sit to decompose. Eventually the grass will die and the sod can be tilled in with the soil beneath it. Add some organic matter to the soil, let it sit, and start planting once the soil is warm enough.

RAISED BEDS

Gardening with **raised beds** is all the rage these days, and for good reason. A raised bed is a garden plot where the soil is situated above ground level, which elevates plants. Some advantages to this style of gardening include:

- **Improved drainage**, which is particularly welcome in areas with heavier than normal rainfall
- **High productivity and more control over soil quality.** If your soil isn't great—especially if you live in a recently built home with sterile backfill dirt surrounding it—add high-quality organic soil to a raised bed and your productivity will increase greatly.
- **Easy access to the garden area**, which is a blessing to elderly or disabled persons
- An **extended growing season**. Soil in a raised bed heats up earlier in the spring, and is often

ready to plant in before the regular soil, which gives gardeners in shorter-summer areas a jump start on the growing season.

To build a raised bed, you need to create a retaining wall to keep soil in place (otherwise it will wash away in heavy rain). Building that retaining wall takes work, cash, or some combination of the two. But if you want to do it, try using old railroad ties and salvaged wood. Some people use landscape timber, though this kind of material is sometimes treated with wood preservatives—and organically minded gardeners might be concerned about chemicals finding their way into the vegetables in the bed. To make a very sturdy raised bed, use stone, brick, or concrete blocks.

Though the process can be labor-intensive and costly (that soil has to come from somewhere!), raised beds can be enjoyed for years once you build them, and they look pretty cool, too.

The Harvest

I love seeing batches of pure, chemical-free produce coming out of our garden. Picking the bounty from my gardens has given me some of the best moments in my life. But there's also a bit of mystery to it, a sort of knack to knowing when to pick each different crop—when to twist the little Brussels sprouts off their stems, when to pluck tomatoes from the vine, or slice leafy greens from the earth, or toss ears of rainbow-colored corn into a giant tub.

Emilee and Sasha enjoying the harvest!

The "right time to pick" depends on where you live, what the weather has been like, and the variety of veggie you're working with. Whatever you do, be prepared once it's time to pick. If fruits stay on their stems for too long, they not only become overly mature, but they'll also signal to the plant that it should shut down. If you want your plants to keep producing through the last frost, pick the fruits regularly.

Here are some crop-by-crop guidelines to keep in mind when you start picking:

Asparagus. Let this plant grow very high for the first two seasons, so it can become strong and establish itself, but don't pick the spears. Only in the third year after planting from seed should you start harvesting. Pick spears when they're six to eight inches tall by snapping them off at ground level. New spears will grow in their place, getting smaller as the season progresses. Stop picking them once they're no thicker than a pencil.

Beans (snap). These can go from tender and delicious to woody and unpalatable in a matter of days, so check frequently and harvest just when you notice that the seeds are getting really plump. Ripe pods will be tender and snap in half easily. Eat them as soon as possible after picking.

Beets. Greens are tasty at any stage, but they're extra tender when very small. The roots are most flavorful when they reach two to four inches across. Once they grow very large, they might start to taste a bit woody.

Broccoli. Harvest when the buds are still very small and tight. Be careful in hot weather, as broccoli will quickly "bolt" (or go to seed) if things get too warm.

Brussels sprouts. Twist these little orbs off starting at the bottom once they're at least one inch across. Smaller sprouts have a richer taste.

Cauliflower. Tie cauliflower leaves around the curd, or head, to blanch it. Harvest heads when you peel the leaves back and see that the head is fully developed and clear white.

Corn. Each corn stalk produces at least one ear, but some will bear two (the second one will be smaller and develop later than the first ear). Pick sweet corn during the "milk" stage, when the juice of a kernel looks milky when you prick it with a fingernail.

Cucumber. Pick fruits at any size, up until

the seeds start to become well developed. Ripe fruits should feel firm when squeezed.

Eggplant. Use a knife or shears to cut eggplants from their stems when they are glossy and slightly soft to the touch, and eat soon after they're harvested.

Kale. You can start harvesting kale soon after the plants bear leaves, when they look green and fresh (they will taste bitter once they turn yellowish); flavors will become milder and sweeter in cooler weather.

Leeks. Grab on to the base of the plant and tug each leek gently from the soil. Use a garden fork to loosen soil if it's not loose enough. They will keep for up to a month in the refrigerator.

Lettuce. Head lettuce such as Bibb, Romaine, and Iceberg is only harvested once, by cutting off the head near the soil. Leaf lettuce can be snipped off throughout the season whenever you feel like making a salad or tossing it into soups or stews.

Melons. This is one that takes some practice. With many varieties, you'll know something is just ripe when the fruit easily slips off of the stem. The ripeness of others is determined by a softening of the skin, a subtle color change, or an intensification of scent. Do a little research with fellow gardeners or the seedsman you're working with to find out what the indicators are for a specific variety.

Onions. Select firm, dry onions with thin skins. A good indicator that it's time to pick them is when about half of the green tops have fallen over. Chop off the leaves just above the bulb and store in a dark, cool place. Sweet red onions keep for four weeks. White and yellow onions are good for up to three months.

Peas. Pods should be bright green and bulging, with satiny pods and seeds that are not yet fully developed. A good rule of thumb is that if the pod looks withered and dry, the peas will taste withered and dry.

Potatoes. New potatoes can be picked at any stage in early growing, such as when tubers are just over an inch across. Larger types can be picked whenever you think they're big enough to eat and their skin is firm. When the tops die, that's a sign that they've grown to maximum size. Harvest them right away once they reach that point.

Pumpkins and winter squash. These should be firm, with unblemished skin. They can be stored in a cool, dark location for weeks, if not longer. Double-check their ripeness by pushing a fingernail into the skin—if it's too soft, they're not ripe yet.

Rhubarb. This should not be harvested in the first season, and only a few stalks should be picked during the second year.

Spinach. Once they grow to three to four inches, pick individual leaves from the center of the plant. Harvest frequently, taking care to not remove all leaves from a specific plant until it sends up a seed stalk, at which point you should get all remaining leaves and then it's done.

Summer squash. Pick fruits when they are very young, a few days after their blossoms fade.

Swiss chard. Harvest leaves whenever they look tasty to eat. The stems taste good once they reach anywhere from one-half inch to a full inch across.

Tomatoes. Pick tomatoes when they're soft to the touch and have reached their final color. Late tomatoes can be picked while still light green and very hard, and then used as fried green tomatoes! Many people think that refrigerating tomatoes adversely affects their taste, so if you can, keep them at room temperature.

Turnips. Harvest young greens as they emerge from the plant's center, and roots once they've reached an inch or two around. In cooler weather, some turnips can get up to four inches around and still taste crisp and fresh.

Watermelon. These are ready to eat when the part of the melon that is resting on the ground turns from white to yellow. Another rule of thumb is to pick when the tendril immediately opposite the spot where the watermelon developed has withered and turned brown. Expect some trial and error with watermelons.

All vegetables have a "window" of ripeness. If you pick them too early, they won't be at their peak flavor, or they might not have reached their optimal size. If you pick them too late, they'll be tough, woody, or just plain inedible.

I've certainly experienced years when a harvest was ruined due to an unexpected cold snap or heat wave, or when everything hit at once and I didn't have enough time to actually get out there and pick everything. To avoid this, pay attention to the weather and practice succession planting, where you plant a few seeds week after week of your favorite crops, to ensure a steady supply rather than a veggie tsunami. If you do end up with more than you can handle at one time, give extras away to a local food bank or family and friends, or can and preserve the excess for use in the winter. You'll be glad you did.

Finally, if you're growing something for the first time and wondering if it's ready, take the plunge and taste it! Just one bite will tell you whether the gamble has paid off. With some crops, like beets, radishes, and salsify, you can pull a sample out of the ground to try, and if it's not there yet, leave the rest in the ground to finish ripening.

Animals

Before you start planting, call your local extension service or talk to a neighbor to find out what pests bother gardens in your area. But be aware that even within a one-mile stretch, conditions can be very different. My parents live just a half mile away, and different animals invade their garden than we get in ours. The more you talk to nearby gardeners, the better prepared you'll be to handle the various scenarios that will pop up.

Deer can be a real problem. They can clean out an entire garden in just a few nights. The most effective way to keep deer away is by erecting a fence so tall that they can't leap over it—eight to twelve feet is recommended.

Cats and dogs are some of the best pest controls available, because they help keep rabbits, small birds, gophers, and mice away. If you don't have a pet, plant your garden close to your neighbor's yard if they do.

Blackbirds and crows love to eat sweet corn and strawberries. Row covers (see sidebar on p. 60) are the best solution for birds. There are specific nettings to keep birds at bay. Scarecrows can also help, but birds get used to them, so don't put them out until veggies start to ripen.

I grew up breeding poultry and have had many chicken friends over the years. These days I keep over twenty-five different kinds of chickens on our land, from Rhode Island Reds to the old

ELEMENTS OF NATURAL GARDENING: WINTER STORAGE

**Root cellars and other ways to
store your bounty through the winter**

Before the days of refrigeration, root cellars were essential to farm families. These underground bunkers were a great place to store veggies, fruit, butter, cheeses, and meat through the winter months.

Even though refrigeration is everywhere today, I still think root cellars are pretty useful, not to mention fun! The idea behind a root cellar is simple: take advantage of cold winter weather and use it in such a way that it keeps your stored foods cold.

In rural areas around America, root cellars were historically dug into the north sides of a hill or bank. The tons of soil moderate temperature shifts and offer ideal humidity. Usually cellars face away from the sun's rays and have a simple system of vents that are adjusted manually to allow cold night air inside and keep out the warmer daytime air. In very cold weather, that process is reversed. If operated properly, a root cellar has high humidity and maintains a temperature of about 35 degrees (but doesn't go below freezing). Cool, damp air is ideal for storing root vegetables, cabbages, and canned preserves. And why shouldn't it be? These are the exact same sort of conditions that vegetables are bred to endure, overwintering quietly to resume their lives in the spring.

Not everyone has the space for a proper root cellar nowadays, and with refrigeration they aren't as necessary. But in many homes refrigerator space is limited, and having extra space in a root cellar makes it possible to buy an entire winter's worth of veggies when prices are low and they're at their peak of ripeness, and store the bounty for later on in the year.

If you don't have the land to create a real root cellar, a great alternative is an **unheated basement**. In a corner of the room, simply build a box of the desired size in one corner, filling it with lightly moistened sand or sawdust, and place the veggies inside. You don't even need a lid, if you don't have one handy. Even just a simple cardboard box, with veggies inside, in an unheated room or closet, will keep most storage veggies in surprisingly good shape. I've stored cabbage, turnips, beets, and carrots this way with great success.

You could also consider **digging a hole** in your backyard. To do this, shovel a hole that is three to four feet deep and a foot or two across. Then, line it with a few inches of hay or sawdust, followed by a metal screen or mesh to deter rodents (they will smell your food and be drawn to it in the fall). Place veggies inside, alternating layers of veggies with layers of straw, until full. Put a sheet of plywood over the whole thing, and insulate it with bales of straw or batches of dead leaves.

If you prefer not to dig a hole, or if you want to create a storage unit on your rooftop, lay four **bales of straw** in a square formation. (Use more bales if you want to store more vegetables.) Place the veggies inside the space and line it with metal screen or mesh, to protect your bounty from hungry mice. Then add more bales over the top. Place them close together to minimize drafts. You can use the hay as mulch in next year's garden!

Some tips to keep in mind when you're storing veggies for long periods of time:

- 🌿 Use a minimum-maximum thermometer to monitor interior temps. Avoid freezing or overheating by allowing or excluding outdoor air, as needed.
- 🌿 Position vegetables in close proximity but not quite touching—they'll keep better that way.
- 🌿 Inspect the contents of your storage unit once every few weeks during the cold months, and remove any veggie that is past its prime or spoiled. This will prevent spoilage from spreading to the rest of the contents.

ELEMENTS OF NATURAL GARDENING: COMPANION PLANTING

Companion planting is a method of organic gardening where you plant certain crops in the same area that have beneficial effects upon one another. Some of the benefits can include hiding or masking another crop from pests, acting as trap crops that lure pests away from certain plants, or creating an environment that beneficial bugs will flock to.

Marigold is one of the most effective pest deterrents you can plant. It helps prevent nematodes (a soil infestation that is prevalent in the South and in which nearly microscopic worms bore into plant roots and rapidly reproduce, destroying the roots in the process) and keeps insects away from leafy greens. Bugs don't like the strong scent, so they stay away.

Amaranth is a trap crop that attracts cucumber beetles. If you plant it near cucumber plants, the beetles go and live on the amaranth instead of in the cucumbers. You can trap or kill the insects on the amaranth plant instead of trying to treat them right on the cucumbers. And as amaranth matures, it seems to release a natural pesticide that will often kill the beetles anyway.

Mint repels aphids and cabbage pests.

Garlic doesn't take up much space and it repels some insects. It's got a strong scent, which I think confuses some bugs.

Another thing you can do is **plant a lot of flowers** that bring in bees to help facilitate healthy pollination. Planting members of the mint family, such as lemon balm, oregano, or mint itself, is a good idea along these lines.

Plant something tall, like **sunflowers**, near shorter, shade-loving crops such as bush beans and squash. This cheerful flower also attracts **birds** and **bumblebees** that will help with pollination.

French La Flèche breed, as well as **black swans**, **peacocks**, and friendly old **turkeys** that we will never eat. Their manure and feathers are great for mulch and compost. Geese are also great. Farmers have long used **weeder geese** in small fields to eat their weeds, which sure beats hoeing! Of course, weeder geese won't work well if you're growing greens, like leafy lettuce, but otherwise, they're great for this task. We also have wonderfully helpful **ducks** living in pens near our gardens. They are our first line of defense against insects. I recommend getting at least a few birds at once, though if you get just one duck, it'll get tame really fast. You will think of it like a cat or a dog, and it will think of you as a friend. You can buy birds at pet stores or feed stores in the springtime. Hardware stores in rural areas also occasionally have them.

Alternative Growing Methods

Some adventurous gardeners experiment with **hydroponic** growing, which is the practice of growing plants without soil. Gravel, rock wool, clay pellets, and other materials support the plant roots while they grow. This detailed method is often favored by folks who have inhospitable gardening climates or little outdoor space, and it's based around the process of pumping nutrient solutions into the root system on a very specific schedule. The results are high-yielding crops that can be harvested very early, because growth happens between 30 and 50 percent more quickly than with conventional gardening methods. And even though it's not my thing, I support all methods that get people excited about growing.

Aquaponics is similar to hydroponics, except instead of using chemical fertilizers, it uses water in which fish have been raised. Such water contains waste from the fish or other aquarium animals suspended within it. These wastes are ideal nutrients for plant maintenance. It's possible to grow both fish and vegetables from the same system. This process, while very interesting, is also very complex and more difficult to implement than hydroponic gardening.

When I garden, my goal is to enhance our environment, not harm it. Simple, old-fashioned methods work best to cultivate safe, delicious crops right in your backyard. You'll notice that I didn't try to tell you about any miracle formula in this primer. That's because you don't need one. The miracle is in the seed itself!

Summary

1. Talk to your neighbors. Ask your fellow local gardeners for tips and hints about what works for them. Gardening books and blogs are helpful resources, but nothing will teach you more than people who are working the same land as you. They know the soil, weather patterns, pests, and animals and are nothing less than an invaluable resource.

2. Rotate your crops. Plant crops in a different place each year to avoid depleting nutrients in the soil. Different plants feed on different nutrients, which will get depleted if you put the same thing in every year. If plants don't get all their nutrients, they'll be weaker and more susceptible to pests and diseases. A good rule of thumb is to avoid placing crops in the same place more often than once every four years.

3. Avoid chemical-based pesticides and fertilizers. Countless toxic soil "tonics" and quick fix "magic cures" are on the market, but instead of blasting leaves and bugs with that poison, it's always best to use organic methods. They might be slightly more expensive, but you'll eventually use less of them, and I believe that the safety benefit is well worth a few extra dollars. In a pinch, you can also make a home remedy for the garden. Popular ingredients for such solutions are garlic, hot pepper, soap, and oils.

4. Try companion planting to deter bugs and pests. See sidebar on p. 66.

5. Mulch, mulch, mulch. You're only as good as your soil, and mulch is the key to good soil. Plants will thrive if they are surrounded with a good supply of organic matter, such as leaves, hay, alfalfa, or compost. Plastic mulches are useful to retain moisture and control weeds.

6. Be creative! In gardening, the key to success is learning to experiment and trust your instincts. It's tempting to get caught up in the minutiae of, How deep do I sow a seed? How often should I water? When is the right time to harvest? How acidic is my soil? But remember: There are no rules in nature, or in gardening. You'll learn more by diving in and trying different methods. Most rules can be bent or broken with a little creativity.

6. Seed Saving ✍

I became interested in saving seeds as a child, when I noticed that my favorite varieties were disappearing from the pages of my seed catalogs. I educated myself about the difference between heirlooms and hybrids, and joined the Seed Savers Exchange in 1996. Since then, I've traded seeds with other collectors across America. Seed saving became an obsessive hobby for me that eventually turned into the business that I now run.

One of the best reasons to grow heirlooms is so you can save the seeds and grow the crop again in the future. Though not many people practice seed saving these days, it used to be a necessity for human survival. For thousands of years, gardeners, farmers, and other folks, in every corner of the globe, had no choice but to save seeds to ensure a reliable food supply.

These days, seeds aren't required for survival, because most everything is available at the grocery store. But raising your own produce from saved seeds is certainly a cost-efficient way to feed your family, since you don't need to pay for seeds or buy produce at the supermarket.

Saving seeds also connects you to our food heritage and helps maintain crop diversity in our food supply. The old varieties that our ancestors cultivated are vanishing these days. It's not because they don't taste great—it's because major seed companies are more interested in selling hybrids and genetically modified varieties, which often won't grow true if you save their seeds and plant them the following year.

Heirlooms that are "pure" should always grow true to type, just like their parents, generation after generation. Hybrids, by contrast, typically differ from their parents in appearance and other traits.

When you save seeds from your tastiest, most productive plants year after year, you are essentially creating your own unique strain of a vegetable that has been adapted specifically to your climate and gardening style.

The simplest crops for beginning seed savers are the ones whose flowers pollinate themselves, sometimes even before they open. These crops seldom cross with other members of the same species, so they require little to no isolation to yield pure seeds—seeds which will produce plants just like their parents, year in and year out.

Six Easy Crops for Seed Savers
Common Beans

Peas

Tomatoes

Eggplant

Lettuce

Cowpeas

Crops in this group will breed true with no crossing, as long as they are separated by fifty feet from other varieties within the same species. In some cases, no crossing can occur even when different varieties are growing right next to each other. (The A to Z Growing Guide starting on p. 83 spells out specific requirements for each crop.) This makes them ideal for saving seeds, even in highly populated areas, where you may not know what is growing in nearby gardens.

Other crops are more challenging to save pure seed from, especially for gardeners in more populated areas. This is because although the plants are easy to collect seed from, their pollination requirements mean that more distance is necessary to ensure pure seeds. Bees spread their pollen around and can fly for surprisingly long distances. For these crops, five hundred feet to a half mile may be required for absolutely pure

Gardeners gather tomatoes from one of our small gardens early in the morning.

seed, though barriers such as solid fences, hills, or buildings do help. Where space is tight, these crops can be protected by a practice known as caging—see sidebar, below. This process is more involved. If you're interested in learning more about this practice, we strongly suggest reading *Seed to Seed: Seed Saving and Growing Techniques for Vegetable Gardeners*. Writer Suzanne Ashworth, along with Seed Savers Exchange cofounder Kent Whealy, wrote this seminal volume, which outlines in close detail the process of preserving more than 160 different kinds of vegetables.

Even within this more challenging group, decent results can be obtained if only one variety of each crop species is grown in your garden. It's certainly well worth a try! With less than the recommended isolation, some crossing may occur when saving seed from these crops; but it often doesn't. It really just depends on the bees and what they are up to at any given time. And it's always possible that no one else will happen to be growing the crop nearby, in which case what's growing in your own garden would be all you'd need to be concerned with. Just remember, even though occasional accidental crossing might yield surprising results, a squash is still a squash, and a cuke, a cuke—they will still be edible.

Crops That Require Greater Isolation

Squash

Melons

Watermelons

Cucumbers

Okra

Peppers

Beets and Chard

Corn

Cabbage Family

Most of the crops on this list are pollinated by insects, primarily bees. A quarter- to a half-mile isolation from other varieties is recommended in order to save pure seed. (Note that peppers are an exception, as they are self-pollinating and do

CAGING

Caging plants to exclude insects can assure pure seed with little or no distance between varieties. Simply fastening a row cover over plants will keep insects from visiting them, although more elaborate cages could be constructed using frames with screen. The practice is effective only on plants that are capable of self-pollination, but that are also crossed by bees. (Plants that require insect pollination cannot be isolated by this method, unless pollinating insects are introduced, which isn't usually practical on a small scale.)

WHAT IS INBREEDING DEPRESSION?

"Inbreeding depression" is a genetic term that is used to describe the detrimental effects of breeding organisms that are too closely related to one another, generation after generation. In gardening, if you save seeds from too small a pool of plants year after year, you run the risk of inbreeding depression. Inbred plants will lack vigor and be generally unproductive. To avoid such a "depression" and ensure that you're saving high-quality seeds, select from a variety of individual plants.

not need insects, though they *can* be pollinated by insects. Pepper pollen is very heavy, and bees don't carry it for long distances, which is why it only needs five hundred feet to maintain purity.)

Wind-pollinated crops, such as beets, chard, corn, and amaranth, require the most isolation for saving pure seeds—up to a mile or more—so these varieties often don't make good seed-saving subjects when growing the plants in town. More details about saving seed from specific crops is included in the A to Z section starting on p. 83.

When you're getting started, here are some basic guidelines:

1. Make sure you're saving the right kind of seeds. As we've mentioned, there are two main kinds: open-pollinated seeds, many of which are considered heirlooms; and hybrid seeds, which are cross-pollinated. Saving seeds from hybrids will often yield disappointing results, because when planted again, hybrids will either be sterile (i.e., they won't grow at all) or will revert to one of

✝✝✝✝✝✝✝✝✝✝✝✝✝✝✝✝✝✝✝✝✝✝✝✝✝✝✝✝

If you live in a humid climate, you may need to increase the drying time.

✝✝✝✝✝✝✝✝✝✝✝✝✝✝✝✝✝✝✝✝✝✝✝✝✝✝✝✝

their parent types. Select types that you can isolate adequately in your situation.

2. Harvest seeds from your best plants. Select from the plants that had early yields, high productivity, and superb taste.

3. Before you start collecting the seeds, clear out a workspace for yourself and organize whatever equipment you'll need, such as paper towels, a knife and cutting board, a colander, jars, and labels. Many seeds look alike, so take care to label each batch of seeds clearly once they are scooped out to dry, to avoid confusion.

4. Cut the fruit open, scoop out the seeds, and let them dry in a well-ventilated area for fourteen to twenty-one days, or until they're totally dry and almost brittle.

Throughout the process, follow directions for crops as specified in the A to Z section (p. 83).

Remember to allow plenty of time for saved seeds to dry; packaging them when they're still moist is a surefire way to get moldy seeds, which usually aren't viable. We like to dry our seeds in front of a fan for one to two weeks.

Seed Storage

Veggie seeds are best sealed in an airtight container, such as a jar or envelope, and stored in a cool, dry place. Select a spot that is located away from heating vents, air conditioners, windows, and sources of moisture or condensation (avoid bathrooms, laundry rooms, sunrooms, and cold garages). We recommend a box or drawer in a bedroom. Make sure no light gets to them, since light could cause seeds to break dormancy prematurely. If stored properly, veggie seeds will be viable for somewhere between four and five years.

To store seeds for even longer, put them in a freezer, where they can remain viable for up to twenty years. But be aware that if you do end up choosing to store seeds in a freezer, you should avoid opening the jar up right away once you take it out. Instead, after you take the jar out, let it rest for a night before opening the lid. Do this because if cold seeds are exposed to warm room air, humidity could condense on the seeds and packaging and compromise their longevity.

7. City Farmer 🌿

Though I'm a country boy at heart, I can't deny that there is something magical about big cities. I love being in a skyscraper and looking out at the rooftop and backyard gardens dotting the cityscape. People get so creative with small spaces! In the Ozarks, there's no shortage of arable land to work with. But not everyone lives in a place with so much space. If you live in a gardenless apartment, or you have just a tiny little yard, it is still possible to harvest delicious vegetables and herbs. If you have a patio, balcony, sunny windowsill, or even access to a rooftop, you can make your own little garden patch.

Pots

Planting vegetables in pots or other containers is a fun way to start a garden in a small space. Most plants like full sun, so place your pots accordingly. If lack of sunlight is an issue on a small patio or in a yard, a dedicated gardener can move the pots once or twice per day, as the sun moves across the sky.

The size of the container is important, and you should choose according to how big the crop will grow.

Small pots (three to six inches across) can grow some plants to maturity, such as smaller lettuce leaf plants and herbs like basil, thyme, chives, rosemary, and lavender. **Medium-size pots**, which range from eight to ten inches across, can hold a few different plants at a time. Planting similar species together, such as a couple of pepper varieties, makes for easier care and a vibrant mix. **Large pots** (twelve inches across or larger) are perfect for big plants, such as tomatoes, squash, eggplant, and cucumbers.

Any **type of container** can work to grow vegetables in, as long as it has a drainage hole. My favorites are terra-cotta, because they're sturdy and classic-looking. There are also metal,

A container gardener's arsenal includes peat pots, a shovel, and any kind of container—as long as it has a hole for drainage.

wooden, ceramic, and more modern man-made materials that can withstand a variety of weather conditions and last for a long time. Pretty much anything that holds soil will work, as long as it has a hole to allow for drainage. I used to make little wooden boxes out of lumber in which to grow strawberries. Figure out what works for you, based on what you're growing and your budget.

For container growing, **soil** should be a mixture of compost, soilless potting mix, and a little sand. This ratio of soil-to-sand is important because it keeps the "soil" loose in your container— real garden dirt tends to get too compacted and hard. Come up to a few inches below the top of the pot. Sow seeds directly in pots, as if you were starting them in a garden. Germination takes five to fifteen days for most vegetables, depending on what you're growing. While you're waiting, keep the soil moist. When the seeds sprout, help them along by keeping the soil damp, but avoid over-watering by checking moisture levels regularly. If soil clumps like cake, wait for it to dry out a bit.

One of the best things about container gar-

dening is that you don't have to deal with weeds, which is a dream for most gardeners. Containers also give you more control over what happens to plants, since there aren't as many pests or random animals crawling around while they're growing, and you can bring them indoors if a frost is expected. As they grow, make sure to harvest your container plants regularly in order to encourage continued production.

Window Boxes and Hanging Baskets

Europeans have been perfecting the art of pretty little windowsill gardens for centuries, and many a fire escape and balcony throughout New York City has a colorful garden hanging from it via window boxes.

There's a dizzying array of different kinds of window boxes to choose from. They range in size from two to six feet long, and they're often pre-drilled so that you can mount them on a wall, add brackets to hang them from a rail (you can purchase brackets at any hardware store), or suspend them directly from a fire escape. Try planting a selection of both lovely and tasty vegetables and edible flowers together in one container. A single box can hold multiple crops at once: salad greens, edible flowers (such as nasturtiums), attractive herbs, and lively little

TYPES OF CONTAINERS

Pots don't need to be fancy or expensive. In a pinch, you can even plant seeds or seedlings in a plastic five-gallon bucket bought for a couple of dollars at a hardware store. I've also seen folks use old galvanized washtubs, wine barrels, and decorative tins. Just make sure whatever you use has a drainage hole. If you don't have a drill handy, ask someone at your local hardware store to make the hole for you.

SIZE MATTERS

Before you go out and buy window boxes, measure the width and height of your window or balcony railing. You don't want to end up with a container that doesn't fit or blocks your view.

HOW TO SELECT VARIETIES FOR CONTAINER GARDENING

Look for plants that are both ornamental and edible. Veggies that are delicious and pretty are ideal for containers. It's even better if you can eat two different parts of a plant. For example, you can eat the leafy greens of beets as well as the root. Intermix tasty ornamentals like colored kale, bright lettuces, and bright peppers throughout the landscape. Strawberries also look charming in little boxes.

Choose high-yielding early bearers. You don't want to wait around all summer for a melon or a giant tomato. Instead, find highly productive varieties of the crops you love that can be harvested throughout the season, such as cherry tomatoes, small peppers, and basil.

Think small. Look for varieties that say "dwarf plant" or "small plant" on the package or in the catalog description. Snow Fairy tomato and Apple Green eggplant are two nice dwarf varieties.

Grow what you and your family like to eat. If you only have enough space to grow one or two kinds of tomatoes, select varieties that your family will enjoy eating.

Don't forget about herbs. Basil is simple to grow, looks beautiful, and is versatile in the kitchen. A wonderful variety is the lilac-colored Purple Opal. Other great-looking and -tasting herbs include thyme, oregano, mint, lavender, chives, and dill. Combine them in one pot for a dynamic visual display.

When in doubt, go for peppers, tomatoes, and eggplant. In my opinion, no garden—not even a container garden!—is complete without tomatoes, peppers, and, if there is room, eggplant. They're all easy to grow, nutritious, and have a zillion culinary uses.

Urban landscapers are making interesting choices these days. Instead of traditional hostas and pansies, I see ornamental edibles like rainbow Swiss chards, vibrant kales, and Crayola-colored peppers popping up in gardens throughout major cities. **Look at the spaces in your neighborhood for planting inspiration.**

peppers. Window boxes are available in a variety of materials, such as wood, metal, iron, and of course, plastic (and you can easily build wooden boxes at home for a fraction of the cost of store-bought ones). Wherever you get your containers, make sure to obtain the proper hardware if any is needed to attach them securely. Once a box is filled with soil, water, and growing plants, it can get very heavy.

Hanging baskets are another fantastic choice for city gardeners—as they are the ultimate space-saving solution and a vibrant addition to a balcony or patio. Though baskets are most commonly used to grow flowering plants and vines, you should also consider putting in peppers or brightly colored lettuces. To avoid soil leakage, line baskets with a layer of attractive, natural-looking coconut husks.

With both window boxes and hanging baskets, keep up with the harvest once it begins. Remove plants right away once they are exhausted, and then put in something else.

Rooftop Gardening

There's no shortage of rooftop space in urban areas, and some cities are experiencing urban

WATER WORKS

The experienced gardener can tell at a glance when a plant needs to be watered. But many beginning gardeners are stuck wondering if they've added too much, or if they should add more.

In general, it's good to err on the side of caution before drenching the soil. Underwatering is almost always less damaging than overwatering.

To see if plants need watering, poke your finger into the soil. If it feels dry deeper than an inch, give it some water. When leaves are slightly wilting, add water right away. If the soil feels like cake dough, it is too moist to water—let it dry out a bit.

Watering is particularly important when you're working with containers, because if a plant needs moisture in a regular garden, it sends its roots deeper to find water—but in a container, the roots are confined. So check moisture levels daily in warm weather.

Before you dive in, take measure of how much light your rooftop gets each day, and note how much shade there is in certain places, before placing your pots or starting your beds.

farming movements, where determined, passionate gardeners are taking over spaces above street level to grow their own food. In Brooklyn, New York, for example, an organization called Eagle Street Rooftop Farm has transformed the rooftop of a warehouse into a 6,000-square-foot organic vegetable farm with 200,000 tons of soil and dozens of crops. And fancy hotels in many big cities around the world have "greened" their rooftops and started organic gardens up there to supply produce for their restaurants.

To try your own rooftop garden, you can bring up containers and work in pots, or you can install raised beds. Using containers allows you to move the plants easily.

Building beds will allow for more plants. With preparation and careful planning, it is also possible to cover a whole roof with beds, soil, and a drainage system. Whatever your goal is, the first step in rooftop gardening is to **consult a structural engineering expert,** who can tell you what is allowed and what will work for your building. A gardening operation—even a small one with a few terra cotta pots—can weigh a lot. Make sure that your rooftop oasis won't cave in or otherwise cause damage to anything below it. After you consult an expert, file any permits necessary before getting started.

Gardening in a Small Yard

If you live in a big city and have a small space, maximize the productivity of your plot by using intensive and succession planting methods. Select plants that yield quickly. Lettuce, spinach, mustards, radishes, and bush beans can all be harvested in fifty days or less. Avoid planting crops that sprawl or get really bushy.

Succession planting in a small space is fun and efficient. Once a crop is exhausted, pull it up and plant a new crop. A great schedule for succession planting in an urban area would be to put in a cool-weather crop such as **lettuce** or **spinach** several weeks before the last frost. By mid-May (or slightly later or earlier, depending on where you live), that crop will be pretty much done producing. Pull the plants up and put in **tomato seedlings.** Tomatoes get big, so stake them as soon as you transplant them, so that as they grow they will climb. You can harvest them through the first frost in the fall. Throw **green beans** in as well around the time you transplant the tomatoes. They'll last through August or so, at which point you can pull them up and put in turnips or rutabagas for the cold months. Succession plant-ing will work best if you understand and plan around how long crops take to mature and which like cooler or warmer weather.

If you notice that your plants are looking a little runty, that might be because they don't have enough nutrients (all plants need nitrogen, phosphorus, and potassium). **Add compost, mulch,** or **natural fertilizer** to the soil between plantings, or spray the plants with fish emulsion.

For sprawling plants, like cucumbers, to-

MY TOP 10 FAVORITE CONTAINER PLANTS

1. **Golden beets** are quick-growing golden-yellow gems that don't bleed (as do red beets) and have an immensely flavorful sweetness.

2. **Fish peppers** are fiery-tasting little fruits that grow in variegated white and green. A must-have for containers because of their stunning white-and-green mottled leaves. A great African-American variety that has superb flavor.

3. **Black cherry tomatoes** look like large, dusky brown grapes and have a magnificent, rich flavor that darker skinned tomatoes are famous for. Twine the large vines up a trellis using bamboo or garden ties.

4. **Ping Tung eggplant** is a wonderful heirloom that is popular in Taiwan and is one of the tastiest and sweetest varieties out there. Fruits grow up to eighteen inches long.

5. **Siam Queen Thai basil** has a very strong clove scent, pretty flowers, and is a great addition to curries and other Asian dishes.

6. **Nasturtium flowers** have peppery-tasting vines and grow in a riotous array of colors, from orange, red, and yellow to fuchsia and ivory. The flowers add a splash of color and creamy texture to salads.

7. **Five Color Silverbeet Swiss chard** is a rainbow chard, with brilliant pink, yellow, orange, red, and ivory stalks, that originated in Australia. This is one of our favorite greens to cook with and a bold pop of color for containers and small spaces.

8. **Giant Red Japanese mustard** is a bold-tasting green that, when eaten raw, tastes like wasabi. The crinkly, deep-purple leaves add some pizzazz to compact flower beds. Also good for pickling.

9. **European Mesclun salad mix** makes one of the tastiest and most vibrant salads ever, and is a favorite for our farmer's market growers! The salad mix that we sell at Baker Creek contains a variety of different lettuces, plus a few greens that originated in Europe, such as kale, chard, and arugula. Flavors range from sweet and mild to hot and tangy.

10. **Alpine strawberries** are a dainty type that produces pointy little berries steadily throughout the season. These berries are very pretty and irresistible for snacking. You won't get a ton if you're growing them in a container (compared to a larger patch or bed), but you can grow enough for fresh eating.

matoes, edible gourds, small-fruited winter squashes, and melons, to keep them from roaming over your plot train vines up a trellis using garden ties, string, or twine. This frees up space and protects the fruits from disease and fungus, which can be more of an issue in compact spaces. Be careful not to secure vines too snugly—you want them to be able to grow freely.

Community Gardens

If I lived in an apartment, the first thing I'd do is look for a community garden in my neighborhood. A community garden is essentially a large "green space" where city residents gather to cultivate small plots of vegetables and other crops.

Most cities have them these days, as they've been sprouting up more frequently in recent years. Members are volunteers who work individual or shared plots. Depending on how big a city is, and how popular a particular garden is, plots may be given to folks on an apprenticeship basis, after they demonstrate commitment to helping maintain the space. But often all you need to do is pay a membership fee to receive your assigned space.

Community gardens are a tremendous resource for novice gardeners, because they provide an environment in which knowledge and camaraderie can be shared with neighbors. Many gardens hold events, including workshops about topics such as composting and harvesting, kids' days, senior center hours, and seed giveaways. To find a garden near you or learn more about starting a plot of your own, visit the American Community Gardening Association (www.communitygarden.org).

Vegetables grow everywhere in Chicago.
The city has replaced many of its flower beds with edible plants.

8. A to Z Growing Guide

With more than three thousand varieties of vegetables in my inventory, there is a lot to choose from in the Baker Creek gardens, but there are some vegetables that we return to year after year for their fabulous taste, beauty, and nutritional benefits. Here is a guide to our favorite fifty, along with some growing tips and seed saving tips. The list may include a few types of vegetables that are new to you. We invite you to plant your old favorites and experiment with new flavors, too, either in your own garden or from a vendor at your local farmer's market. With each new heirloom vegetable you incorporate into your garden and your diet, you're expanding your appreciation for nature's bounty and helping preserve the safety of our food supply.

Amaranth
Amaranthus species

Golden Giant Amaranth has lovely, sunny-gold-colored flowers and delicious grain.

Easy to cook, utterly delicious, and versatile, it's no wonder that amaranth has become popular in recent years. Like other grains such as spelt, quinoa, and millet, amaranth is a staple at health food stores and at some supermarkets. Americans are embracing its many uses and numerous health benefits. It can be cultivated as both a leafy green vegetable and as a high-protein grain.

I remember seeing "pigweed," which is another name for wild amaranth, growing profusely all over my childhood gardens. I always love seeing bright amaranth fields in the moun-tainous highlands outside of Mexico City, where it thrived when the Aztecs cultivated it back in the fourteenth century. Amaranth was a staple of early Mayan and Aztec civilizations, until the Spanish missionaries and conquistadors arrived and forbade the natives from planting it, which helped bring about the end of those great civilizations and led to dependence on the colonial government.

For nearly five hundred years after that, amaranth more or less faded into obscurity in the Americas, while corn and wheat became the go-to grains. But in 1974, the influential organic farmer and publisher Robert Rodale brought it to the attention of newly health-conscious Americans, who liked the nutty taste of the seeds. Since then, it's become a staple of vegetarian and vegan diets, and an alternative to flour for people who are sensitive to gluten.

Horticulturists also love it as an ornamental plant—the cascading red tassels of the Love-Lies-Bleeding have brightened many a cottage garden since the nineteenth century.

Growing Tips

Amaranth is by far one of the easiest vegetables to grow from seed, and it thrives in most climates, even those with short growing seasons. Two weeks after the last frost, sprinkle the tiny seeds onto the soil and keep moist. Within ten to twelve days, small seedlings will sprout. There will probably be far too many to keep up with, so thin them to about one foot apart for smaller varieties, like Joseph's Coat, Green Calaloo, and Thai types, and two to three feet apart for larger varieties. Amaranth is rather drought-resistant and doesn't need a lot of water. Most gardeners are able to harvest delicious greens within forty days or so after planting.

Pests and Disease

Almost all pests steer clear of amaranth, except for the striped cucumber beetle, which is a major threat in the early growing stages. Use organic controls to keep this beetle at bay, including spinosad, pyrethrins, and netting. Once the plant reaches maturity, it is thought to produce a chemical that kills—or at least deters—cucumber beetles, and the problem usually goes away.

Seed Saving

Amaranth is wind-pollinated, so if you want to save pure seeds, make sure to separate varieties by planting them at least a half mile apart. If you don't have that much space to separate them, just cultivate one variety at a time. To harvest the seeds, let flower heads grow until maturity and then, about eighty days after sowing, cut them at the stem and place them in the bottom of a cardboard box to store in a cool, dry place. Once they are dry, winnow the chaff from the seeds by pouring the mix, a little at a time, into a bucket placed three to five feet below. As you pour the seeds, the chaff will blow away, because it is lighter than the seeds. If you have trouble, vary the distance that you are pouring, depending on the speed of wind; sometimes it helps to use an electric fan. Store seeds in jars in a cool, dry place. They should remain viable for up to five years.

In the Kitchen

You can do so many things with amaranth. Many folks enjoy it as porridge, in place of oat-

Amaranth is very popular with gardeners for eating and as an ornamental. But it's also a highly beneficial crop when planted strategically. Try planting it near melons and cucumbers—as it will lure cucumber beetles away from them.

meal for breakfast in the morning. To prepare, bring five cups of water mixed with two cups of dry amaranth grain to a boil in a saucepan. Turn to low heat and let simmer for twenty minutes, then serve in a bowl with a drizzle of maple syrup and some fresh fruit, like blueberries or raspberries.

Young, leafy greens can be added to soups, stews, and stir-fries, or simply sautéed in olive oil with salt and pepper. On the Caribbean islands of Trinidad and Tobago, one of the most popular dishes is Callaloo, a hearty soup of pureed amaranth leaves, okra, and seasonings. And in Southern Asia and parts of Africa, the mineral- and folate-packed leaves are picked young and tossed into salads and stir-fries. The seeds are most versatile when ground into flour and used as the basis for gluten-free cookies and other baked goods.

Amaranth deserves its superfood status because it's loaded with protein, fiber, calcium, magnesium, and lysine. It actually has one of the most perfect balances of amino acids found anywhere in the plant kingdom, making its seed a complete protein. That's why it's so valuable for vegetarians, as well as in the developing parts of the world, where protein is often not readily available to everyone.

Artichoke
Cynara scolymus

Is there a vegetable more unique and fun to grow than the artichoke? This complex crop has been a favorite of discriminating gardeners for centuries. Part of why artichokes are so alluring is because they can prove difficult to grow in some areas. They love mild, moist growing climates and won't grow well in extreme heat or cold. So it's not surprising that coastal California, with its unbeatable temperate climate, dominates the artichoke industry. Nearly all commercial artichokes come from in or around Castroville, California, which some refer to as the "artichoke capital of the world." That said, plenty of gardeners in other states have success with artichokes, and I encourage you to give them a try and see for yourself.

When I was growing up, it was such an act of patience for me to wait for the first flower bud to appear among the young artichokes' leaves, but always worth the wait. The only thing more fun than growing artichokes is eating them—I vividly remember the first time I ate a fleshy artichoke steamed and served with lemon juice and salt. Heavenly, rich tasting, so fun for kids to open them up, petal by petal.

A favored crop of the ancient Romans and Greeks, artichokes have long adorned the tables of the wealthy and ruling classes. First cultivated in the coastal regions of Northern Africa and the Mediterranean, they're still very popular throughout Europe. In America, Thomas Jefferson grew them at Monticello in the mid-eighteenth century, but they didn't catch on with the masses until the early twentieth cen-

tury, when a pair of Italian immigrant brothers planted a few hundred acres of them on the California coast.

Growing Tips

The preferred growing regions for artichokes are mild coastal areas such as California, Oregon, and Long Island in New York, where temperatures usually top out around seventy-five degrees. Artichokes struggle to grow in hot climates. In order to flower and produce their chokes, the seedlings must be "vernalized," or exposed to cooler temperatures, to "trick" the plants into "thinking" that they've gone through a winter.

Artichokes grow best when started from seed indoors a good amount of time before the last frost. Then you can transfer them to the garden after a root system is established. About twelve weeks before the last frost, sow the seeds in three-inch pots. Once they've developed at least four true leaves, expose them to cool temperatures, meaning lower than 50 degrees. They need about twelve to twenty days at this cooler temperature. Artichokes are hardy to as low as twenty degrees, so vernalization could be achieved by setting out transplants for two to four weeks before the last frost. Otherwise, transplant the seedlings to the garden two weeks after the last frost, gently covering the root balls with soil, at three feet apart, in rows that are five feet apart. Though well-drained, fertile, and deep soil is preferred, artichokes can adapt to other soil types as well.

Growth can be relatively slow, so you should expect just one harvest, in late summer, in most areas. As the seedlings grow, mulch them with

Artichokes growing in a field near Santa Cruz, California.

compost or straw to keep pests and predators away, and keep the soil moist with regular watering. Buds will start growing sometime between 60 and 120 days after transplanting outdoors, depending on your climate.

Harvest buds when they are still very tight and firm; they'll taste bitter if you wait too long and they have opened really far. If you do wait too long, however, you'll get gorgeous, bright purple flowers.

To overwinter, trim plants back to the ground in late fall, following the last harvest, then cover them with a three-inch-thick layer of leaf and straw mulch to protect the roots from freezing (unless you live in a climate with a warm winter, in which case mulching isn't necessary). Exposure to excessive moisture is one of the most frequent causes of death for artichoke plants during winter. To keep this from happening, place a bushel basket or a medium- to large-size bucket over the crown during heavy frosts, snow, or rainstorms. Crowns can also be stored in pots. Keep them dry and cool, around forty degrees, but not below freezing.

Pests and Disease

Most people manage to cultivate artichokes without worries from pests. But when problems do arise, it's usually from slugs and snails, and the problems are minor and easy to take care of. To get rid of these pests, walk through the garden in the mornings and handpick them off by flicking the critters from the leaves into a bucket filled with soapy water. Or set a saucer of beer into the ground so that the edges are level with the soil—the creatures will be drawn to the beer, fall in, and drown. Another option is to sprinkle diatomaceous earth on and around the plants.

Seed Saving

To harvest seeds, allow the artichoke heads to grow beyond full bloom. Once the flowers turn brownish and brittle, cut them off with a sharp knife or gardening shears and store them in a box, at room temperature, for three to four weeks, until they are fully dry. Make sure you only let one variety flower if you want to save pure seed.

In the Kitchen

Artichokes are a great source of calcium, magnesium, phosphorus, and potassium. The tastiest way to enjoy them is to pick the tight, tender flower buds fresh from the garden, then steam them until the individual "petals" are tender. You'll know they're done when the petals can be pulled out fairly easily (about twenty-five minutes for a large-size head). Once they're done, drain the artichokes upside down on a paper towel and serve them on a plate with salt, olive oil, and lemon juice.

Asparagus
Asparagus officinalis

One of my favorite things to do as a kid was to take walks with my mother through the Boise Valley to harvest wild asparagus. Hundreds of canals crisscross this region, and the rich soil along their banks had sandy patches where tender green asparagus spears thrived in April and May. I'd dutifully study the banks and toss spears into a basket I'd brought along just for this occasion. Once we returned home to the kitchen, my mother lightly steamed the bright green spears and served them warm, with mushroom soup, or on their own with a little salt and olive oil. Twenty-five years later, asparagus is still one of my favorite vegetables. Nothing quite compares to it in early spring. Along with green onions, it's usually the first vegetable to make a debut at our table marking the beginning of spring.

A member of the lily family, asparagus first gained popularity in ancient Greece and Rome more than two thousand years ago. The word "asparagus" actually comes from the Greek word *asparagos,* meaning "sprout" or "shoot." Though it is native to the Mediterranean and parts of Asia, it was introduced to the New World by early colonists, who planted it in New England, and it has since gone wild across much of the country.

Growing Tips

When it comes to asparagus growing, there's good news and not-so-great news. First, the not-so-great news, which is that asparagus takes up to three years to be ready for harvest. That means that while you're watching those tasty spears peek out through the soil for the first year or two, you must resist the temptation to harvest them. They need to store up energy so they're strong enough to grow in a robust manner.

The good news? Once established, this perennial keeps producing for between fifteen and twenty years. If three years is too long for you to wait, buy "crowns" from a nursery. This cuts a year off the wait.

But if you do decide to grow asparagus from seed, soak the seeds for a day in warm water to speed up germination, and then sow them indoors in trays or flats, a half inch deep into the soil and two inches apart. Seeds germinate in ten days to two weeks at the ideal temperature of between seventy-five and eighty-five degrees. Germination will take longer if temperatures are outside of this ideal range. Sometime between ten and twelve weeks, harden off the plants (see sidebar on p. 54), and then transplant them into your garden at fourteen inches apart. You can also sow directly in the soil following the last frost, expecting the same speed of germination as mentioned above.

For best results, soil should be sandy, loose, and well-drained—asparagus won't grow if the

Though you'll often see it at farmer's markets and on the menu at restaurants, a truly "white" variety of asparagus doesn't really exist. Rather, white asparagus is achieved by hilling up earth over green spears just as they emerge from the soil. When you block exposure to sunlight this way, the spears are prevented from developing a green skin, which can make them more mild and tender.

soil is too wet or too cold. To help control weeds and retain moisture, mulch the plants with straw.

Once they're in full production, harvest spears once a day, and twice a day if temperatures are above eighty degrees. Keep on picking the stalks as long as they are growing fairly large. Stop harvesting when the new stems decline to about the width of a pencil. Let these grow into feathery fronds, which will nourish the root for the next year's crop.

Pests and Disease

Asparagus is not bothered by many pests and is a cinch to grow organically, because it will happily grow wild in decent conditions. Blue-

A handful of fresh-picked asparagus.

black and yellow asparagus beetles sometimes chew on the spears, but to avoid this, spray spinosad and use row covers (see sidebar on p. 60) in spring, and mulch the plants generously in winter. Aphids and other small insects will also occasionally be bothersome, but an application of neem oil or Safer Soap can help take care of that issue.

Seed Saving

This is a rather easy crop to save seed from, provided you are only growing one variety (otherwise there is a risk of cross-pollination between varieties). Let stalks mature beyond the typical harvest stage, until they are woody and fern-like. These feathery stalks will produce small red berries that are filled with medium-size black seeds. Once the fruit has dried, harvest and crush each berry individually with your fingers to extract the seeds. Be sure that the seeds are very dry—the seeds will be tough and firm, the berries will feel leathery—and store in a cool, dry place. They should remain viable for three years.

In the Kitchen

Asparagus is most commonly prepared steamed and sprinkled with oil and salt—it cooks very quickly, though, so be careful not to overdo it. It's also a perfect addition to stir-fries, soups, casseroles, and curries, and served raw with a dipping sauce. Eat asparagus soon after picking, as it is rather perishable. Nutritionally speaking, it's a powerhouse, a good source of antioxidants as well as vitamins A, C, B, and K; folate; fiber; minerals; calcium; and some protein.

Beans

Dragon Tongue bush bean—
a European favorite with striking speckled pods.

Beans are one of the most important types of food on earth and are packed with fiber, protein, calcium, iron, and potassium. Dried beans can be prepared in myriad ways and are a great, inexpensive pantry staple at Baker Creek.

This is one of the first vegetables I recommend to people just starting out, because of how simple they are to grow. There is a kaleidoscopic variety available, and Emilee and I eat beans nearly every day.

What we call "beans" are actually a diverse assemblage of related plants, all of which yield an abundance of large, high-protein seeds. They all belong to a single plant family, the Fabaceae family, which formerly was known as the Leguminosae.

Beans are grown for both dried seeds as well as tender young pods that can be eaten raw. Though at first glance it might seem overwhelming to try and understand them, due to the sheer volume of varieties and types of beans, there are

a lot of similarities between types, and they're all grown in a similar way. Here's a look at some of my favorite kinds.

Common beans (*Phaseolus vulgaris*), such as the pinto, red kidney, and green beans, are the most well known of all beans, and you've seen them in many different dishes, most famously the pinto beans in frijoles refritos; plump kidneys in a spicy Mexican chili; and green, purple, or yellow fresh pods sautéed and simmered in tomato sauce, or even in salads and with dipping sauces on vegetable plates. This type of bean originated in Mexico, the great center of early agricultural development, and the colors of the seeds never cease to delight me, as they come in blood-red, white, blue-black, green, yellow, and every conceivable shade of beige, tan, brown, and pink. Some are solid-colored, and others have stripes and speckles. They grow in one of two ways: as bush beans, which are stocky plants that grow up to one or two feet high, and as pole beans, which vine upward along a trellis, fence, or anything else vertical. Pole beans can grow anywhere from four to fifteen feet high.

The **scarlet runner bean** (*Phaseolus coccineus*) is another type from Mexico, so-called because of its bright red flower, which is showy enough to earn it a place as an ornamental in many gardens. These beans are *big*—they can get up to an inch in diameter! Some varieties have white or pink flowers, and the seeds themselves may be white, purple, mottled pink and brown, or some spectacular combination of all those in one! These beans should be trellised, as they are climbers. They prefer temperatures that are slightly cooler than many beans (they do best in sixty to seventy-five degrees) and so grow best along the coasts,

Red-flowered fava beans.
Attractive flowers are
followed by wholesome beans.

in the northern states, and at higher elevations. The seeds are edible at all stages, and the pods, despite their size and somewhat coarse appearance, are tender and juicy, perfect French-cut or julienned.

Lima beans (*Phaseolus lunatus*) are from South America. They work well in warmer climates and have flat, angular seeds. The Christmas pole lima can get very large. Limas grow in both pole and bush varieties.

Long beans (*Vigna unquiculata* var. *sesquipedalis*), are one of my all-time favorites. Related to cowpeas, long beans are hot-weather beans that are grown primarily as snap beans. When summer heat has shut down common beans, long beans will yield stalwartly. And the name is literal—some pods are known to grow up to three feet in length. Yet, for all their great length, these beans are still very tender and mild-tasting until nearly fully grown. Varieties include green, red, purple, and lavender colors that are stunning in the garden and on the plate.

One of the finest, richest sources of human food on earth, **soybeans** (*Glycine max*) are bush beans that are indigenous to northern China, where they were domesticated more than three thousand years ago. There are two types of soybeans: the "oil" type, which is grown for its oil content, and "edible" or edamame beans, which are also called soya beans, and are the best kind for eating fresh. The soya bean is one of the most popular of all beans in the world. On my travels in Asia, I've seen how important this crop is to the diet of more than a billion people.

Sadly, in America, soya beans have been genetically engineered and patented, and the safety of modern soy varieties from companies like Monsanto is in question. As a result, many small soy product manufacturers have started to use traditional varieties only. To make sure you aren't consuming genetically engineered soy, which may have unknown health risks, read the label before consuming soy products.

One of the most interesting beans is the spectacular **winged bean** (*Psophocarpus tetragonolobus*). Also known as the asparagus bean, the winged bean is native to New Guinea and is an important crop that grows abundantly in the twenty-five thousand or so islands that make up the Pacific Islands region, including the Philippines, Indonesia, and Micronesia. I tried this remarkable bean when I first visited Thailand, and I was instantly drawn to its great taste and its unique appearance and waxy texture. I've tried many times to grow winged beans here in Missouri but have met with only moderate success because they prefer areas with shorter days than we have here. This bean does well in Gulf Coast states and Southern California. If they have the right conditions, wing bean plants will grow up to twelve feet tall, flower, and also develop pods with four curious "wings." The pods are the main crop, but the stems, leaves, and high-protein tubers are also delicious. Before planting, nick the rock-hard seed coats with a knife or a file and soak them overnight to help germination along.

The **hyacinth bean** (*Lablab purpureus*) is grown throughout the tropics, mainly for its pods. If they're picked young, the pods have a robust flavor, but we recommend growing this bean as an ornamental. Lavish, fragrant, violet-purple or white sweet pea–like flowers bloom on its climbing vines. It's easy to see why these plants were

TOP: *Chinese Red Noodle bean—this Asian specialty has fantastic-looking, long red pods.*
BOTTOM LEFT: *Purple Podded Pole bean—this Ozark heirloom has delicious pods.*
BOTTOM RIGHT: *Hunan Winged beans—a nutty-tasting tropical bean.*

popular in the Victorian era. Be careful about this bean, because if it's not properly prepared, it can be poisonous.

The cold-weather-loving **fava bean** (*Vicia faba*) marches to the beat of a different drummer. Hardy to temperatures as low as fifteen degrees, this versatile bean withers in the heat. If planted in the fall, it has a good chance of overwintering successfully, at least as far north as Zone 7 and often in Zone 6 as well. Though the pods aren't edible, they do set high yields of medium- to large-sized beans, which can be dried for winter or eaten fresh in a puree or casserole, or added to soups.

Many health-conscious hippie-types would starve without **garbanzo beans** (*Cicer arietinum*), which are also known as chickpeas. These heat-loving Mediterranean natives have been culti-vated since before the days of Babylon and are an indispensable part of Middle Eastern cuisine, as they're the main ingredient in hummus and falafel. The entire two-foot-tall plant is edible, including the pods and the finely cut compound leaves. The seeds can be sprouted in a jar or col-ander indoors, and the sprouts are a delicious ad-dition to salads and stir-fries.

Growing Tips

With the exception of fava beans, all the types of beans that are listed above like full sun and should be sown one inch deep into well-worked, well-drained soil after the danger of frost has passed. If you haven't grown beans before in your garden, inoculate seeds with proper soil bacteria to enable the process of nitrogen fixa-tion (see sidebar on this page). (Inoculants are available at nurseries and hardware stores in the spring. They consist of a simple, organic powder in which the beans are merely tossed and rolled about immediately prior to planting.) It's best to keep the soil watered, though many beans can tolerate some drought. As always, weeds will need to be kept under control.

Provide support for climbing types with a trellis or by winding them around a nearby fence. Or you can make your own teepee trellis, with three or four long stakes, up to twelve feet long, depending on how much space you have. Lash them together at one end and spread them out at

When growing beans from seed, the soil doesn't need to be especially rich, because legumes can draw nitrogen from the air and convert it into plant food, which is a pretty amazing feat that few other plants are capable of. Beneficial bac-teria live in the roots and enable the process.

the other, teepee-style, then poke them into the soft earth. Any vining bean can be planted at the base of the "teepee," three to six seeds at the foot of each stake. The vines will climb and fill in, and they make a great shady spot for kids to play in during hot weather. If you're going for the pods, harvest them as soon as pods have grown up to about four to eight inches. Don't wait too long, or else the pods will get tough and stringy. After you do your first harvest, plants will need to be picked every two or three days.

Shell beans are beans that have reached ma-ture size while inside of the pods but haven't yet gotten their mature coloration. They're still quite moist at this stage and will cook very quickly. Harvest the entire pods and pull them open to reveal the young beans. Remove these and dis-card the pods, which will be tough and inedible by the time this stage is reached.

To harvest dry beans, if possible you should allow the pods to remain on the plant until they're fully dried. If frost or prolonged wet weather threatens, it is better to pick the pods when they're a bit immature and allow them to dry indoors. The seed is viable anytime after it has reached its mature coloration. When fully dry, seeds may be hand-shelled, or larger quanti-ties may be threshed out—which is actually kind of fun to do: Place the pods in a clean pillowcase, fasten it tightly with a string, put it on the floor, and stomp the daylights out of it. The pressure will cause the pods to pop open, and then you can dump the whole mess into a shallow pan or basket. The beans will fall to the bottom, and voilà, there you have it. (You can winnow the remaining chaff in front of a fan, or outdoors in a good breeze.)

Pests and Disease

Beans are occasionally bothered by aphids, cucumber beetles, and bean leaf beetles. When those pests arise, we recommend applying spinosad or pyrethrin sprays. One insect that can be a real problem is the bean weevil, which lay eggs on the beans when they are in the garden. The eggs usually hatch on the dried beans, often after you have them stored a few weeks; the weevils then eat many holes in the seeds. To avoid this happening, freeze your dry beans for at least five days after harvesting them—this will kill the larva.

Seed Saving

When it comes to beans, of course, the seed is actually the mature bean. So if you have beans, then you have the basis for future crops.

Depending on the species, you may need to isolate varieties in order to avoid cross-pollination. Common beans, long beans, and soybeans are self-pollinating and rarely get pollinated by insects. Ten to twenty-five feet is usually enough isolation between varieties to assure purity. Favas, limas, hyacinth beans, and runner beans are frequently pollinated by bees, espe-

cially bumblebees, so a half mile of isolation is recommended if you are trying to save seeds. The winged bean's propensity for crossing is a little unclear, but since there are very few winged bean varieties in the United States, crossing is probably not likely.

Planting other flowers nearby, such as lemon balm or basil, will often divert the bees away from the bean flowers, which really aren't their favorite, leaving the latter to self-pollinate and thus reducing the chance of unwanted crossing.

In the Kitchen

I could write a whole book about cooking with beans, as they are immensely nutritious and have so much culinary potential. Fava beans can be used either dry, as shell beans, or in ragouts—and they're also delicious in leek soup, minestrone, and in artichoke dishes (with or without fennel). Garbanzos can be ground up with lemon, tahini, and herbs to make hummus and falafel, or added to an endless variety of Indian curries. Long beans taste fabulous in stir-fries, as do the immature pods of hyacinth and winged beans. Common beans have myriad uses. One of our favorite methods is to make refried beans, which is essentially mashed and fried pinto beans with a little bit of cumin and sliced onion. To make a creamy soy milk, grind dry soybeans in water and drain off the "milk," which you can either drink as is, or process further to make tofu. Fermented black soybeans are the basis of the famous Chinese "black bean" dishes. The Japanese love to boil immature soybeans, pods and all, and then pop the cooked beans into their mouths—a simple and classic style of edamame.

Beets and Chard

Beta vulgaris

For delicious, mineral-rich roots and nu-tritious leaves, you just can't beat a beet. Chard and Swiss chard are also the same species as beets. The difference is that regular beets are grown mainly for their fleshy roots, and chard is grown for its tasty, colorful leaves and stems—which are larger than those of beets.

Nearly half of the world's sugar comes from the cultivation of sugar beets, which are one of the most popular beet varieties and consist of up to 20 percent sugar. My German ancestors grew sugar beets in the fertile plains of Colorado in the 1930s and 1940s. Unfortunately, these days, America's sugar beet production is mostly controlled by Monsanto. They offer Roundup-Resistant varieties, which are gene-altered so they can be sprayed with massive amounts of weed killer. Not only has this led to fewer independent farmers—like my grandparents—cultivating sugar beets; it has also contaminated traditional, non-hybrid varieties through inadvertent cross-pollination.

Chioggia beets are also called Candy-Stripe beets due to their sugary, red-and-white stripes.

NATURAL BEAUTY

In ancient times, women used the juice from red beets as blush and lip stain. You could even try this today at home. Slice the end off of a beet and apply it to your cheeks and lips for a natural glow.

Beets are wind-pollinated and their pollen carries for up to two miles. This means that if pollen blows from a gene-altered beet of one variety, it may carry to a non-hybrid variety and contaminate it with the foreign genes—which can never be separated back out. Written record of the cultivation of this plant dates back to the fourth century B.C., when Aristotle mentioned the red variety of chard. Beets were first mentioned six hundred years later, when Romans mentioned eating the root. For much of the last two thousand years, however, both plants have been mostly grown for their leaves. And according to ancient Greek texts, these were used as an herbal medicine rather than for sustenance. Beets are believed to be originally from the Mediterranean region, where wild plants still grow to this day, and the greens were once gathered by ancient Europeans as a popular "potherb."

Growing Tips

Growing beets and chard could not be easier. They work pretty much anywhere that has decent soil, light, and moisture, so an open garden, containers, and traditional flower beds would all work. You can avoid transplanting them, though, because they take cold weather fine and they grow pretty quickly.

To get started, scatter seeds and cover lightly with one-third inch of loosened soil. It's best to start beets when daytime temperatures are between fifty-five and ninety degrees, anytime from early spring to late summer in most areas. If you are growing in containers or raised beds, make sure the soil is at least eight to ten inches deep to allow bulbs sufficient room to develop. If you're planting directly in the garden, the soil should be well worked, deeply dug, and moderately rich.

Within seven to fourteen days, young seedlings will peep out through the soil. Once they reach three to six inches tall, or start crowding their neighbors, thin them out so that plants are spaced about four inches apart. Beets should be harvested when they are young and tender—no more than three to four inches in diameter. Otherwise, they may become woody and fibrous.

Keep well watered, but make sure to avoid excessive watering. Young plants can usually handle temperatures as low as twenty-five degrees, and mature roots will last through much colder weather if they are well mulched with leaves or straw.

Pests and Disease

Beets and chard are seldom troubled by pests of any kind. Occasionally, however, aphids will appear. Apply insecticidal soap. Likewise, if flea

Most varieties of chard will survive in warm areas when other greens have already withered and turned yellow from the summer's heat—and they're cold-hardy enough to overwinter in many areas.

beetles become pesky, spray alternating applications of spinosad and neem oil, or apply a floating row cover (see sidebar on p. 60). The cutworm sometimes severs the leaves and stems of very young seedlings at ground level, but organic controls are inconsistent in treating this.

Seed Saving

Start beets for seed saving in mid-summer or early autumn, so that the roots will have grown to at least medium-size before the first frost. Once winter arrives, the goal is to keep the roots alive until spring.

Beets are notorious for crossing with other beet and chard varieties. They need at least two miles of isolation to ensure purity. So if you're going to save beet seeds, just grow one kind. Most people aren't going to be saving beet seeds anyway, so this won't be much of a problem, since beets grown for eating are usually harvested long before they flower. (If you do live in an area where sugar beets are grown for seed, just be aware of their propensity toward wind pollination.)

To overwinter beets in a mild climate, just leave them in the ground, covered with a few inches of mulch. In colder northern climates,

Sasha just picked a big Yellow Mangel beet.

where temps often drop below ten degrees, there are two options. Before the ground freezes, you can cut off the leafy tops at about a half inch from the top of the root, then place the roots into a wood or heavy cardboard box filled with sand or sawdust—make sure the roots are separate and not touching each other—and store in a cool, humid place. A root cellar is ideal, though most people won't have access to one, in which case a medium- to large-size ice chest or cooler will suffice. Keep the temperature between thirty-three and forty degrees and the humidity around 95 percent for long storage. Another option, for moderately cold climates, is to leave the roots in the garden but cover them with a generous layer of leaves or straw, which should be pulled back in early spring, two to four weeks before the last frost date, so plants can start growing again. Whichever method of overwintering you use, once the weather warms and the roots are back in the ground, they will quickly send up tall flower stalks that will eventually yield lots of seeds. Harvest the seed heads, stalks and all, by hand when they are a light tan color, dry them inside for a week or so, then strip the seeds from the stalk and store them in a cool, dry place. Beet seed should remain viable for approximately five years.

In the Kitchen

One of the persnickety things about beets is the fact that they bleed during cooking; they'll stain your fingertips, your apron, and the other food they're cooked with. They can be steamed, roasted, baked, eaten raw, deep-fried, or dried in the oven as "beet chips." After cooking, their skins slip off easily.

The first beets of spring are a glorious tonic to us after long winters—never do roots taste so sweet and delicious. I always grew the standard red beets like Detroit Dark Red, and then I discovered the colored varieties that grow in yellow and white, and the stunning striped Chioggia from Italy. The only bad beet memory I have is from childhood, when my well-meaning aunt or grandmother would prepare a mountain of pickled beets. Even now as a full-fledged beet lover, I find pickled beets sour and foul-tasting. I've always wondered what would compel someone to turn such a tasty vegetable into such an epicurean monstrosity.

There is no doubt that the beet is one of the healthiest vegetables—our ancestors used them as a cure for myriad ailments. And indeed, beets are loaded with folic acid, potassium, calcium, betacyanin, iodine, sulfur, and vitamins B1, B2, and C.

It is their sweetness and earthy flavor that makes me crave beets almost daily. The greens can be prepared much like spinach, in a crisp salad or blanched and served on crostini with roasted beet roots, drizzled with balsamic vinegar, lemon juice, pepper, and fresh herbs. Beets also taste delicious grilled. Slice the roots in half, brush them with olive oil or walnut oil, and grill them for eight to ten minutes on each side, then sprinkle more oil and some salt on them.

My favorite variety is the Golden beet, which is a beautiful golden yellow. These beets are particularly great because, unlike regular red beets, they don't turn everything they touch crimson. Their leaves are tasty when lightly steamed and served with a little bit of fried garlic and shallots. We like to grow all different colors of beets—then serve them sliced and arranged for a marvelous display.

Broccoli

Brassica oleracea var. *botrytis*

I love broccoli, and over the years, I've eaten a ton of it. This cool-weather crop resembles a green-headed cauliflower, but it's faster and easier to grow than its ivory-hued cousin. A member of the cabbage family—like turnips and Brussels sprouts—the tall, hardy broccoli plant finds its origins in the Mediterranean and became popular in America after World War I, when a pair of Italian immigrant brothers, Stefano and Andrea D'Arrigo, brought it from Sicily to San Jose, California.

In 1922, they shipped it to Boston's North End to see how people responded in the restaurants and markets—it was accepted enthusiastically by the neighborhood's burgeoning Italian community. It started appearing in seed catalogs, along with meticulous explanations of what it was and how to prepare it, since most gardeners were seeing it for the first time. From there,

Calabrese broccoli is a standard old-time strain that has superb taste.

the broccoli business boomed, and within fifty years it was the vegetable of choice for health-conscious consumers and widely recommended by health professionals as one of the most beneficial vegetables available.

We love broccoli and eat more than our fair share of it at Baker Creek. Plant a little and you will find it easy to grow anywhere there is cool weather and a decent amount of sunshine.

Growing Tips

Sow broccoli seeds indoors six to eight weeks before the last frost, in trays or cups, and cover with a quarter inch of potting soil. After the plants are five to seven inches tall, set them into the garden about twenty inches apart. We set plants out before the last frost because we want to eat the broccoli before the pests do, and getting them into the garden early allows us to beat the insects to the harvest.

Young broccoli plants can usually take a light frost, but if you are expecting a hard freeze, cover them with a blanket, newspaper, or an upside-down bucket—anything, really, that will help protect them from the cold snap—as a precaution. In my garden I set broccoli seedlings outside four weeks before the final spring frost. It is very important to grow broccoli in cooler temperatures, because it won't thrive in the hot summer—so plant it in the spring or fall in most areas. Gardeners who live in cooler coastal climates can sometimes plan for year-round harvests, but far-northern climates may only be able to do one cycle, in the summer. Broccoli likes rich soil, so we spread two inches of composted poultry manure over the ground and mix it into the soil before planting. If poultry manure isn't avail-

Original varieties of broccoli only produced small flowering shoots—as opposed to the large-headed, modern kinds that we know today. An old sprouting broccoli variety called the Early Purple Sprouting is finding favor again with chefs and home cooks who love the little florets, which have unique zip and crisp flavor that newer hybrids just can't match.

able to you, any other kind of manure or compost will do.

To harvest, cut the heads when they are still tight and compact, with no opened flowers, sixty to one hundred days after setting plants outdoors. After you harvest the central head, side shoots will often appear in the following four to six weeks to produce smaller heads that can be harvested each week. The entire harvest period typically runs from forty to eighty days, depending on where you live (areas in milder climates will produce for a longer time).

Pests and Disease

There are myriad biting and chewing beetles, worms, aphids, and other creatures that love broccoli. But I can't blame them—it is so delicious! To keep the little critters from feasting,

BROCCOLI TIP

Most people just prepare the florets, but the entire broccoli plant is actually edible. You can cook the leaves like cabbage (see Cabbage, p. 106). So don't let anything go to waste.

here's a good trick: Most insects don't hatch until after the weather is warm and hospitable, so plant broccoli as early as possible after winter starts to ease up. Secondly, never plant a brassica in the same area of the garden year after year. Always rotate on a three-year cycle (see p. 59). If you still have problems, use a floating row cover (see sidebar on p. 60) and spray with spinosad and diatomaceous earth.

Seed Saving

Sometimes when broccoli is planted early, it goes to seed in the first summer, but often it's a biennial crop that goes to seed in its second season. It will cross with other members of the cabbage family, so if you are saving seed, be sure to isolate your crop by at least a half mile from other flowering brassica varieties.

Overwintering for seed production is easy in mild or warm climates, but much more difficult in cold zones and the north. If you live in an area with winter temperatures that drop below twenty degrees, keep plants from freezing by transferring them into a cold frame, an unheated garage, or a greenhouse before the first hard frost. In springtime, once the hard frosts are past, you can replant the broccoli plants (they will be quite large by then) in the garden. Eventually they will send up shoots of cheery, four-petaled flowers that will yield slim, pointy seedpods. Harvest seeds after the seedpods have become a golden-brown color, and store them in a cool, dry place. Broccoli seeds should last for about five years.

In the Kitchen

Though it can be creamed, as in broccoli soup, or eaten raw sliced into salads or as a crudité with a dipping sauce, broccoli shines best when it is lightly steamed. The secret to this vegetable is to not overcook it. The florets should still be crisp and bright green when you're finished cooking, rather than soft and pale green. My favorite way to prepare broccoli is to cook it like the Chinese do: In a wok, heat up sesame oil, soy sauce, sweet-chili sauce, and six or seven large cloves of minced garlic, and cook the broccoli in the mixture for six to eight minutes. I also love it steamed with olive oil and sea salt. The best part about broccoli is that it contains more than ten vitamins, loads of minerals, and is also fairly high in protein.

Brussels Sprouts

Brassica oleracea var. *gemmifera*

Brussels sprouts are thought to be a relatively new vegetable. They were first documented in 1587, although some authorities believe them to have been around much longer. They are yet another member of the amazing brassica family, which also gives us cabbage, broccoli, and cauliflower. The "sprouts" look like tiny cabbage heads that are usually smaller than two inches wide and which grow abundantly up a main stem. They do indeed hail from Brussels, which is the capital of the small country of Belgium. In America, Brussels sprouts are a popular side at Thanksgiving, and they first reached this land when French settlers brought them to Louisiana, where the cool, mild winters are ideal for growing Brussels sprouts.

Growing Tips

This cool-season biennial yields "sprouts" the first year, about four months after sowing. Brussels sprouts will taste odd and strong if they're grown in hot weather, so it's best to plant them as a fall and winter crop, unless you live somewhere with a mild climate.

Sow in early to mid-summer so that they will be able to mature in cool weather. Mild frosts improve the flavor of this crop. Plant one-quarter to one-half inch deep in well-drained, moist soil. Thin or transplant seedlings to stand about two feet apart in the row. As Brussels sprouts grow, sprouts form on the stem, and the plants will look like a mini tree with tiny cabbages growing on it. Smaller sprouts taste best. The average yield for Brussels sprouts is between one and two pounds per plant.

Pests and Disease

The usual brassica pests afflict Brussels sprouts. Eliminate aphids with a strong jet of water from the garden hose, or spray insecticidal soap or neem oil. To take care of cabbage loopers and other caterpillars, spray spinosad or Bt spray upon discovery, before they get a foothold.

Seed Saving

Brussels sprouts are a biennial that blooms in its second year. They will cross with other members of the brassica family, including cabbage, kale, cauliflower, and broccoli, so make sure to keep them away from those crops if you want to save Brussels sprouts seeds. Follow the seed saving guidelines for cabbage (see p. 107). If stored properly, Brussels sprouts seeds are viable for five years.

In the Kitchen

Brussels sprouts get a bad rap because in the past, people tended to overcook them. But sautéed and roasted with some hot sauce and salt and pepper, with a squirt of lime—they're dynamite. To prepare as a side, sauté the sprouts in a little olive oil over medium heat for three minutes, then pop them into an oven that's been preheated to 400 degrees. Roast them for 15 to 20 minutes, or until they are bright green. Season with salt and pepper and hot sauce, to taste. Delicious.

Long Island Improved Brussels sprouts are perfect when roasted with olive oil.

Cabbage
Brassica oleracea var. *capitata*

Cabbage is thought to have been carried by the Celts, in its original form, from western Asia throughout Europe on their migrations, and early versions measured as big as one foot across. I love growing hearty-tasting green and deep purple varieties. It's one of the most beautiful crops in the garden. It's also great because it stores for months and provides us with fresh food throughout the winter and well into early spring. I think that more people should grow cabbage.

There are two main types—flat-leaved and savoy (crinkle-leaved)—but they both taste pretty similar. Cabbage has historically been popular with people of modest incomes. This is partly because the odd odor it gives off when it's cooking made it less appealing to the wealthy, and partly because it's inexpensive and easy to cultivate even in less-than-perfect growing conditions. In ancient times, Roman soldiers carried cabbage as sustenance during battle and also used the leaves to bind wounds—the leaves contain the amino acid glutamine, which is an anti-inflammatory.

Growing Tips

Cabbage tastes best when it is grown in cool temperatures and will probably not thrive if it is grown in very hot areas where daytime temperatures don't dip below seventy degrees.

Start seeds indoors in pots, in an area with full sun, eight to twelve weeks before the last frost of spring. Transplant seedlings into the garden when they have four to six true leaves, two to four weeks before the last frost.

Pick a spot that gets full sun and has rich, moist soil, and plant seedlings twelve to eighteen inches apart, in rows that are two to three feet apart. Apply a layer of mulch after transplanting to minimize weeds and conserve soil moisture. After the plants have grown outside for a couple of months, the head begins to form at the center. At this stage, if the plants are suddenly soaked, as with an unusually heavy rain, the inner leaves will grow faster than the outer leaves can accommodate, and splitting of the heads will be the result. Split heads are still okay to eat, but they don't keep well. Avoid letting your cabbage split by grasping the entire plant by its head and turning one quarter turn, ninety degrees, clockwise in the soil after a heavy rain. This breaks some of the roots just enough to slow the growth down.

Harvest the head by cutting the heavy central stem with a sharp knife and allowing as many leaves as possible to remain on the stem. Leave the remaining stem in place in the soil. Occasionally, a small secondary head will form, for a second harvest.

Cabbage may be grown in late summer and fall for fall harvest and winter storage. Late types like Late Flat Dutch and Perfection Drumhead are ideal for this use. The same method is followed for growing these late varieties: Just make sure to start the seed in June, before the weather gets so hot that germination is inhibited. Alternately, seeds can be started in an air-conditioned room with temps of around seventy degrees.

Pests and Diseases

Aphids are a major pest for cabbage, though they do more harm to the appearance of the plant than to the actual cabbage itself. Use insecticidal soap or neem oil on them. To get rid of caterpillar-type pests, like the bright green-and-white cabbage looper, which appears early in the season and has a telltale "hump" in the middle of its body, use Bt spray. If red-and-black harlequin bugs appear, carefully remove them by hand and dispose of them in soapy water.

But keep in mind that row covers (see sidebar on p. 60) are always the best for cabbage— you won't have any pests at all if you put up row covers after planting.

Seed Saving

Cabbage must be overwintered before it blooms and sets seed. If you live in an area with moderately cold winters, then you need to transport the plants from the garden, roots and all, and store them in moist sand, in a cold environment like a root cellar or an unheated room—the plants must be kept cool (below forty degrees) but really shouldn't freeze, either.

As winter wanes, four to six weeks before the final frost, replant cabbage plants in the garden. If the head is still intact, make a deep, X-shaped cut in the top of it so that the seed stalk has an easy path to poke up through the head as it grows.

The flower stalk will emerge through this cut and grow four to five feet in height, before setting on hundreds of four-petaled yellow flowers. These will eventually turn into long, slim, pointed seedpods, which can be picked individually, when they turn brown but before they split open. (Otherwise, the seed will be scattered and lost.) For larger amounts, the entire seed head is cut off near the ground, carried indoors, and hung upside down. A sheet or tarp is placed un-derneath. Then, as the seed heads mature and dry, they will split open and drop the seeds onto the sheet, where they are easily gathered. After a final indoor drying period of seven to fourteen days, store the seeds in a jar, envelope, or plastic bag. Cabbage seeds will last for five years.

In the Kitchen

This is one of the most used vegetables in our kitchen, being easy both to grow and to store. It lends itself to a variety of delicious dishes and salads; you can use it to make sauerkraut, and it is also great fried or just steamed. This vegetable is a good source for vitamins, which vary a little depending on the color.

Savoy di Verona cabbages have unique, purple-tinged heads.

Carrots
Daucus carota

Atomic Red is my favorite carrot variety for cooking.

There are only a few vegetables that taste delicious—and look colorful—even in the dead of winter, and carrots are one of them. One of our tastiest traditions during winters in Oregon was roasting carrots over an open fire. We ate them right in the field, in the afternoons on winter days, roasting them in the coals. Just the basics—food, fire, and eating. Think rustic, no seasonings, no utensils, just dirty, earthy fingers and carrots cooked on the ground and eaten with delight.

Though the orange variety is most common in America, there are also purple, red, white, and yellow carrots. The darker colors contain even higher amounts of bioflavenoids than the orange ones. Red and purple varieties are said to be the oldest and are native to Afghanistan circa the tenth century A.D. It wasn't until the seventeenth century, when plant breeders in the Netherlands began working with them, that orange carrots were developed. Purple and red carrots are most commonly found these days throughout India, Japan, and other parts of Asia, and they have recently begun popping up in markets around

America and Europe, where chefs and home gardeners like their crisp, rich taste and the pop of color they bring to the table, as well as the standard nutritional benefits of carrots, which include immunity-boosting beta-carotenoids, potassium, and vitamins C and K.

Growing Tips

Carrots are a cool-season crop, so they should be planted in spring or fall in most areas. They germinate within two weeks in a soil temperature of fifty degrees. In hot climates, try starting them in March or April and again in September. In colder areas they may grow throughout the summer. To overwinter in northern climates, cover the roots with a thick layer of straw or leaves to help prevent them from freezing.

Carrots will work well in small gardens, but keep in mind that long, slender carrots, like St. Valery or Berlicum varieties that are commonly seen in supermarkets, need very deep, loose soil (twelve to sixteen inches deep) that is free from rocks and filled with humus. If your soil isn't quite deep or loose enough, try shorter and rounder varieties, like Tonda di Parigi, which is round and harvested at one to two inches in diameter, or Chantenay Red Core, which is a short, stump-rooted variety.

To start from seed, sprinkle the tiny seeds over well-worked, loosened earth and cover with a very fine layer of soil. One of the most important things about growing carrots is to avoid heavily watering the delicate seeds during germination. Mist the soil lightly instead, and keep it uniformly moist until tiny sprouts appear. Growth may be slow at first, so be patient, and once the young seedlings begin to crowd each other in the row, thin to three inches apart so that roots can grow larger. (The best part of thinning out the baby carrots is you can eat them as a snack.)

Pests and Disease

A variety of beetles and caterpillars are attracted to carrot leaves. They usually only cause negligible damage, but sometimes a dose of spinosad or pyrethrum may be necessary if you have a heavy problem.

In some areas, the carrot rust fly can be a major problem. The flies lay their eggs at the base of the plants and then their wormlike larvae tunnel into the roots. The damage they do won't be noticed until the roots are harvested, but the flies themselves are about a quarter-inch long, with a shiny black body, reddish-brown head, and yellow legs. If they land in your carrot patch, cover the patch with a row cover (see sidebar on p. 60). And be sure to rotate your crops the following year (see p. 59).

Cosmic Purple carrots are stunning purple-skinned roots with spicy-sweet, yellow flesh.

Wireworms, another carrot pest, are actually the larvae of the click beetle, a slender, hard-shelled brown grub that grows to be about an inch long. To combat these pesky critters, use row covers or trap them by placing a section of carrot or potato in the ground, with a portion just above the soil level, and marking the location with a stake. Every three days or so, pull up the piece of carrot, remove the grubs, and replace the carrot to catch another group.

Seed Saving

The carrot is a biennial seed crop, so it doesn't usually go to seed until the second growing season. To help this process along, leave some of autumn's crop in the ground over the winter, with a heavy layer of mulch on it to protect the roots from severe cold. The next spring, those roots will send up flower heads, which will eventually yield seeds.

In Montana, our neighbor Eddie Schmidt used to keep huge carrots alive through the frigid Rocky Mountain winters by putting down a layer of straw. An eighty-year-old man, he was so proud of his carrots, which he had grown in loose, deep soil, that he took great pride in taking us out to his garden, where he would push back the snow and straw to pull fresh carrots as big as two pounds out of the ground for us to take home.

If you live very far north, dig up carrot roots in the fall and store them over the winter in a cool location (such as a root cellar), in sawdust or sand, at a temperature between thirty-three and forty-two degrees. If you don't have a root cellar, put the carrots in the crisper drawer of a refrigerator, or in a box of damp sand or saw-dust in the garage, basement, or an unheated room. In the early spring, replant them in the garden and the roots will quickly sprout, bloom, and go to seed.

When growing carrots for seed, leave only one variety in the ground when the roots start to flower; otherwise varieties may get cross-pollinated by insects, and your seed will be mixed, unless you separate varieties by a half mile or more.

Harvest the seed heads when the flowers are yellowish-brown and dry but before seeds begin to drop from the heads. Put the seed heads inside to dry for a couple more weeks, then pluck the seeds free from the stems, discard the latter, and store them in a jar.

In the Kitchen

Carrots taste great raw but also work well in soups and stews and stir-fries. They're a nutritional powerhouse, packed with antioxidants, vitamins, and beta-carotene. Each different color has a distinctly different taste—I first tasted purple carrots in Bangkok, where they make delicious, violet carrot juice, a beverage and tonic.

At home, I prefer the extra-juicy yellow, purple, orange, and white varieties for fresh eating. Orange and purple types are perfect for juicing. All of these colors are also great for cooking, but red carrots are my favorite cooked, as these are extra flavorful, with a spicy taste that makes them superb in a variety of dishes or just roasted and spiced with chili and thyme and splashed with olive oil. The are also great shredded into carrot cake. The red color gives them good amounts of lycopene.

Cauliflower

Brassica oleracea var. *botrytis*

Though the sensitive cauliflower has a reputation for being a bit bland and high-maintenance, when grown and prepared properly, it can be a surprisingly interesting addition to many recipes. A member of the same family as broccoli and cabbage, cauliflower is similar to broccoli but has firmer flower heads. And unlike broccoli, which was rarely found in America until the 1920s, cauliflower has a long history in America. It was cherished as far back as the eighteenth century. In 1883, the New York Experiment station, which is an organization that conducted breeding experiments and trials, grew twenty-two varieties. In 1888, Massachusetts senator James J. H. Gregory grew twenty-one varieties.

The word "cauliflower" is derived from Latin, meaning "cabbage flower"—which is exactly what it is: a giant cluster of flower buds. The large size of these heads (which typically grow to between four and six inches in diameter) has been selected over hundreds of years of breeding by gardeners of Europe and, later on, America. It is said to be from the Mediterranean, possibly from the island of Cyprus, and has enjoyed long cultivation in Europe and the Near East. But it's most synonymous with Indian cuisine, in dishes like Aloo Gobi, various curries, and even cauliflower tandoori.

Growing Tips

Like other brassicas, this cool-season crop matures properly when temperatures are in the sixties, and it is great to grow in the fall. If you do want to try growing cauliflower in spring, start seeds indoors at eight to twelve weeks before the last frost. Harden them off for a week or two by gradually exposing the plants to more and more sunshine and wind, and then transfer the seedlings to the garden a week or two before the last frost date, at a distance of fifteen to eighteen inches from one another.

White cauliflower varieties need to be blanched. This is what it's called when you restrict sunshine from the curd, so that it grows pale and sweet-tasting. When the flower head is about the size of a small egg, start the blanching process. To do this, first make sure the plant is

Snowball cauliflower—this old favorite is still popular in home gardens.

fully dry (to avoid rot), and then gently gather the leaves around the central head and fasten them with twine or a garden tie. This keeps pests and diseases away, and also keeps moisture and light out; air will still be able to circulate, helping the heads to continue to develop.

Cauliflower doesn't handle excessive heat well, so make sure the soil is moist when temperatures go above normal for more than a day. Test for moisture by sticking a finger into the soil, and add more water if it feels dry.

Harvest cauliflower by cutting off the heads while they are still firm and taut but before they start to separate.

Pests and Disease

The same pests and diseases that bother broccoli also afflict cauliflower. To control them, plant as early as possible, use row covers (see sidebar on p. 60), and rotate the location of these crops every year, since brassica-loving bugs get very established in soil and can last through even very cold winters.

Seed Saving

It's difficult to save seed from cauliflower in extremely hot or cold areas. Folks living in milder coastal areas, like California, Oregon, Washington, British Columbia, and Long Island, will have the most luck saving these seeds.

The part you eat, if left alone, eventually develops into a large flower head. You could let the flowers go to seed, but it takes such a long time that growers usually overwinter young plants for seed production in the second year. So apply a thick mulch in fall (or lift and store, as for broccoli, and replant the next spring). Allow the plants to grow and bloom in their second year and then harvest seedpods in the fall, once they have become light brown. Extract seeds from their pods and store in a cool, dry place.

If you live in an area with winter temperatures that drop below twenty degrees, keep the plants from freezing by replanting them in a greenhouse or cold frame.

In the Kitchen

Cauliflower is an abundant source of vitamin C. Besides the usual white, this superb veggie is also sometimes available in striking colors like pale orange and lavender. My favorite cauliflower dish is Aloo Gobi, a flavorful Indian mixture of potatoes and cauliflower.

I also love the full, rich flavor of roasted cauliflower. To prepare, chop up the florets of a head of cauliflower into two-inch pieces and toss them with a mixture of olive oil, garlic, curry powder, and salt. Then roast on a baking sheet at 425 degrees for fifteen minutes, or until they are light golden-brown.

Chinese Cabbage

Brassica rapa

To me, Chinese cabbage conjures up images of the Orient, and little ladies in crowded restaurants cooking it up in giant woks. And indeed, these delicious greens have been on pretty much every plate of Chinese food I've ever eaten, in some form or other. Though they're native to China, they are also popular in Korea, Japan, and North America. The two main types of Chinese cabbage belong to the *Brassica rapa* species and are close cousins to the common turnip, although Chinese cabbage has a great variety of textures and flavors. I grow a dozen or so different kinds each year.

Bok choy is a loose-leaf plant that grows between three and eighteen inches in height, depending on the variety. Usually ready to be harvested within sixty days after planting, almost all parts of the plant are edible, including the green leaves, the crisp white stems (also called petioles), and even the flower buds. Tat soi is one of the tastiest kinds of bok choy, about mid-size and with smaller, smoother, spoon-shaped leaves.

Napa cabbage is a tender, nutty tasting head that grows bullet-shaped or cylindrical in shape. Known most commonly in America as a main ingredient for kimchi, its pale green leaves are blanched naturally by the puckered outer leaves, which are crinkled and deliciously retain sauce. All parts of this cabbage are both edible and delicious. Somehow they manage to be delicate as well as firm and possess remarkable crunch.

Extra Dwarf bok choy has tiny, tender heads that are delicious, and so cute.

Growing Tips

Being brassicas, or members of the cabbage family, Chinese cabbages are generally a cool-season crop and can be planted early in spring or in the fall. Both bok choy and napa cabbage are very hardy, though too much exposure to cold can cause premature bolting (blooming and going to seed), even among very young plants. So be sure to protect these plants with blankets or inverted buckets if you anticipate a cold snap.

Unlike most brassicas, however, Chinese cabbage does not like being transplanted, so you should sow seeds directly in the garden. Soil should be rich, moist, well drained, and worked very fine.

Plant seeds a half inch deep (less in very heavy soil), at a distance of two to three inches apart. Once the seedlings are peeping out of the soil, thin them to eight to ten inches apart, depending on the size of the variety, allowing more space for larger varieties and less space for smaller varieties. Apply mulch to control weeds and retain soil temperature and moisture.

Chinese cabbage likes full sun, but afternoon shade may prevent it from bolting in summer heat. Bok choy will be ready to harvest about fifty days from sprouting. Napa cabbage takes another few weeks, about seventy days. This is a great crop for succession planting, which prolongs the harvest. And it stores well in the refrigerator for three to five weeks.

Pests and Disease

Flea beetles and root maggots sometimes attack Chinese cabbage if left to their own devices. Combat them by using row covers (see sidebar on p. 60), which repel pests but retain some heat, making them ideal for very early or very late season extension.

Aphids can be blasted from the plants by a jet of water from a hose, or they can be killed using insecticidal soap or vegetable oil–based organic insecticides.

Seed Saving

Isolate napa cabbage and bok choy from other members of the *Brassica rapa* family (such as turnips or broccoli rabe) by a half mile, or cage the plants and hand-pollinate.

Save seed from a minimum of six plants at a time to avoid inbreeding depression, or the succeeding generations will become weak, slow-growing, and unproductive. Make sure to avoid saving seed from plants that bolted early—otherwise you're likely to get that trait again. Instead, save seed from large, well-grown specimens. Allow stalks to grow and flower, reaching about three feet in height. After the flowers fade, long, slender, pointed seedpods will emerge. When these begin to dry and turn brown, pick the pods individually, or cut the entire seed head and hang it upside down, indoors, over a sheet or a plastic drop cloth spread over the floor. The tiny seeds, as they come free from the pods, will fall onto the sheet and you can then gather them. If not collected in this way, the seedpods will shatter and volunteer seedlings will eventually appear in the garden, often at amazing distances from the parent!

In the Kitchen

As with most greens, Chinese cabbage is a low-calorie vegetable (a typical serving has just twelve calories) particularly rich in folate as well as vitamins A and C, and it can easily be steamed, stir-fried, braised, added to dumplings and soups, or used anywhere, really, that normal cabbage is used in recipes. I love steaming baby bok choy on its own, or sautéeing it with shiitake mushrooms, garlic, and a dash of hot pepper sauce. You can also throw the leaves into salads—they're much more tender than regular cabbage.

Corn

Zea mays

Corn is a truly American vegetable that originated in Mexico and was developed into a staple crop over the course of thousands of years from a wild grass called *teosinte*. It is one of the main botanical backbones of many cultures around the globe, for its taste, nutrition, and how easy it is to grow.

As a child, I loved peeling back the husks and seeing what was inside an ear of corn—it was like flipping open a crayon box and encountering that rainbow of possibilities. One of my favorites is Hopi Blue, a very dark, midnight-blue native strain that you can whip up into a tasty cornbread. Strawberry Popcorn has ears that look like giant red strawberries. I also treasure the multicolored ears of the Rainbow Indian corn for their sheer beauty, though I don't cook with it too often. As one part of the "three sisters" of Native American agriculture (along with squash and beans), corn was traded widely throughout North and South America long before the time of the explorers, and it was loved by Europeans, who quickly realized that it gives much higher yields than other grains, in a variety of climate conditions.

Corn comes in a spectacular array of colors, from blue-violet, blood-red, yellow, pink, and orange, to ivory, periwinkle blues, rich chocolate-brown, and even shades of green. And many different types have been used in different ways over the years. Sweet corn—so-named because its kernels are loaded with sugar—is the most popular kind of corn for eating in America. When corn is eaten on the cob, for example, it's usually sweet corn. Our favorites are Black Aztec and Golden Bantam. Dent and flour corn varieties, like Thompson Prolific and Pencil Cob, have soft kernels that are easy to grind up, so they're commonly used for flour and feed. Flint corn is the granddaddy of all corns. Varieties like Wade's Giant and Rainbow Indian are hard, shiny, and gorgeously glassy. Popcorn is also a type of flint corn.

As agriculture developed in the United States, corn quickly became king. And it's become the most popular grain crop produced in America. Sadly, along with this mass production, many traditional varieties have been lost. Older corns with a higher protein and mineral content fell out of favor because they had smaller yields and because they weren't as uniform.

This is a major problem, because the prevalence of genetically modified corn is leading to the demise of diversity. Most corn that is grown in America can now survive being sprayed with huge amounts of Roundup, Monsanto's chemical weed controller.

The big agribusiness companies have also created corn that actually produces its own toxic insecticide, so that if a corn borer eats it, it will get sick within a matter of hours and die off. This may be good for higher yields for the big growers, but there are many unknowns about the safety of such engineering. It is believed that GM corn leads to health problems in lab animals, such as lesions, birth defects, and cancer.

At Baker Creek, we are very wary of anything genetically modified—especially a crop that has its own poisons. We have been testing corn varieties for GM contamination since 2006. When we first started testing, we were startled

Zapotec Green corn is a delicious corn that was recently discovered in Mexico.

and disappointed to find that nearly half of our corn varieties had some degree of genetic contamination.

It has become increasingly difficult to find pure corn seed and keep it that way. We aim for extreme isolation of our varieties. And every day I try to find ways to educate people about this potentially dangerous technology. I have deep ties to corn, since my father used to grow acres of it on our farm in Oregon. As a child, I spent a lot of time running through the green fields and harvesting the plump yellow ears. I love the beauty, history, and taste of corn and feel connected to my Mexican ancestors by growing their native crop. I'm driven to defend it against patents, modification, and corporate control, and I feel gardeners have the right to pure, unadulterated seed, just like my ancient ancestors had.

Growing Tips

Corn is fairly easy to grow, but it needs a lot of feeding. To obtain maximum yields, make sure the soil is very rich and amended with manure, compost, or other high-nitrogen fertilizer. Soil should be deeply worked but not too fine—corn grows well in a rough seedbed. Plant seeds directly in the soil, as corn doesn't care much for transplanting. Place seeds a half inch to four inches deep—deeper plantings are best if you have dry summers.

Timing is flexible with this crop. You can sow it anywhere from two weeks before the last frost up until June, as long as you allow enough time for the crop to reach maturity before the first frost. Plant seeds six to twelve inches apart. Since wind is the main pollinator for corn, plant the seeds in a block that is at least four rows deep, rather than in a single long row, to encourage good pollination between the different plants.

Mulch or hoe regularly to control weeds. Corn can handle considerable drought because of its deep, robust root system. But regular watering is preferred, especially when tassels and silk first appear; otherwise pollination may be compromised and the ears may not fill out.

If you're growing sweet corn, and we recommend that you do, harvest it at what is called the "milk stage"—this is the point at which if you pop a kernel with your fingernail or a sharp object, milky-looking juice is released. If the juice is clear, the ear isn't ready to harvest. If no juice is released, the ear is past its prime for eating as sweet corn. (Timing is crucial, as the ears do not remain in the "milk stage" for very long, so it's best to check ripeness frequently.) All other types of corn should be dried on the stalks if possible, but in very moist climates, the ears may have to be picked green and dried indoors or under artificial heat; otherwise seeds may mold or even sprout right on the ear.

Pests and Disease

Corn is susceptible to a variety of pests and bugs. When they are young, seedlings are vulnerable to white grubs, cutworms, flea beetles, and wireworms. Corn borers and corn earworms infest more mature plants. For earworms, try injecting drops of mineral oil into the silks of each ear, just as they emerge from the husks. Keep pests in check by practicing proper crop rotation each season. You can also spray borers and earworms with Bt, or *Bacillus thuringiensis* (not to be confused with "Bt corn," which is a gene-altered type of corn).

Seed Saving

A wind-pollinated crop, corn is notorious for crossing between varieties. The chances of crossing does decrease significantly after you're farther away than a thousand feet, but varieties have been known to cross up to several miles away. To avoid inbreeding depression, it's best to sow fifty to two hundred plants at a time. Seed corn should definitely be allowed to mature and dry on the plants to get seeds of the highest quality.

If you want to save seed, make sure that none of your nearby neighbors are planting gene-altered varieties; otherwise your seeds won't "come true," or they may taste like bland, homogenized Frankenfood (plus, if you were to save such seed, you'd actually be propagating GMOs).

In the Kitchen

There are a lot of great ways to prepare this energizing, high-protein crop. Eat corn fresh off the cob. Grind it up into cornmeal and make grits or muffins. Bake it into cornbread and serve it as a side, with a bowl of three-bean chili. You can also toast it into corn-nuts, pickle it, and throw it into soups. Some open-pollinated varieties, such as Painted Mountain, are particularly high in protein. And of course, there's always popcorn! We pop our kernels in a cast-iron skillet on the stove and season with salt and coconut oil.

Corn that has been treated with lye is called hominy; the skins are easily removed, and the kernels can be boiled in stew or ground for masa, from which corn tortillas and tamales are made. This treatment makes the corn more nutritious and gives it the familiar flavor that is usually found in Mexican cooking.

Cowpeas
Vigna unquiculata

Cowpeas are a heat-tolerant crop that is once again coming into its own in the West, with cultivation having increased dramatically here since the 1980s. Indigenous to Nigeria, they were originally transported to the New World aboard slave ships in the eighteenth century. I find these little beans to be tastier than most common beans—with a finer, more earthy texture and a richer flavor. In America, pioneers often planted cowpeas early on in the development of a homestead, because they tolerate poor, acidic soil and can produce an abundant hay crop in as little as sixty days. I was first attracted to this beanlike crop after I realized that it comes in a showy rainbow of colors—including red, white, yellow, green, brown, black, and varieties with deep purplish and red speckled and mottled pods that add a splash of color to a backyard garden.

Growing Tips

Cowpeas are a great crop for beginning gardeners who have a bit of room to accommodate their vigorous growth. Bush types can be grown in rows two feet apart, but runner varieties have vigorous vines and spread out five feet or more from where the seed was planted.

Two to three weeks after the last frost, plant seeds three to four inches apart, about one inch deep in the soil. If you are planting in soil that hasn't grown cowpeas previously, inoculate the seed with the beneficial bacteria that help this crop add nitrogen to the soil, even while it produces a crop that can be removed from the land.

(An inoculant is an organic powder that you toss the beans in prior to planting.) Cowpeas tolerate dry conditions but grow faster with good soil moisture. Check soil moisture by poking your finger into the dirt—if the soil seems dry one to two inches below the surface, water the plants.

Space vining types, like Texas Longhorn or Monkey Tail, as much as five feet apart to give them room to run, or plant the seeds at the base of a trellis or wire fence to give them something to climb. Growing bush types is great if you don't have that much room or don't want to deal with vines. My favorite bush types are Six-Day Purple Hull and Old Timer.

The Purple Hull Pink Eye is a great cowpea to grow for snaps, because its pods stay extra tender and succulent for a long time. But most cowpea varieties are grown for dry peas—pods are allowed to stay on the vine until they're brown and dry. Then they're picked and the seeds are removed and stored for eating.

Pests and Disease

In North America, cowpeas don't have many pests or diseases while growing. However, if you are saving seeds for this crop, weevils and tiny beetles love to eat those seeds, so it is advisable to store them in a plastic bag, coffee can, or Mason jar, in the freezer.

Seed Saving

Cowpeas are self-pollinating, so crossing will seldom happen between varieties. We recommend separating varieties by fifty to one hundred feet.

To harvest seeds, let the pods grow to maturity and remove them from the vine when they

Purple Hull Pinkeye pods are great steamed as "green beans," not to mention beautiful.

are just dry. If the pods are left too long, they will eventually split open and the seeds will drop out of them. Fall precipitation can cause the seeds to mold or even sprout inside of their pods, so it's good to harvest pods just after the seeds develop their final color. Spread the pods out on newspaper or a drying rack, in a location with good circulation, away from heat and moisture. Allow them to dry until they pop open under slight pressure from a thumb and forefinger. Peas may either be shelled or stored still in their pods. Seeds will keep for four to five years.

In the Kitchen

Hoppin' John is a simple, traditional cowpea dish that is popular in the South and loaded with protein. To prepare, simmer cowpeas with rice and chopped white onion and serve with cornbread. Young cowpea shoots also make fine greens—they impart a taste that is similar to that of mung bean sprouts (a close relative) in stir-fries or salads.

Cowpeas are a high-energy carbohydrate that is loaded with protein, calcium, and minerals, along with modest amounts of vitamins B_6 and K.

Cucumber

Cucumis sativus

Richmond Green Apple cucumbers have tender, light-green fruits that are very sweet.

Mountains. Others believe varieties like Sikkim may be close to the original wild type, and it was the Sikkim variety that was first discovered by explorers of that region.

The cucumber is one of a number of vegetables native to India and has been cultivated in Western Asia for three thousand years. Pliny the Elder, the ancient Roman naturalist and military commander, wrote about how Romans grew cucumbers in greenhouses in order to make them available throughout the year for Emperor Tiberius. King Charlemagne loved them in France, as well, and in 1494 Christopher Columbus introduced them to Haiti, where they were traded widely. They were soon growing throughout much of North America.

Cucumbers come in many shapes and colors, and some varieties can grow up to two feet long. If planted properly, they're typically one of the first crops of summer. They've always held a

A member of the same family as squashes, melons, and watermelons, the cucumber is widely thought to be a cultigen, which means it doesn't grow as a wild species. Rather, it is said to have been developed throughout centuries of painstaking selection from a wild species in the foothills of the Himalayan

In Roman times, women wishing for children used to wear cucumbers tied around their waists to help encourage fertility. Other historic uses were as treatment for scorpion bites and poor eyesight, and to scare away rodents.

In Victorian England, many raw vegetables and fruits were regarded as unhealthful and even dangerous. Pamphlets urged people to keep uncooked veggies away from children, explaining that they could bring about weird diseases. Cucumbers came to be regarded as "fit only for consumption by cows," which ended up leading to their nickname, the "cowcumber."

prominent space in my garden. I love them for their abundant yields and refreshing taste—they consist mostly of water. This keeps them cool and moist and might be where the phrase "cool as a cucumber" came from. As a child, I grew Suyo Long, White Wonder, and little, yellow Lemon cucumbers, and I still love these old varieties—their distinctly sweet, tangy flavor is just not equaled in most modern cucumber varieties.

Cucumbers are easy to slice and eat raw in salads, and great for pickling. Every summer my mother used to fill our cellar shelves with jar upon jar of crispy little dill pickles, which we then enjoyed all year.

Growing Tips

Cucumbers work best when they are sown directly in the earth. After danger of frost has passed, plant seeds a half inch deep in well-drained soil, in rows that are eight feet apart. Space seeds six inches apart within rows. Once the seeds germinate, thin to eighteen inches apart to allow adequate space for vines, which will create a canopy over the fruits. If you want straight fruit, trellis the vines as they grow; otherwise the cucumbers will be slightly curved. A trellis also makes the fruits easier to pick.

This crop grows very quickly, spreading either up on a trellis or out on the ground. It thrives

Dragon's Egg cucumber is a unique Croatian heirloom that is white and egg-shaped, hence the name.

Hmong Red cucumber—this variety from Asia's Hmong tribe keeps for more than a month and is stunning in color.

in full sun, though in very hot or dry climates it will benefit from a few hours of afternoon shade. You can harvest the cucumbers at any size, but most often they taste best when picked young. Each variety has its own size at which the fruit tastes best—trial and error will help you figure it out. Harvesting early and often also encourages the vines to keep producing.

Pests and Disease

The cucumber's main predator is the cucumber beetle, and the crop will be susceptible to assorted wilts and blights if the beetles are not controlled. Watch carefully for these small, yellow-green bugs with either stripes or black spots—they will fly around the plant when disturbed. Early detection of this pest is a must, as you have to get rid of the beetles before they chew into the vines. Apply spinosad at the first hint of an infestation. If you can manage to control this beetle, cucumbers are pretty easy to grow.

Seed Saving

Cucumbers are pollinated by bees. To assure pure seed, isolate different varieties by a quarter mile if possible, though a few hundred feet is better than no isolation at all. Saving seed from cucumbers is very simple. Let fruits grow to full maturity. They'll be large and deep yellow or brown, instead of green. Harvest the ripe fruit by cutting or pulling it off the vine. Then cut in half lengthwise and scoop the seeds into a bucket or large bowl. Add enough water to cover the pulp, and let the mixture ferment for three days, stirring daily (be careful not to leave the mixture out too long, as the seeds might sprout). Once fermentation is complete, add a lot more water,

stir vigorously for two minutes, and wash away the fermented pulp by rinsing in several changes of water. Pour off the rotted pulp and bad seeds that float to the top, and discard. The seeds are clean when the rinse water is clear; the good seeds will sink to the bottom.

Spread seeds on a piece of cardboard to dry. After two weeks, put them into a jar and store in a cool dry place. Cucumber seeds should keep for five years.

In the Kitchen

Cucumbers are a healthy, refreshing snack that tastes delicious raw, pickled, or cooked into chutneys, stir-fries, and curries.

The first time I tried a cooked cucumber was in Bangkok, where cucumbers are fried with tomatoes, carrots, and other veggies and served over fragrant jasmine rice. Although steaming or frying cucumbers isn't done much in the West, both are actually pretty tasty—though there's still nothing quite like a home-grown cuke picked small and eaten right there in the garden. That's truly one of the joys of summer.

Pickling types have thin skins that allow easy absorption of brine or vinegar. Slicing types are large-fruited, with thicker skins. They can be stored longer than the pickling varieties. Greenhouse or "forcing" types tend to be even larger in size; some varieties of these can set seedless fruit without pollination. There are also several types of mild, sweet storage cucumbers, like Sikkim and Hmong Red, which are mostly from Asia, usually picked when large and brown, and are known for their ability to be stored for up to two months. Cucumbers are a great source of vitamins C and K and potassium.

Eggplant
Solanum melongena

Eggplants come in a great diversity of colors and shapes.

Colorful, versatile, and easy to grow, eggplant is a member of the nightshade family, which also includes potatoes, peppers, and tomatoes. It's known as *aubergine* in Britain, and *brinjal* in India, and is one of our favorite things to grow at Baker Creek. There are hundreds of different varieties that you can grow in every color of the rainbow, from white to orange to green to deep, dark purple. In flavor, they range from mild and sweet to acidic and slightly bitter. In shape, they range from pea-size, to small and round, to long and slim, to massive, four-pound Italian varieties that could feed a whole family. Interestingly, eggplant is not a vegetable—rather, its botanical classification is actually that of berry.

Eggplant originated in Sri Lanka and southern India, where to this day it is considered the "king of vegetables," and has been found in southern and eastern Asian countries for more than twenty-five hundred years. It remains a staple of Asian, Middle Eastern, and Mediterranean cuisines, with China being the top producer of the crop in the world, followed by India. Back in the days of the old Orient, eggplant was used in myriad ways. Ladies of high fashion used pigment from the shiny, purple skin to dye their teeth what they believed was a most beautiful shade of gray (it's hard to believe this gesture has yet to make a comeback in today's fashion world!). Eggplant is thought to have gotten its name because one of the early varieties of the crop produced light-colored fruit that resembled goose eggs. It was introduced to Europe in the Middle Ages in Spain (via Arab lands), where, in the sixteenth century, people called it the "mad apple"—it was believed that it would drive you insane if you ate it.

In the eighteenth century, Thomas Jefferson, one of the most well-known gardeners in the history of America, was among the earliest eggplant fans in the United States, and grew many different kinds in his gardens at Monticello. By the 1860s, several varieties of eggplant were offered by American seedsmen. Some people may have childhood memories of an unpleasant encounter with eggplant—often this is a result of the strong, acidic taste that is common to big, black grocery store varieties. But skeptics, take note: Commercial varieties of eggplant don't reflect the vast variety of flavors that are available. Go ahead and try a long, slender Oriental eggplant, and you'll enjoy its sweet and mild taste.

I planted my first eggplant back in 1990, and within a few years, we were raising up to fifty varieties at a time. Eggplant is easy to grow, ornamental, delicious, and doesn't attract too many pests. Upon traveling to Southeast Asia, I encountered dozens of new dishes using eggplant, and loved seeing it piled up high at street markets in every shape, size, and color.

Growing Tips

Gardeners in long-season areas, such as the Gulf Coast or Southern California, can sow eggplant seed directly in the ground. Seed may be sown in rich, mellow garden soil, no more than a quarter inch deep, when the soil temperature has reached at least seventy degrees. Farther north, eggplant is best grown from transplants started indoors. Start seeds in pots eight to twelve weeks before the anticipated date of the last frost. Plant a quarter inch deep in a soilless seed-starting mix. Keep your newly planted seeds on a bright windowsill or use a grow lamp. The area should be warm, at a temperature of around eighty degrees.

Seedlings often appear within one to two weeks, but keep in mind eggplant germination can be erratic, so maintain good moisture and a proper warm temperature, and be patient. Once shoots appear, feed them occasionally with a balanced, organic fertilizer to maintain good growth and productivity throughout their lives.

Before transferring eggplant seedlings outdoors, set the young plants outside for a few hours each day. This hardens off the plants and prepares their stems to withstand the elements—direct light, wind, rain—generally getting them ready for life outside a protected environment. Bring them outside for good when the weather has stabilized. This means mid-seventies during the daytime and at least fifty degrees at night. In the garden, set the plants into the soil two feet apart, in rows that are approximately five to six feet apart. Soil should be well drained and moderately fertile.

Sasha with some big Italian eggplants.

Avoid growing eggplant or its relatives of the Solanum family in the same space year after year, because that's how pests and fungal diseases establish a foothold. Instead, move your eggplant patch every year—and don't grow it in the same spot more frequently than every four years.

Eggplant needs a minimum of six hours of direct sunlight per day. Once planted, keep the plants watered and fertilized, stay on the lookout for pests, and wait for harvest. We recommend picking fruits when they are on the smallish side, so that production continues until frost.

Eggplants mature seventy to eighty-five days after being transplanted into the ground and one hundred and fifty days from sowing seed.

The fruits should be harvested when they are quite firm to the touch and glossy in color, but still technically immature—so that their taste is still mild and tender. If fruits feel flabby or if the skin has gone dull, you are probably too late, and prime condition has passed. In such a scenario, remove those fruits to encourage the plant to set on more, or leave them to produce seed.

Pests and Disease

Like other solanaceous vegetables, eggplant is commonly bothered by the potato beetle, aphids, spider mites, and in particular, tiny black flea beetles. These pesky insects eat hundreds of holes in the leaves, which stunts growth and occasionally kills the entire plant. Infestation with

Malaysian Dark Red eggplant is sweet and tender.

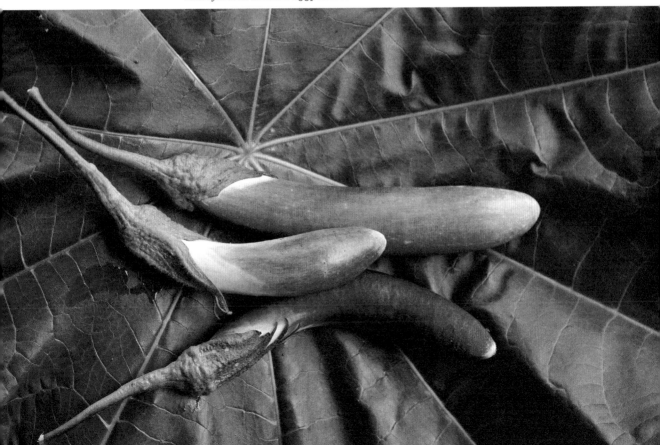

the potato beetle can lead to fungal diseases, like *Verticillium* wilt. The adults of many bugs can be carefully removed by hand, one by one, but many of these beetles can be treated with a good spray. You can also use spinosad, pyrethrum, cloth mesh, or floating row covers (see sidebar on p. 60).

Saving Seed

Eggplants are a self-pollinating crop, so insects are not necessary for the production of fruit and seeds. This is a real benefit for seed collectors, because it means that different varieties can be grown relatively close together without fear of cross-pollination. But bees will occasionally visit the flowers, so for the home gardener, we recommend separating varieties at least forty feet, which, for eggplant, is sufficient to maintain adequate genetic purity.

The fruit of an eggplant holds many small, soft, edible seeds. To save eggplant seed, allow several fruit on at least six plants to ripen far past the edible stage—this means the smooth skin will go beyond the deep, glossy purple or white color and change to dark yellow or yellowish-brown. (Another way to know a fruit is fully mature is when you see brown or soft spots, or push your finger into the skin, and if the indentation stays, the fruit is mature.) Once it's fully mature, harvest the fruit and grind it up the best you can, grating the pulp by hand or using an old-fashioned meat grinder. You can use a strong hand in this process—eggplant seeds are hard, smooth, and plump, and they don't damage easily.

Toss the pulp and seeds into a bucket and fill it with water, then stir this murky mixture until it separates. Once the pulp floats to the top and the seeds sink to the bottom, discard the pulp and clean the seeds in a water bath until the rinse water comes off clear. Pour the seeds onto a screen or large piece of paper, spread in a thin layer, and let them dry for fourteen to eighteen days. Once they are dry, store them in a cool, dry place. The seeds should remain viable for three to six years.

In the Kitchen

It's easy to fall in love with this delicious vegetable, because of its remarkable colors, nutritional benefits, low-caloric count, and versatility in so many dishes. The fruit can be a bit bitter until it is cooked, but it is a staple of vegetarian diets because it can be used as a substitute for meat in main dishes and is jam-packed with vitamins and nutrients: It's a great source of potassium, calcium, vitamin C, and protein. A little-known fact about eggplant is that it contains traces of nicotine—because of traces of nicotinoid alkaloids in the seeds, but have no fear; you'd have to eat twenty pounds of eggplant to equal the amount in just one cigarette.

Eggplant is used in a variety of cuisines, from Italy to Asia. It shines in Greek moussaka; sliced and baked in eggplant Parmesan; roasted and mixed with lemon, tahini, and garlic in baba ghanoush; simmered into delicious green curries; and stewed into a ratatouille with tomatoes, peppers, onions, and zucchini. At Baker Creek we are always baking eggplant in the oven or battering and deep-frying it in vegetable oil with basil and seasonings. We even have developed a recipe for a delectable eggplant cake!

Eggplant cake.

Endive and Escarole

Chicorium endivia,
Chicorium intybus

Endive Extra.

Endive and escarole are similar greens that are both part of the same family and grow best in slightly cooler weather; they will bolt in extreme heat. Endive, which is sometimes called frisee, has narrow, frilly leaves, while escarole has broad, flat leaves. Both crops have a bit of a strong flavor to them, but are delicious in salads and stews. The plants originated in India, and Northern Europeans grew them by A.D. 1200. Directions for using them appeared in English cookbooks in the 1500s, and in American volumes by 1806.

Growing Tips

This cool-season plant should be planted in spring or fall, or as a winter crop in mild cli-mates. Sprinkle seeds on the surface of rich or even mucky soil that is moist and has good drain-age. Rake seeds into the soil, just lightly covering them. Tiny seedlings will appear within a few days. When the seedlings have grown enough that they begin to look crowded, thin them to six to twelve inches apart. Control weeds by hoeing very shallowly or hand-pulling. A mulch is good, especially since the plants will be more bitter when they are drought-stressed, but mulching may encourage slugs in gardens already prone to them. Harvest by cutting the plant off at soil level with a sharp knife.

Mature endive and escarole leaves tend to be bitter unless blanched. If you choose not to blanch, harvest them at eighty-five to a hundred days, or whenever the plants look big enough to eat. Both crops are often blanched to make the leaves milder. To do this, when the plants are nearly full-size (two to three weeks before har-vest), pull the outer leaves over the heart of each plant and tie them together with string, a rubber band, or twine. The leaves must be dry when you do this, or the whole plant may rot. Or simply in-vert a bucket or large flowerpot over the entire plant. After seven to fourteen days, the plant will produce new white or pale green leaves that are delicate and mild. Colder weather concentrates the sugars in the leaves, making them extra sweet.

Pests and Disease

Cutworms attack young seedlings of these plants. Foil them by wrapping a piece of a drinking straw completely around young stems where they emerge from the soil, to act as a col-lar. Aphids can be controlled by blasting them from the leaves with a forceful stream of water. If you notice slugs, hand pick them or bait them with beer in shallow containers, nestled into the soil. The slugs are drawn to the beer and then drown.

Seed Saving

Endive and escarole are biennial, so overwinter them to obtain seed. They may sometimes bolt to seed the first year, especially if they are stressed. Don't save seed from premature bolters, though. In its second year, the plant sends up a stalk of lovely, sky-blue flowers that in time yield the seeds. Watch the developing seedpods, and harvest the entire flower stalk when the seedpods begin to dry. Crush the pods and sift them with a screen to remove chaff, or remove the seeds by hand. Larger quantities can be winnowed in a steady breeze or in front of a fan.

In the Kitchen

Brush endive leaves with oil and grill them. Squeeze the juice from half a lemon, and sprinkle salt and pepper on top and serve the endive as a side dish. Or you can use the leaves as a salad base: Toss with pine nuts, olives, artichoke hearts, oregano, basil, and a dressing of red wine vinegar or lemon juice for a tangy, Greek-inspired salad fix. These greens are high in vitamin A, iron, and potassium.

BELGIAN ENDIVE 101

Belgian endive is a chicory that is grown for its mild, pale green shoots, called chicons. It grows throughout the season, just like any chicory or endive, but the harvesting process is very different. To harvest Belgian endive, lift the entire plant out of the ground—roots and all—in autumn. Cut off the leaves a couple of inches above the base, and trim the roots back to just their major, central portions, leaving 7 to 10 inches of root on the plant. Then lay that in a box filled with moist sand, and keep it in a cool spot (below forty degrees is ideal) until you want to plant it again.

To restart growth, bring roots indoors to a warmer location. A dark cellar at about fifty-five degrees is ideal. The roots are forced into growth in the dark, so the heads are automatically blanched. The warmer temperature makes the plants begin to send up new leaves, which emerge from the soil in a very tight, pointed head that somewhat resembles the heart of a Romaine lettuce. You should be able to harvest them when they reach approximately six inches in length, usually a week or two after bringing them inside. These succulent, mild-tasting chicons have a bitter snap to them and are superb slowly braised with a splash of lemon or lime juice, or lightly steamed.

Florence Fennel

Foeniculum vulgare

Though it is closely related to parsley, dill, carrots, and coriander, fennel has a unique aroma and taste that is similar to anise seed. Indigenous to the shores of the Mediterranean, this herb is used regularly in Italian and French cooking and holds an interesting place in Greek and Roman mythology. Prometheus is said to have used a fennel stalk to steal fire from the gods, and the Bacchanalian wands that Dionysus and his followers used were actually giant fennel stalks. Ancient Greek warriors used to eat fennel before battle, believing it would give them courage. At Baker Creek, we love it because of its multiple uses and sweet, delicious crunch.

Fennel often thrives in the wild in coastal climates. When I'm out on walks in Sonoma County in California, I often see patches of it and grab a few sprigs for a sweet-tasting snack.

Growing Tips

Around the time of the last frost, sow seeds directly in the soil a quarter inch deep. Fennel likes full sun and rich, moist, well-drained soil.

FENNEL POLLEN 101

Fennel pollen is the most potent—and pricey—form of fennel. It's almost as expensive as saffron, and very popular in Italy, where they make it into pesto and add it to olive oil. If you happen to get your hands on some, sprinkle it into salad dressings or add it to a potato gratin for a special treat.

Thin the plants to eight to twelve inches apart once growth is vigorous. (You can use thinnings in salads or as garnishes, at any size.) When the bulbs start to swell, hill the soil or mulch around the base to blanch the stalks, which will keep them milder-tasting. Fennel is a great crop to succession-plant through late spring and again starting in late summer, to secure a continuous harvest. Apply mulch and water well to ensure large, tender bulbs.

Pests and Disease

Fennel isn't bothered by too many pests, but the larvae of swallowtail butterflies can be an issue for some gardeners. These chubby critters have huge appetites, and they love to gorge on fennel's aromatic, fernlike leaves. I always have a terrible time killing them, though, because I can't help but want to enjoy them when they turn into magnificent butterflies. . . . Gardening is about more than just food, right?

Seed Saving

It's easy to save seed from fennel. The crop is a biennial, so the first step is to overwinter the plants (although spring-sown or stressed plants may bolt the first year). If you live in a mild climate, you might be able to safely leave the fennel in the ground through winter, but if you expect hard freezes, dig the plants up to store in a root cellar, and replant them in the spring, a few weeks before the last frost. The plants will send up flower stalks resembling dill. Leave them alone until they begin to dry, at which point you should cut off the heads with gardening shears (do this before the heads shatter and lose all their seed).

Simply allowing the seeds to drop would

Florence fennel was developed in seventeenth-century Italy and is grown for its anise-flavored leaf stems, which are swollen and cling together in what looks like a bulb. This variety of fennel is delightfully versatile—the seeds, bulbs, and leaves are all so tasty. And it attracts many beneficial insects to the garden, especially lacewings, ladybugs, and syrphid flies, all of which are great because they help keep away the bad guys.

In the Kitchen

Fennel is a low-calorie vegetable that is high in antioxidants, vitamin C, fiber, and potassium and is also a great source of manganese and folate.

Add fennel seeds to Indian curries and chai, or chew on a sprig as a breath freshener after eating. Grilling sliced fennel bulbs makes them really tender and brings out their sweet flavor. To prepare, wash and trim fennel bulbs and remove the stalks and leaves (you can put them into a salad or soup later). Slice off an inch or so of the rough bottom of the bulb. Brush the slices with oil and put them on the grill to cook until browned.

save the trouble of collecting them, but beware: Fennel is considered by many to be a weed, and it is known to self-sow a little too freely if too many seed heads go unharvested in the garden.

Florence fennel is delicious, easy to grow, and perfect for flavoring a variety of dishes.

Garlic
Allium sativum

Heirloom garlic varieties are numerous and range from mild and almost sweet, to blazing hot and fiery.

Fresh garlic adds indispensable flavor that injects flavor to a variety of dishes. It takes a while to grow—between eight and ten months—but the flavor is much better when it's harvested fresh instead of shipped thousands of miles. I've always loved the rich, mellow spiciness and intoxicating aroma of this crop, and I appreciate that it's simple and fun to grow. The seeds for garlic are actually the cloves. When you plant one clove, it grows into a bulb with many cloves, each of which can be planted and cultivated into another bulb. This means you can multiply the size of your garlic harvest many times over within just a couple of seasons.

Garlic is a *cultigen,* or a species that isn't found in the wild, having originated in cultivation in Asia several thousand years ago. Unlike most cultigens, garlic very seldom sets seed, and it is therefore dependent on humans to cultivate and distribute it. And so humans have done, for millennia: Garlic is mentioned in the Bible and the Koran, and it was found in King Tut's tomb. It was traded throughout the New World by Spanish, Portuguese, and French explorers, and today it is grown across the globe. In India, it has long been used in ayurvedic medicine, to help with ailments such as asthma and bronchitis—though Indian people actually frown upon it as a foodstuff, especially high-caste Hindus, as they have historically regarded its pungent odor as vulgar. It is also a staple of Asian food, often prepared in tandem with ginger, onions, and basil.

There are hundreds of different kinds of garlic, but they can all be categorized as either **soft-neck** or **hard-neck**. Soft-neck is the most common type, the easiest to grow, and it keeps longest. Hard-neck garlic should be used shortly after growing because it has a thinner skin. It also has larger cloves. Hard-neck varieties are popular with chefs for their more complex flavor palette.

Growing Tips

Soil for garlic should be deeply worked, crumbly, well drained, and rich in organic matter. Plant plump cloves in the fall, for harvest the following year. To prepare beds, apply a three-inch layer of manure over the soil. On top of that, work amendments such as bone meal or phosphate rock to add much-needed phosphorous, and maybe some wood ashes for potassium. These nutrients are necessary to produce large, plump bulbs.

If you get a lot of rain in springtime, rake soil upward so that the beds are slightly raised (this facilitates drainage, so that the cloves don't stay too wet and rot in the soil). Push cloves into the soil with the pointy end upward and the blunt end on the bottom, at six to eight inches apart. I get them deep enough so that the top of the clove is barely covered by loose soil. Once they are all in, cover them with five inches of hay or straw mulch, which will hold the cloves in place throughout the winter months, while their roots develop (winter rain and snows will push the mulch down, compressing this layer to a thickness of one to two inches, which is fine). Young garlic shoots will poke through the mulch in spring, but little else will.

In order to get good-size bulbs, it's critical to control weeds, as just a few weeds will stunt garlic growth. Mulch helps, but you should also pull any stray weeds you might see. In the spring, green sprouts will emerge—a cheerful sign in many climates that spring is on its way. As the shoots start growing, put down a dose of compost tea (see sidebar on p. 55) and water regularly. Should the soil get too dry, administer a deeper watering. The green garlic shoots grow to between twenty and twenty-four inches, and then, at some point between early and mid-summer (depending on your climate and the weather, because it is always different), the outer leaves will turn brown and begin to die back. When at least four of those leaves have turned, it's time to dig the bulbs.

To harvest garlic, use your hands or a garden fork to gently maneuver a bulb free from the soil. Once you've dug them all, shake off the extra dirt and leave them to dry in a spot that's away from sun and rain, on a wire rack, for three to five days, or longer if temperatures are on the cooler side. Once the bulbs are dry, cut off the tops with gardening shears and store them at cool room temperature (fifty to sixty degrees is ideal).

Pests and Disease

Garlic has no pests to speak of, usually. Proper crop rotation is sufficient against the few diseases.

Seed Saving

For garlic, the clove is the "seed," so propagation is achieved by replanting cloves. It is generally agreed that the largest cloves planted this year make the largest bulbs next year. Store garlic that you want to hold for seed at room temperature, rather than in the refrigerator, because exposure to temperatures lower than forty degrees may cause cloves to sprout prematurely.

Some varieties send up shoots that contain many tiny bulbs, where a flower might be more expected. These tiny bulbs, called *bulbils,* can be planted and will yield true-to-type garlic eventually, but it may take two seasons to get large bulbs. So planting cloves instead of bulbils is recommended. These bulbils, however, together

In recent years, **green garlic** has become popular in gourmet circles. To harvest this milder form of garlic, pick regular garlic when it is very young, before the bulb is fully formed, when it resembles an overgrown green onion or scallion. The leaves can then be chopped up and added to stir-fries, salads, and pestos.

with the stem that supports them, are a gourmet treat called "scapes" and can cost up to $12 or $15 per pound in some areas. Scapes are delicious harvested very young (before they become tough and fibrous) and can be eaten raw, steamed, as a delicious topping to baked potatoes, or mixed into pesto. These intense little treats are beloved in organic food circles and much sought-after at local farmer's markets each spring.

In the Kitchen

Due to its robust flavor and seemingly endless health benefits, garlic is beloved around the world and has been called the "key to life." The rich, sulfuric compounds in garlic give it its distinct fragrance. One of the easiest ways to prepare it is to put a full head of peeled garlic cloves into a pan, add about a quarter cup of olive oil and a pinch of salt, then mix well. Cover the pan with a lid or metal foil and bake until the cloves are tender. Roasted cloves are also a delicious addition to pizza, pasta, sandwiches, and salads. You can also roast a garlic head and serve it whole as a vegetable in its own right.

Gouprds

Lagenaria longissima

Edible and ornamental gourds are some of the oldest—and most peculiar—plants known to man. Gourds belong to the same family as pumpkins and squash and are similarly low-maintenance and easy to grow.

Ornamental gourds are highly useful and have long been cultivated—long before plastic and metal were available everywhere—as bottles, bowls, birdhouses, musical instruments, and for countless other uses. As for edible gourds, Italians are fans of the slender, snake-like Cucuzzi gourds, which they eat much like zucchini. In Asia a multitude of long, round, pear-shaped, and cylindrical varieties are on display in huge mounds in markets from Japan to India.

I planted Italian Cucuzzi shortly after we moved to Missouri, and one thing I noticed right away was how vigorous the vines were, along with the lotus-like leaves; they not only grew through the garden and up the fence, but even high up into the trees, so we had tasty gourds hanging just above my reach. I also love the fact that this is one of the few vines in my garden that stays nearly pest free! But what really draws me to this plant is the delicious fruit, which is used like zucchini squash, but has a deeper, more intense flavor. It is well worth growing, as you not only get lots of edible fruit, but also, if you leave some fruits on the vine until late fall, you should have some hard gourds for use in craft projects.

Thai Bottle gourds are tender and tasty if cooked when young, or they make great craft projects when dried.

True gourds have very large seeds and white blooms (rather than yellow like squash) and bloom at night.

Growing Tips

Gourds can be fussy about germination. Sometimes they take up to three weeks to sprout. To help them along, make sure soil is warm (above seventy degrees) and well drained. I sow gourd seeds directly in the soil about a week after putting my squash in. If you have a shorter growing season, start seeds indoors three to four weeks before the last frost. Before planting, soak the seeds in water for about twelve hours to encourage germination and then plant them about one inch deep in soil that is rich and amended with organic matter.

The quick-growing vines will naturally climb over anything in their path, so be sure to give them space to grow and plant them twenty-four inches apart, in rows that are ten feet apart. Plant gourds in full sun, and make sure they are well watered.

Most gourds reach maturity in one hundred to one hundred and twenty days. Pick them when their stems are dry and brown. If you want to use them for craft projects or as carrying vessels, allow them to mature on the vines and remove them just before threat of any hard frost. Then let them dry, whole, until the skins are tough and hard like wood and the seeds rattle when the fruits are shaken. Be patient—large gourds can take several months to dry out completely! The skins will turn tan, but may show some black mold on the surface. The fruits can then be cleaned with a scratchy pad like the kind you use when washing dishes and maybe a mild bleach solution, which usually takes care of the discoloration and leaves a clean, buff-colored fruit, all ready for winter craft projects. If needed, the hard shells can be cut with a handsaw or electric jigsaw.

Pests and Disease

Though they are susceptible to similar pests and diseases as other Cucurbita family members, like squash and pumpkins, I've never had much of a pest problem with gourds. Their vines are so vigorous, they're almost impervious to insect assaults.

Seed Saving

It is very easy for bees, moths, and even cucumber beetles to cross-pollinate among the different varieties in this species, *Lagenaria longissima*. So if you want to save pure seed, just grow one at a time or separate varieties by at least half a mile. A minimum population of about fifteen plants should be grown to help avoid inbreeding depression (see sidebar on p. 71). Harvest the fruits as soon as their skin is very tough and hard (you should just barely be able to mark it with your thumbnail), though it may still be a rich apple-green in color. Then cut the gourd open with a very sharp knife and scoop out the seeds to dry.

In the Kitchen

Though they don't show up on dinner tables in America too often, if you pick the edible varieties of gourd when they're young and tender, they're perfect for a variety of dishes, just like zucchini and squash. Add one-inch cubes to soups and stews, or slice and bake them as a pizza topping. Edible gourds are fairly high in vitamin C and also contain a lot of fiber.

Ground Cherry

Physalis pruinosa

Chinese Lanterns are a beautiful member of the ground cherry family.

These unique, refreshing little fruits are also known as "husk tomatoes" and grow inside of a crinkly paper husk. Their taste is almost tropical, like pineapple, and they grow wild in fields and along roadsides throughout America, Asia, and Europe. As members of the nightshade family, they like growing conditions similar to tomatoes and eggplants. My daughter, Sasha, and other children get so excited when they encounter ground cherries—they love how each little gift is wrapped up like a piece of candy, just for them.

Native American tribes and early American settlers thought of these fleshy fruits as a delicacy, with their sweet-tart flavor. The high concentration of pectin in ground cherries means they lend themselves well to use in jams and preserves. I first grew ground cherries in my garden as a teenager, and I still enjoy having a patch of them in my garden each year. Often they never even make it into the house; we just sit by the plants and eat a few at a time.

The plants of the different species all look pretty much the same, with sprawling, bushy leaves, soft stems, and tan husks. All are close relatives of the tomatillo (*P. ixocarpa*), but unlike tomatillos, ground cherries are sweet enough to be used in preserves, pies, and for eating out of hand. They also taste delicious when dried.

Growing Tips

Ground cherries are easy to grow, under the same conditions as tomatoes and eggplants, but they prefer to sprawl along the ground, so refrain from using stakes or tomato cages with them. Start the tiny seeds in small pots indoors six to eight weeks prior to the last expected frost and cover just barely with soil. Keep them warm and moist and you should have sprouts in ten to fourteen days. Once the danger of frost has passed, transplant the tender seedlings into the garden, eighteen to twenty-four inches apart. Harvest when the fruit falls off upon a gentle touch—the calyx will be a golden-tan color, and berries will be a golden yellow.

Pests and Disease

Most gardeners have few pest problems, if any, with this crop. However, cutworms may destroy young seedlings. One clever organic remedy is to create a barrier around the plant by slitting a toilet paper roll lengthwise to slip over the seedling and nestle down into the soil. Other occasional pests include white flies, flea beetles, caterpillars, and spider mites. If we have problems, we apply insecticidal soap and spinosad to the leaves upon discovery of infestations.

Seed Saving

All varieties of ground cherry are self-pollinating, but they can cross via insect as well. It's rare that you'd plant more than one variety, but if you do, isolate each by two hundred feet to insure purity in the seeds. To save seeds, wait until the fruit is very ripe. Then cut it in half and squeeze into a bowl. The seeds will squirt out. Rinse the tiny seeds through a window screen, using the screen like a colander. Experiment to see whether the seeds wash through, and whether the pulp can be worked through also. Or use the fermentation technique, as explained in the tomato Seed Saving section (p. 201). Lay the clean seeds out to dry on newspaper for a week before storing. Seeds will keep for three to five years.

In the Kitchen

All ground cherries, particularly the Cape Gooseberry, have high concentrations of pectin, so they're a superb addition to jams, preserves, and pies. You can also add them to salsas and chutneys, or dry and store them to eat later like raisins. But I still think they can't be beat served fresh.

Ground cherries have long been used in Chinese medicine to help heal abscesses, coughs, and sore throats, and to bring down a fever.

Here are some of our favorite kinds.

Old-time homesteaders planted the **traditional ground cherry** (*Physalis pruinosa*) early on when they were establishing their farms, to get fruit in the early years, while other bigger fruits were still growing. Though it's small—this variety gets to only about a half inch in diameter—it packs a wollop of citrus and pineapple taste. While growing, the plants sprawl out a few feet, and when fully ripe, the fruits fall to the ground, tightly enclosed in their papery husk, which keeps them fresh for weeks.

One of the tastiest of all ground cherries, the giant **Cape Gooseberry** (*P. peruviana*), originated in South America, but was the basis of a lively agricultural industry in South Africa, hence the reference to Capetown in its name. These golden fruits grow to one-half to one inch.

Chinese Lantern (*Physalis alkekengii*) has stunning, reddish-orange husks and tolerates cold better than any other ground cherry variety. The small, scarlet berry isn't quite as sweet or flavorful as its cousins, but florists love the plants' tall, slender stems for the pop of texture and color they add to arrangements. The Chinese Lantern is also a perennial. It spreads rather aggressively, so do plant it like a vegetable, in a place where the ground will be tilled following its season. And collect all the fruits—don't allow a lot of seed into the garden.

Kale and Collard Greens

Brassica oleracea var. *acephala*

Nero di Toscana kale, sometimes called "Dinosaur kale," is a popular item at many farmer's markets.

I love kale and collard greens (which are basically the same crop with different names) so much that I grow them year-round. They belong to the same absolutely amazing species as cabbage, broccoli, cauliflower, and Brussels sprouts. What other species gives rise to so many diverse forms? It hails from Asia Minor and the eastern Mediterranean, and both kale and collards were known as early as classical Greek times (fifth century B.C.). Kale and collards are, in fact, more or less like the primitive form of cabbage. By Roman times all the modern forms of kale and collards were known, including the wavy-leafed types we now commonly refer to as kale and the smooth-leaved varieties now known as collards. The Romans introduced them everywhere in Europe, where they were previously unknown, including, possibly, the British Isles, whose climate suited the crop perfectly and where it became a staple. It was first mentioned in America as "colewort," about 1669.

The word "collards" comes from a corruption of the Anglo-Saxon *colewyrts,* which simply means "cabbage plants." "Kale," in turn, is a variant of the Scottish *cole* or *caulis,* which in turn derived from the Latin word for cabbage. (Incidentally, kohlrabi and cauliflower are names also related to these words, and the plants are related as well!)

These cooking greens thrive in chilly weather and can be harvested through December in many areas, and year-round in more mild climates. Lower temperatures make their wild, crinkly leaves taste even sweeter and more tender, but once the deepest of freezes arrive in winter and nothing is growing outdoors, there are

Morris Heading collards is a true southern favorite that is a staple on our table.

always bunches ready to harvest in the greenhouse so that I don't have to miss out. I just plain feel healthier when I'm eating this vegetable.

And indeed, this is literally one of the most healthful things you can grow. In just one serving, you'll get more than the recommended daily dose of vitamins A and K, as well as a ton of vitamin C, calcium, fiber, and protein.

Growing Tips

I grow kale and collards as both spring and fall crops. If you're planting in spring, start seeds indoors eight to ten weeks before the last frost date. For a fall harvest, sow seeds directly in the garden in June or July, and you will enjoy yields right up until the really cold weather of winter. In mild climates, they will continue right through spring.

Sprinkle seeds and cover with a fine layer of soil, which should be very rich, evenly moist, and well drained. They need full sun, so place accordingly. Kale and collards mature quickly, within sixty days, and grow to between twelve and thirty-six inches across, and between twelve and forty-eight inches in height. So thin them out to at least twelve to eighteen inches apart to avoid crowding. Keep the soil moist, and once the plants are growing well, add two to four inches of mulch to help maintain an even soil moisture and keep much-needed nutrients close to the roots.

Pests and Disease

Beware of the same pests that other brassicas are susceptible to. In particular, be on the lookout for red-and-black speckled harlequin bugs, which grow to be quite large (they can get as big as a pinky fingernail). These are the most disastrous and will wreak havoc on leaves once they establish themselves. The best defense is to provide good soil and keep the plants healthy. The only natural control we've found for harlequins is to pick them off by hand and drop them into a bucket of soapy water. Moth larvae can also be a problem—the cabbage looper moth is particularly fond of kale—but we've always been able to control them with Bt or spinosad.

Seed Saving

Kale and collards are insect-pollinated and therefore cross easily within their type as well as with other brassicas. If your goal is to maintain a pure strain for seed saving, take care to isolate this crop from broccoli, Brussels sprouts, cabbage, and other brassicas by at least a half a mile.

As biennials, they must experience winter's chill before they will throw up branched spikes of cheerful-looking yellow blossoms. Allow these flowers to grow, and they will give way to long, pointed seedpods.

Collect the seeds just as the pods dry and turn brown, by, picking the pods and shelling out the tiny seeds. Another method is you can cut off the seed head and hang it upside down over a basket or tub to catch the seeds, which will drop free as they ripen.

In the Kitchen

Curly kale tends to be more popular in the North; collards are a staple in the South, as well as in Africa. You can do a lot with these greens, but the most healthy way to enjoy them is to cut the leaves into bite-size pieces and steam for a few minutes, or until tender. Sprinkle the pieces with garlic salt and olive oil; a splash of lemon; or balsamic vinegar.

Kohlrabi
Brassica oleracea

A flowering White Vienna kohlrabi.

In the '60s and '70s, gardeners compared the peculiar shape of kohlrabi—with its stems jutting out from a giant round "root"—to Sputnik, the Russian satellite that used to hover over the earth transmitting secret data to the Soviets. Unusual though its shape may be, I think of kohlrabi as a superior vegetable, and a deliciously tender and sweet one at that. My father always planted a small row of it just for fresh snacking right in the garden, and it's a standard in our garden today.

Some people call it a German turnip, and indeed, the German word *kohlrabi* translates as "cabbage turnip." But unlike root vegetables, kohlrabi grows aboveground and has a mild and pleasant flavor. Tender, fine-textured, crisp, and juicy, it has the crunch of an apple and a taste that is similar to cabbage. We believe it was first mentioned in the first century A.D., and then again by the Roman statesman and naturalist Pliny the Elder, who wrote of a Corinthian turnip. We think he was referring to this vegetable, which would place its provenance in Greece, where Corinth was an important city. It wasn't mentioned again until the sixteenth century, and soon after that it was growing in India. It was wildly popular in Kashmir—and is still a staple in Kashmiri cuisine—presumably because the climate there is perfect for growing this crop.

Although the whole plant is edible, the "root" or aboveground bulb is the part that's usually eaten. Early White Vienna is pale green and Early Purple Vienna is purple, but all kohlrabis have pure, white flesh. And they can grow huge—some varieties, like the humongous Superschmelz, can get up to ten pounds or more!

Growing Tips

Kohlrabi does best in cool conditions, but it can handle more heat than other cabbage-family veggies. Plant new batches of seeds every few weeks, starting three to four weeks before the last frost of spring and continuing up to six weeks before the first frost in autumn. This succession planting will ensure a continuous harvest spring through fall in all but the warmest climates. Sow the seeds one-quarter to one-half inch deep, in rich soil that is moist but well drained, in full sun.

Rows should be twelve to twenty-four inches apart. After thinning, plants should be twelve to eighteen inches apart from one another.

To control weeds, lay down plastic mulch or a three-inch layer of straw to keep soil conditions consistent. The key to quality kohlrabi "roots" is quick, healthy growth with no hiccups in development, such as those caused by dry conditions or competition from weeds.

A side dressing of manure or compost, or an occasional drink of manure tea (p. 55) will keep the growth rate high and the crop tender and succulent.

Harvest kohlrabi when it is young. Most varieties taste best when they're about the size of a baseball. If they grow too big, the flesh becomes fibrous and unpalatable.

Pests and Disease

Similar to other brassicas, kohlrabi is afflicted by flea beetles, root maggots, aphids, cabbage loopers, and harlequin bugs. Foil the flea beetle and root maggot by growing kohlrabi under a row cover (see sidebar on p. 60), which keeps out pests while retaining heat, making it helpful in very early and very late season extension. Blast aphids from the plants with a hose, or kill them using insecticidal soap or vegetable oil–based organic insecticides. This is a class of oil-based insecticides that also has a mild fungicidal effect. Each of them is based on different ingredients. I use Organocide, which contains sesame oil, refined fish oil, and emulsifiers. The large, red-and-black harlequin bug can usually be controlled by

handpicking, if you get it early. Use spinosad or Bt spray to kill the larvae of various moths, such as the cabbage looper.

Seed Saving

Kohlrabi is a biennial that must be overwintered before it throws up branches of cheerful, four-petaled yellow flowers that turn into long, pointed seedpods. Seeds must be collected just as the pods dry and turn brown. Pods may be harvested individually, or the entire inflorescence may be cut and hung upside down over a basket or tub to catch the seeds, which will drop free as they ripen.

When planting kohlrabi for seed, isolate different varieties by at least a half mile, or cage and hand-pollinate the plants to maintain a pure strain. Kohlrabi will cross with other brassicas, including broccoli, kale, cabbage, and Brussels sprouts.

In the Kitchen

Don't be afraid to experiment with kohlrabi. Besides being eaten as a raw snack, it can be sautéed, steamed, or even boiled. One popular way to serve it is mashed kohlrabi, as an alternative to mashed potatoes. To prepare, peel and slice kohlrabi into two-inch squares and boil for ten minutes or so in salted water, until tender. Drain. Mash with a fork and add two to three tablespoons of olive oil, one-eighth of a cup of chives, and salt and spices to taste.

Kohlrabi is a rich source of vitamin C and fiber. It also contains protein and a variety of minerals.

Leeks
Allium ampeloprasum

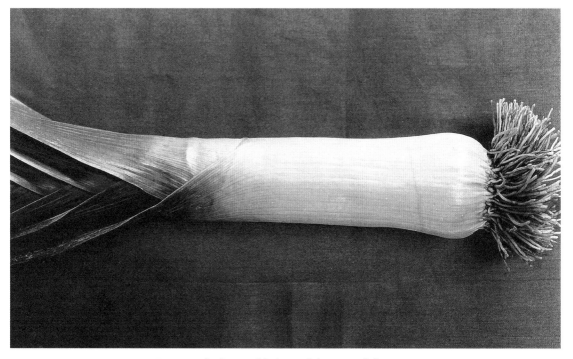

Carentan leek—an old photo of this French favorite.

Leeks are a member of the onion, or *Allium,* genus, which means they're closely related to garlic, shallots, and chives. The flavor of these green-and-white cylindrical stalks is similar to onions but sweeter and more subtle. The most famous leek dish is vichyssoise, an elegant, cold soup of potatoes, leeks, and cream that was invented in 1917 at New York City's Ritz Carlton Hotel. French chef Louis Diat is often credited as its creator. This pureed soup has a mild, creamy taste that was inspired by Diat's childhood. He was quoted as saying that he and his brother poured milk on their hot soups to cool them down, and he remembered how delicious it tasted. In the garden, leeks will grow to about twelve to twenty inches in length and one to two inches in diameter. If you plant leeks in the summer and leave them to grow through the cooler months of fall, they'll develop a richer, sweeter flavor than those picked earlier in the year.

Leeks are said to have originated in Central Asia, but they also have been found in ancient Egyptian archaeological sites. In Rome, leeks were a favorite of Emperor Nero, who believed that eating them helped improve his singing voice. Though often available year-round in regular grocery stores, as with other *Alliums,*

✿✿✿✿✿✿✿✿✿✿✿✿✿✿✿✿✿✿✿✿✿✿✿

> Aside from regular leeks, ramps (which are also known as wild leeks) are stronger tasting leeks that grow in damp, shady areas throughout eastern North America—they're particularly popular in Appalachia, where they're a wild native plant—during early spring. Foragers are known to sell them by the pound to hard-core foodies and chefs, and then suddenly they vanish until the following spring. Smaller and more delicate than regular leeks, ramps also have a stronger flavor and aroma than their domesticated cousin.

✿✿✿✿✿✿✿✿✿✿✿✿✿✿✿✿✿✿✿✿✿✿✿

it's best to harvest the sweet, flavorsome roots when they're in season, September through May. Add leeks to autumn soups and stews. They store well in the refrigerator and have many of the same nutrients as onions and garlic, such as allyl sulfide, which may have cancer-fighting attributes; calcium; folic acid; vitamin C; and potassium.

Growing Tips

Leeks thrive in fertile, well-drained soil, with a lot of sunshine. When starting from seed, plant seeds one-third of an inch deep in small pots and cover lightly with soil, about ten weeks before the last frost. Transplant seedlings to the garden two to four weeks before the last frost. Space the plants approximately five inches apart. As they get bigger, mound dirt up around the stems, which will exclude the sunshine and keep the stalks white and tender. Throughout the growing season, add straw mulch to help minimize weeds and maintain moisture. Mulch protects against the cold, allowing leeks to stand in the garden until late November or December in temperate climates.

Pests and Disease

Leeks are generally pest-resistant and benefit from annual crop rotation, which is the main way they'll stay pest-resistant—so make sure to avoid planting them in the same part of the garden where a member of the onion family has grown in the past three years.

Seed Saving

Leeks do not cross-pollinate with other onion family members, but they will cross with other leeks, so grow only one variety of leek for seed saving. Allow some of the best specimens to flower and the seed balls to mature; then harvest.

This crop is biennial and must overwinter before it'll go to seed. Most varieties last through cold months with minimal care, but if there are hard frosts where you live, lay down a four- to six-inch layer of mulch. Leek seeds can be saved for two years.

In the Kitchen

The mild, sweet taste of leeks lends itself to a variety of dishes. During growing, dirt is mounded around leek stalks and gets into all of the plant's layers, so take care to wash leeks very thoroughly before you start cooking. After trimming off the hard ends, slice each leek lengthwise and fan out the layers under running water to get rid of any excess dirt from the garden. The white stalk is the tastiest part, and when chopped into half-inch pieces, it is a superb substitute for onions in many dishes.

Lettuce

Lactuca sativa

Devil Ears lettuce has pointed, "ear-shaped" leaves that are tender and flavorful.

Iceberg, Bibb, Romaine . . . Americans love their lettuce. It's a staple in our salads, and we are second only to the Chinese in our growing and consumption of it. This ancient crop, which is believed to have originated as a weed in the Mediterranean basin region more than four thousand years ago (images of lettuce were painted on the walls of Egyptian tombs), was brought to America by Christopher Columbus and became popular with the early settlers.

The darker the leaf, the more vitamin C, beta-carotene, calcium, iron, folate, and dietary fiber you'll get, which is why the pale green iceberg varieties are inferior to others in nutrition, as well as flavor.

Growing Tips

Lettuce is a cool-weather crop that is easy to grow from seed. Mucky soil and afternoon shade are preferred, along with daily high temperatures between fifty and seventy degrees, though some varieties can handle extremes on either end. Some butterhead varieties, like Big Boston and Brunė d'Hiver, can handle severe cold, for example, and so are great to plant in the fall for salad greens through winter. We love planting the colorful varieties like Flame and Forellenschluss, for their different tastes and brilliant hues, and as ornamentals to brighten the landscape. Varieties such as Mascara and Lollo Rossa give actual flowers a run for their money when it comes to producing a lot of color very early in the season.

In cooler climates you can succession-plant lettuce throughout the summer, and in areas with warm winters, it's possible to harvest through the winter. For spring planting and summer harvests, sow seeds two to four weeks before the last frost. If you're planting in the fall, do it after the summer's heat has started to wane, four to seven weeks before the first frost date in fall. To start, sprinkle seeds over a well-worked, loose bed of garden soil, then cover with about an eighth of an inch of fine, damp soil.

Tiny green shoots will appear three to seven days after sowing. When the seedlings begin to crowd one another, thin to four inches apart for

Marvel of Four Seasons lettuce is a great old favorite with tasty, red-tinged leaves.

> All varieties of lettuce contain an opiate-like substance called lactucarium. Romans and Egyptians ate lettuce after dinner, to help bring about sleepiness.

> In the refrigerator, keep lettuce separate from apples, which produce ethylene gas, which will lead to brown spots on lettuce leaves and accelerated spoilage.

smaller-leaf lettuces and up to twelve inches apart for larger varieties and head lettuces such as robust Romaines, which prefer wider spacing. When thinning, you'll get baby greens that are great to throw into salads. Lettuce is also very easy to grow in pots. Make sure the containers are at least eight inches deep and have good sun.

If you have a problem with slugs, avoid applying mulch (slugs love mulch!) and handpick your weeds instead. To harvest lettuce, use a sharp knife to cut off the leaves or the head about an inch above the root. Or harvest only a few leaves at a time; often a healthy plant will yield for several weeks handled this way.

Pests and Disease

The number one enemy for lettuce is slugs, who snack on the outer leaves. They make their appearance on leaves on foggy, drizzly days. To control them, put on a gardening glove and pick them off one by one. Or you can trap them in open containers of beer. Aphids can also be a bother; they will feed between the folds of the leaves. Rinse these away by spraying the leaves with cool water, or spray with insecticidal soap or neem oil.

Seed Saving

It's very easy to save lettuce seed, as long as the climate doesn't get too hot too early, which kills lettuce before it goes to seed. Lettuce is self-pollinating, meaning it rarely crosses with other varieties.

To prepare, allow a dozen lettuce plants to grow, unharvested, through the spring and summer, at which point they will "bolt" or send up seed heads. Once the seed heads are a yellowish-tan color and very dry, cut at the bottom with a sharp knife and place them in a paper bag. Then crush the heads using your hands and sift to separate the seeds from the chaff. Store lettuce seeds in a cool, dry place. They should last two to four years.

In the Kitchen

Because of how it is grown, it's very important to wash lettuce carefully before eating it—to make sure it's free from bugs and sand. For extended freshness, store lettuce, roots and all, in a glass of water with a plastic bag over the leaves, in the refrigerator.

Though it is most popular in sandwiches and salads in America, some varieties, like Celtuce, also taste great steamed, sautéed, or braised. The Chinese especially love cooking lettuce. But for me, not much compares to the crunchy freshness of Romaine leaves, either alone or sprinkled with a sweet salad dressing—either Thai Peanut or a Sweet Chili dressing is perfect for me! The leafy lettuce varieties are a decent source of vitamin A and K and contain a small amount of other minerals and vitamins, as well.

Melon
Cucumis melo

Melon is a crop that comes in thousands of varieties, some of which can be grown in nearly any climate, producing among the sweetest fruits you can grow and doing so in as soon as sixty-five days.

When I was growing up in eastern Oregon, we lived in one of the best melon-growing climates in America, with warm, dry summers, much like the areas where melons are believed to have first been cultivated, in Central Asia and the Middle East, regions that have thousands of melon varieties to this day. Melons are one of my all-time favorite things to grow. They go by many names, including honeydew, casaba, Crenshaw, muskmelon, cantaloupe, Persian, banana, and rockmelon, and come in many sizes and colors.

The history of the melon goes far back into our past. It was popular in ancient Egypt, Persia, and Armenia and was mentioned in the book of Exodus in the Bible, in which the Israelites long for this fruit. The Romans imported melons from Armenia, but it was not until around the fif-

The Rich Sweetness melon. I recently acquired this tiny melon from Russia; it is the perfect size for a single serving!

*Our friend Dave Kaiser with Banana melons.
This great melon is among our favorites.*

teenth century that they gained popularity as a garden crop in Italy and Spain. The term "cantaloupe" is derived from melons that were planted in the city of Cantalupo, near Tivoli, Italy, in the papal gardens there.

Christopher Columbus brought the fruit to the New World on his second voyage, and within a couple hundred years, the melons were growing throughout the Americas. It became a favorite of many Native American tribes, and many old strains can still be found growing among the native peoples in Arizona, New Mexico, Guatemala, and Mexico.

Melons range in size from tiny, egg-size fruits that weigh just two ounces, to a 64.8-pound monster grown by Scott Robb, a renowned giant produce grower who lives in Alaska. That area has very long days, which may have helped the fruit gain such astounding weight.

Types of melons vary greatly. Round to oblong, netted-skinned Persian melons are thought to be the parent of the modern-day orange-flesh melons that are common in American markets. The Casaba melon is an ancient melon that was named for a town in Turkey and was very common in early America. The sugary sweet honeydew actually originated in France and was called White Antibes, but American seedsmen changed it to the more down home–sounding "honeydew" as a marketing ploy.

One of the most interesting melons is the Armenian cucumber, which is also called snake melon. The slow-growing fruits are ribbed, so slices have beautiful, scalloped edges. The "snake" moniker comes from how the vines coil on the ground. Flavor of this melon is always mild, and usually sweeter than regular cucum-

bers. The texture is unfailingly crisp, like that of an actual cucumber, but even more crunchy.

In China they grow a melon called Hami, which originated in the province of Xinjiang more than seven hundred years ago. It has delightfully crisp flesh, and comes in more than one hundred varieties. The Hami is said to have been used as tribute that King Hami would send the Qing emperor.

Pickling melons are everywhere in Japan. And then there are my favorite melons, which are European cantaloupes. I especially love Charentais, a round, smooth-skinned melon, with thick, firm flesh and a delicious, tropical fragrance, that is becoming more popular with American chefs and backyard gardeners. Other types of European melons come in an array of colors, including green, red, yellow, brown, orange, white, and almost black. Inside, the flesh can be white, yellow, orange, or green. European melons are great eating, and many types produce fruit fairly quickly.

Growing Tips

Melons are easiest to grow in areas with warm, dry climates, but they can thrive almost anywhere with proper care. Soil should be loose and fairly rich, with good drainage.

Wait to plant this crop in the garden until the soil has warmed. Daytime temperatures should be at least seventy degrees, and nighttime temps should be no lower than fifty degrees. Plant the seeds a half inch deep and twelve inches apart, in rows that are six feet apart.

When the seedlings are four to six inches tall, thin them to twenty-four inches apart. Mulch around the plants with straw, or in cool areas use a black plastic mulch, as this helps to warm the

If you live in an area with a short season, select varieties like Minnesota Midget or Far North, as these will ensure that you get ripe fruit, even in many cool northern areas.

soil and produce more melons in cool northern areas. Then just water when the soil starts to feel dry, but not too often, as melons don't like to be soaked! Standard American muskmelons like Hale's Best and Jenny Lind will pop right off the vine with a little tug when ripe, but many European and Asian varieties are trickier, so you may have to watch for slight changes in color and a slight softening of the fruit before picking them. It may take a few mistakes before you become an ace at selecting ripe melons.

Pests and Disease

Melons can be victims of a variety of diseases, including powdery mildew, downy mildew, Alternaria leaf spot, and anthracnose. To help control these issues, plant melons in a new part of your garden each year, and select an area with excellent drainage. If you're in a rainy climate, consider creating mini raised beds by raking the soil up six to eight inches. If your soil is more on the heavy clay side, add sand or coarse compost to improve drainage (melons can't stand "wet feet"). Finally, make sure to not overwater. To check and see if you need to water, poke a finger into the soil. If it seems dry a couple of inches deep, it's time to water.

The real insect pest for melons is the striped and spotted cucumber beetle. This insect will not only eat the plants but also spread many of the above diseases, and it will likely kill all your melon vines if left unchecked! Apply spinosad or a pyrethrum spray at the first hint of an infestation. Covering plants with row covers (see sidebar on p. 60) can also prove effective, provided these are removed when the plants begin to flower, as the bees need to pollinate them in order for fruit set to occur.

Seed Saving

Melon seeds are simple to save. Let fruits grow to full maturity, when the flesh is soft and sweet. Harvest the ripe fruit by cutting or pulling it off the vine. Then cut in half and, with a spoon, scoop the seeds into a two-gallon bucket—or anything big enough to accommodate the amount of pulp that is being processed. Then add just enough water to cover the pulp. Allow the seeds to ferment for two to three days, stirring the mixture daily. Be careful not to leave the mixture out too long, as the seeds might start to sprout. After the seeds have fermented, add water, stir vigorously for a minute or two, and drain off the pulp. The good seeds will sink to the bottom. Discard the rotted pulp and the bad seeds that float to the top. Several changes of water will probably be needed; keep rinsing until the water runs off clear.

Rinse the good seeds with water, drain, and spread the seeds out on a piece of cardboard to dry for twelve to fifteen days. Once they are fully dry, put them into a jar and store them in a cool, dry place. Melon seeds will sprout for around five years if stored this way.

Melons are pollinated by bees and therefore cross easily with one another (though they will not cross with watermelon, cucumbers, or squash). Isolating from other varieties by one-half mile assures purity. If you don't have that much space, cage and hand-pollinate (see sidebar on p. 71).

In the Kitchen

Melons are easy to enjoy and excellent for fruit salads and fresh eating. In my mind, there's no better way to eat this fruit than when it's sun-warmed from the garden and freshly harvested, although some "winter" varieties are grown for storage and, if stored in a cool, dry location, can stay fresh until around Christmastime, providing a great fall and winter treat (in fact, they develop their full sweetness while in storage). Melons contain good amounts of vitamins A and C and are great made into jams and on fresh tarts. This fruit is truly a great luxury of summer and is a favorite on our table each year.

Boule d'Or melon is a luscious French heirloom honeydew variety.

Mustard

Brassica species

There are several different types of mustard. Some types are grown for their leaves, others for seeds. All are cool-weather crops, which means they are ideal for areas with cooler summer climates and in very early spring and late fall gardens. All possess a unique pungency, beyond that of turnips and sometimes almost like horseradish in its intensity. Mustard was grown in ancient Egypt for the oil that can be extracted from its seed, as is still done in many countries, especially Asian ones, to this day. The Romans introduced mustard cultivation into the rest of Europe, including France, which excels in modern times at producing gourmet mustard spreads. Mustard was later introduced into the Americas by the Spanish. Mustard is such a fast-growing, obliging plant, that it has been grown nearly everywhere, as its value is easily appreciated by all who encounter it.

India mustard, *B. juncea,* originated in the foothills of the Himalayas and is grown for its turnipy-garlicky-horseradishy-peppery-tasting leaves. It is the principal type of mustard grown in America.

Black mustard seed, *B. nigra,* is the basis for familiar yellow and brown spreads. Its seeds are ground and give prepared mustard its sharp, stimulating pungency.

Growing Tips

Mustard plants are very fast growers with a short lifespan. Sow seeds directly into the ground in very early spring. In areas where the soil is dry enough to be loosened, the seeds can even be planted in late winter, to sprout as soon as the cold lessens. Mustard revels in cool weather and tolerates quite a hard frost with ease, although some varieties tolerate warm conditions as well. Pick a location with full sun and rich, moist, well-drained soil.

Rows should be two feet apart. Once they are growing well, thin young seedlings to six inches apart within the rows; use the thinnings for a very early mess of greens.

To harvest, pick individual leaves or cut the entire plant off with a sharp knife right at the ground level.

Mustard grows more quickly than most weeds, so hand pick weeds or hoe instead of mulching this crop. Once each plant sends up its flower stalk, its leaf harvest is exhausted, as the leaves will become strong-tasting and tough at this time, though by that point in the season, you'll have spinach and lettuce ready to harvest in its stead.

If you're planting mustard as a fall crop, sow seeds directly in the four to eight weeks before the first frost date. Mustard can make a leaf crop in only forty days or so and can tolerate occasional light freezes in the garden.

Pests and Disease

All usual brassica pests may affect mustard. But it is normally planted very early (or, alternately, late) in the season, at times when leaf-chomping pests and burrowing insects aren't very active. The major exception is aphids, which are easily thwarted with a hard blast of water from the hose or with an application of insecticidal soap or neem oil. If you have problems with other leaf-chewing pests, try applying a spinosad spray.

Japanese Giant Red mustard—stunning red leaves are fiery-hot tasting.

Seed Saving

The two mustard species won't cross with each other, but varieties within each species certainly will cross with other members of the same species. If you are planning on saving seeds and you have planted more than one variety, you must isolate each type by at least a half mile or cage and hand-pollinate them to ensure purity.

Mustard leaves will eventually give way to yellow flowers, which eventually give way to seedpods. Pick pods individually and shell out the seeds, or harvest the entire seed stalk and bring it indoors to dry. The pods release their seeds as they start to dry, so place a sheet or tarp under the hanging seed stalks, to catch the seeds as they drop.

In the Kitchen

I am especially fond of the Japanese Giant Red variety of mustard greens. Its reddish-purple leaves have a pungent, garlicky flavor that add a kick to Asian dishes and pickled preparations. Milder varieties, such as Tendergreen, have a smoothness that cooks nicely, and they are also a fresh alternative to spinach as a salad green. Mustard greens are vitamin-packed, and one serving of them provides a day's supply of vitamins A, C, and K. This vegetable also delivers some protein and a broad variety of minerals in fair to modest amounts.

Okra
Hibiscus esculentus

Vidrines Midget Cowhorn okra—an old Louisiana favorite that we are trying to save from extinction.

Okra, or gumbo, as it is sometimes called, is grown for its mucilaginous immature seedpods, which are battered and deep-fried or used in soups and stews. Believed to have originated in the Ethiopian highlands, okra is said to have been carried to Egypt and India, where it is a staple crop to this day. It still grows wild in the Upper Delta of the Nile River.

One of the earliest known accounts of okra was written by a Spanish Moor who visited Egypt in A.D. 1216, some six hundred years after the Islamic conquest. The plant was introduced to South America directly from Africa, perhaps being carried aboard slave ships bringing their cargos to Brazil, where it was grown as early as 1658. It made its appearance in this country first in French Louisiana and was grown later in the English colonies, including Philadelphia, in the mid-eighteenth century. It wasn't grown widely in the United States until after 1800. Since that time it has gradually become a traditional Southern crop, being well suited to the heat of Southern summers, when few other vegetables will thrive.

I grow this delicious crop for beauty, as it produces lovely, yellow hibiscuslike flowers on stately, tropical-looking plants. The blossoms are followed by pods that can be the normal green or several shades of red. Red-podded varieties such as Jing Orange or Bowling Red also have brilliant red stems, which are gorgeous for bouquets.

Growing Tips

Okra loves hot sun. Plant seeds directly in the garden two or three weeks following the last frost date (if the season is long enough). Okra tolerates poor, dry soil, but will be more productive with some compost worked in and some irrigation in very dry weather. However, the soil should not be excessively rich.

Before planting, soak okra seeds in a bowl of water overnight to encourage germination. Sow in full sun, a few inches apart, in rows that are five to six feet apart, in soil that is at least seventy degrees. If you live in an area with a shorter growing season, planting seeds indoors three to four weeks before the desired transplant date is the only way to grow this vegetable. Just make sure seedlings don't become root-bound in the pots, and handle them carefully, as okra doesn't really transplant well.

Set transplants about 15 inches apart in the row, or thin the seedlings to allow this much room once the seedlings are up. Hand-pull or hoe incipient weeds and apply mulch. Irrigate occasionally if the soil becomes dry enough that the plants wilt in the afternoons. Large yellow flowers will appear in roughly six to eight weeks. The pods may be harvested immediately after the flowers have faded, or they may be allowed to grow for a few days. But definitely pick them no more than a week after blooming, otherwise they become woody and inedible. It's worth noting that cowhorn types, such as Fife Creek Cowhorn, produce much longer pods, which are still tender even though they're large at five to seven inches long.

When weather conditions are optimal, okra produces heavily and rapidly. So once production is under way, harvest at least twice per week, and more often in hot weather. The plants may be small in northerly climates and yield only a few pods each, but in the lower Midwest and the South, the plants reach five to ten feet tall and yield dozens and dozens of pods.

Use sharp gardening shears or handheld clippers to harvest, as the stems are very strong. And wear long sleeves and gloves to protect your arms and hands: The fruit, leaves, and stems of okra are very prickly and can irritate skin.

Pests and Disease

The main insect pests are various beetles, which may be controlled by weekly applications of spinosad. In our area, we have never had pest problems, and the plants are vigorous enough to outgrow moderate damage.

Seed Saving

Okra is a self-pollinating crop, but the showy blossoms are attractive to bees. This means that crossing can happen. If you are growing several varieties and want to save seed, bag individual flowers or cover entire plants with a row cover (see sidebar on p. 60). The pods should be left on the plants until fully mature. They will turn brown, dry out, and begin to split. In our experience, they should be picked just as the splitting begins; pods are often not fully dry at this point, and we like to finish drying them indoors. Once dry, the individual pods are twisted and the seeds drop out, taking only a minimal amount of chaff with them. Larger quantities may be placed in a bag and stomped on to free the seeds. The seeds are then spread out and dried further for a couple of weeks to ensure complete curing. Stored seed may be expected to last at least three years.

In the Kitchen

Okra is really popular in the Ozarks, where we deep-fry, pickle, and eat it raw. In the far South, it's synonymous with gumbos and a frequent ingredient in other soups as well. I've been eating okra since I was a small child, as my dad would often plant some even in our northern gardens in Oregon and Montana. It is a vegetable that always goes into much of our summer cooking, a favorite no matter how it is cooked. Okra is a terrific source of fiber, vitamins C and K, and small amounts of minerals.

Onion

Allium species

Onions are members of the *Allium* genus, which makes them close relatives of garlic, chives, leeks, and dozens of ornamental types. Numerous wild species are cultivated by inhabitants of the regions they hail from, and several species and crosses are grown in the West and in Japan. They all share a similar pungency due to the presence of volatile sulfur compounds.

Onions come in several types: the ordinary bulbing type in hues of red, yellow, or white; slim scallions or bunching types that never develop a bulb; and multipliers, which are propagated from small offsets, or secondary bulbs, replanted just like garlic, in lieu of seed. Then there are the top-setting onions, also called Egyptian or walking onions, which make new bulbs atop what would otherwise be a flower stem. These stems fall over in autumn rains, which brings the tiny bulbs into contact with the soil, and there they grow; since the stems are two to three feet tall, the onion planting does indeed spread quickly, or "walk."

Common onions, *Allium cepa,* originated in Central Asia. They were known to the Egyptians at the time of the building of the pyramids. The Bible mentions them in Exodus, when the Israelites hunger for the onions they knew in Egypt. This vegetable was grown for around four thousand years in Mesopotamia, but it was universally the province of peasants and disdained by the upper classes, and this did not change until the Middle Ages, when Charlemagne ordered onions planted in his royal garden.

Onions arrived in the New World with the

Flat of Italy onion—flattened red roots are lightly spicy and easy to grow.

first Europeans and caught on with the natives, who in many cases had been eating local wild onions previously. The Pilgrims brought onions with them, and onions have been a favorite in North America ever since.

Growing Tips

The most important consideration when plant-ing onions is to select the right varieties for your particular growing climate. Bulb formation in onions is triggered by longer daylight hours, which happen during spring. There are two main types of onions. **Short-day** onions get the signal to bulb up when days have reached about twelve hours long. **Long-day** types bulb up in the long days of summer in the higher latitudes; they won't bulb up until days are running fourteen to sixteen hours long.

Long-day varieties include Ailsa Craig or Noordhollandaise Blooderode. Southern garden-ers need short-day types, such as Red Creole or Texas Early Grano. A few types, like Golden Princess, aren't too sensitive to day length and are good choices to plant in the summer and grow fall onions for winter storage.

When grown from seeds, onions are usually sown indoors in containers, as much as three months before the last frost date of spring. They don't need a lot of heat to sprout, so the tiny seeds will germinate at room temperature. Once they start growing, they'll be slow at first. Transplant them outdoors four weeks before the last frost. Select a space with full sun and place them six inches apart, in rows that are twelve inches apart, in finely worked, moist, rich soil that has decent drainage. The onion row is a fine place to use any compost you may have to spare.

After transplanting lay down two to three inches of mulch (preferably compost or straw) for weed control—onions can't stand competition and won't amount to much if even a few weeds are present to suck up moisture and nutrients.

Pull any stray weeds that make it past the mulch, and water regularly.

To harvest, wait until the green tops fall over and see how your onions have grown. Ei-ther they will have bulbed up large and plump, or they might be smaller and more restrained if the conditions weren't optimal.

No matter what size or shape they are, they'll still taste like onions. When they're ready, pull them from the soil and cure them by allow-ing their skins to dry out in a warm and shady location for ten to fourteen days.

Once they have been cured, pull the tops off the bulbs and clip the roots. Now your onions are ready to be stored. During storage, handle them carefully, because every bruise or scratch is an opportunity for spoilage organisms to enter the bulb.

Pests and Disease

Onions are rarely bothered by pests, but onion thrips can become a nuisance in some areas. These small brown worms are only a millimeter long, but they can wreak havoc with their rasp-ing mouthparts that tear small holes into leaves and allow the pest to drink up the sap. Signs of an infestation include bent leaves with silvery-gray flecks. Leaf damage from thrips can lead to foliar diseases, so be vigilant about these little guys. Insecticidal soap and spinosad will control them.

Seed Saving

Onions cross with other onions, including occa-sional crosses between bulbing types and scallion types like Welsh onions and Hi Shi Ko, which are grown for green onions and never form a bulb.

Bianca di Maggio onion—sweet and tender, these little roots are sought out by chefs.

Onions never cross with garlic, leeks, or chives. They need a mile of isolation, though even several hundred feet is better than no isolation at all. As a seed crop, onions are biennial.

To save onion seeds, you must get a crop through the winter. Unless you have very mild winters, this means you need to lift the bulbs from the ground and store them in a cool room, at sixty degrees. They keep best if they are exposed to some air circulation—don't close them in, and avoid storing them in plastic, which doesn't breathe. Sweet or mild onions are a bit more problematic because the compounds that make onions pungent are also the ones that resist spoilage. These types should be grown as late in the season as possible and refrigerated after harvest.

In spring, review the bulbs that you overwintered and select the highest-quality ones—with smooth skin, free from blemishes, and on the larger side—to be replanted in the garden. Four to five weeks before the last frost date, put them into the garden (make sure to plant them in a different place than where they grew during the previous summer), in loose, well-worked soil that has good drainage.

Set the bulbs so that the "neck" (the part on top, where the greens sprout), is just above ground level, and apply a layer of mulch.

At that point, there isn't much to do until the seeds are ripe, so watch as the bulbs send up green leaves (a few of which may be harvested and eaten like scallions, if you like). Eventually, the stems will throw up a spherical ball of tiny blue and purple flowers. These will fall off after pollination, leaving just the seeds.

Onion seeds are enclosed in a filmy husk. They are ripe when they become hard and dark black, at which time you should pick off the seed head and allow the seeds to complete drying indoors. Once they're dry, you need to separate the seeds from the husks. To do this, place the seed balls in a paper bag and shake it around for thirty seconds or so. You can also use a mesh strainer to separate them. Or just plant them, husks and all. They'll sprout happily either way.

Store them carefully in an airtight container, in a cool, dry place away from heat and humidity. Onion seeds are viable for two years.

In the Kitchen

There are so many important uses for onions. They liven up stews and soups, are wonderful sautéed into sauces, fried into onion rings, pickled, and of course added to salads and sandwiches. Freshly harvested onions are a mainstay on our spring and summer table and seem to always improve our health. Doctors recommend onions for a number of health reasons; the sulfide compounds may help battle cardiovascular problems, among other ailments. Onions are also a good source of fiber and vitamin C.

Parsnip
Pastinaca sativa

The parsnip is an old-fashioned root vegetable that was popular in American gardens for winter eating throughout the nineteenth and much of the twentieth century, though it has fallen out of favor in recent decades. Parsnips look like big white carrots and smell a bit carroty, as well, but with a stronger, earthier aroma.

Parsnips originated in the eastern Mediterranean and the Caucasus and were popular as a sweetener before sugar became more prevalent. The Romans called both carrots and parsnips by the same name, *pastinaca,* and indeed, the two are close relatives.

It is said that the emperor Tiberius was so fond of parsnips that for his table he had them imported annually from Germany, where they grew in profusion along the Rhine. By the end of the Middle Ages, parsnips were cultivated throughout Europe, with the first known illustration appearing in Germany in 1542. (The early pictures show parsnips just like the ones we like today, but there is also a round, turniplike form.) They were evidently cultivated in England in the same period, and when early American settlers arrived in Jamestown in 1609 and in Plymouth in 1620, parsnips were there, as well, humbly feeding the colonists while other crops, like maize and squash, received all the glory.

Jere with some large, sweet parsnips.

Growing Tips

Parsnips are one of the more persnickety crops to grow, and they don't do well in hot weather. In the South, they are best planted in the fall, for harvest in the spring. Everywhere else throughout America, you can plant them in the spring, two to four weeks before the last frost. Soil should be very rich, well worked up to twelve inches deep (similar to carrots) in full sun, with good drainage and free from dirt clods or stones.

Sow seeds a half inch deep and very thickly (one every half inch), because germination is slow and not always reliable. It may take two to four weeks, so mark the row and start picking weeds even before parsnips sprout. Some gardeners plant a few radish seeds in the row with the parsnips; these sprout in only a very few days, showing where the row is, and may be harvested long before the parsnips need the space.

Let the rows stand eighteen inches apart, and once they are growing steadily, thin parsnips to four inches apart within the rows.

Control weeds with mulch or careful hoeing, but avoid hoeing too close to the young plants, as feeder roots may otherwise be damaged.

After four to five months in the ground, the roots should be mature. They frequently reach twelve inches and longer, with a width at the shoulder of two inches or so. They may be lifted when mature, and stored under refrigeration (as they should be if the weather is still hot). The best parsnips mature after the heat of summer wanes. These are stored right in the ground, covered by several inches of coarse mulch, such as straw. The parsnips actually taste better after exposure to cold, even freezing, temperatures, because the cold turns some of the roots' starch into sugars.

Pests and Disease

The multicolored swallowtail butterfly's caterpillar likes parsnips, just as it likes its relatives, dill and fennel. Leaf miner is an occasional pest; removal and destruction of affected leaves is usually sufficient.

Seed Saving

Parsnips are biennial, which means that the roots must experience a winter chill before they will send up a four- to five-foot flower stalk in their second spring. Allow the lacy cream-colored flowers to bloom, set seed, and mature. Pick the seeds off by hand when mature—brown and dry—but before they come loose from the stalk. (Their papery "wings" sometimes carry the new seeds astonishing distances, and if a few should take root and grow the following spring, they may be left in place if they're not in the way. Indeed, the plant has already naturalized throughout the moister third of the United States.) Bring the harvested seed indoors, allow it to dry a bit, and store. Parsnip seed has a very short shelf life and cannot be counted on after it has reached a year or two old.

In the Kitchen

This vegetable has been a staple on our tables ever since I was a child; I remember harvesting the roots and frying them in a pan like potatoes. The roots of this crop are lightly sweet and have a spicy taste all their own. They taste wonderful when sliced, sprinkled with oil, and baked in the oven until tender. Another way to use them is in parsnip cake. To make this, just whip up a recipe for carrot cake, but substitute more flavorful parsnip roots instead of shredded carrots. I just adore this root and hope it finds a place in more gardens and kitchens across America. It's nutrient-dense, and a particularly good source of fiber, manganese, vitamins C and K, and folate, as well as a decent source of protein, calcium, and potassium.

Peas

Pisum sativum

Oregon Sugar Pod peas—the big, tender pods are delicious, but never last long.

Peas are a delicious crop and one of the first planted each spring. This little dynamo dates back to the very beginnings of agriculture. Peas were cultivated in the Middle East, Ethiopia, and Western Asia, but their exact origins have been lost in the mists of time. Wild peas grow in those regions to this day.

Though they were originally cultivated for their dried seeds, Europeans started eating the young and green seeds as a sweet, juicy delicacy in the 1600s. Dried peas are starchy, with a somewhat grainy texture when cooked. But being a legume, they contain a lot of protein, which is why they made such an important winter staple in the Old World, where, remember, they had

no true beans prior to the discovery of America. Peas made the journey to North America with the earliest colonists. Thomas Jefferson grew thirty different types at Monticello.

As a child, I was very fond of snow and snap peas, and I still am. These edible podded types are excellent for backyard gardens, because they are heavy producers that grow quickly. Snow peas are grown for their flat, edible pods, which are used fresh in Asian cooking, although they were first developed in Holland. They are typically bright green, but I also enjoy growing varieties with yellow and purplish-blue pods.

Snap peas are a modern development, a cross between snow and regular peas. They have edible, round pods like snap beans and are used in similar ways.

Pea shoots are a fun little vegetable secret. These flavorful baby leaves of pea plants are wonderful as well. When they're picked young, you can add them raw to salads or noodle soups, or use them as an edible garnish on pasta. Later on in the growing season, their flavor is richer, and they can be sautéed with garlic and oil as a lovely side dish.

Growing Tips

Peas are a cool-weather crop that should be planted in very early spring or in the fall.

For spring planting, sow seeds directly in the garden four to six weeks before the last frost date in spring. Most pea varieties have vines and will need to be trellised, staked, or given some other form of support as they grow. Some bush types, such as Sugar Ann or Oregon Sugar Pod II, don't grow as high as regular peas. But a small trellis may still be helpful, to keep things tidy.

For a fall planting, sow seeds directly in the garden about sixty days before the first fall frost is expected. However, if you live in an area where temperatures are still above seventy-five degrees at that time, your climate might be too warm for a fall planting, so just stick with peas as a spring crop.

Plant pea seeds one half to one inch deep in finely worked soil, one to two inches apart in rows that are at least a foot apart, and wider if you're using a trellis—make sure you have room to walk between rows to tend the peas. Thin the plants to two to three inches apart within the rows.

Remove weeds as soon as you see them. If you let them get too big, pulling or hoeing will harm the shallow, delicate pea roots, too.

When applying mulch to a spring planting, try hay or straw. A very fine mulch could retain too much moisture, which isn't optimal, because a lot of rain is still to come. Fall-planted peas might benefit from a finer mulch, since the weather tends to be drier then in many areas.

When harvesting, pick pods when they're plump and bright green, before they become tough and stringy. Work carefully to avoid harming other parts of the plant. To shell your peas, simply grasp the stem and pull it down toward the blossom end of the pod—it should come free, allowing the pod to be split open and peas to spill into a waiting bowl. If you are harvesting large quantities for freezing or canning, consider purchasing an inexpensive hand-cranked sheller, as it is a great time-saving tool.

Pests and Disease

The pea-leaf weevil is the only pest of any significance. You know it's present if you see scal-loped edges on the pea leaves. It's only young plants that are affected, so good rich soil, or a dose of fish emulsion or manure tea, may help the plant outgrow the damage this pest causes. Rotating planting location from year to year may also help.

Seed Saving

Peas are self-pollinating but may occasionally be crossed by bees if they happen to visit the flowers. Isolation of twenty-five to fifty feet between varieties is considered adequate unless there is a lot of bee traffic in the beds. If that proves to be the case, and it may vary from year to year, securing row covers (see sidebar on p. 60) over the planting will exclude the bees. Or, in the future, plant only a single variety if you want to save seed.

The pods are allowed to dry on the plants, which happens by early summer. They are then picked and either opened individually or threshed out just like beans or cowpeas. After a final, indoor drying period, the seeds may be stored in jars, plastic bags, or envelopes, and can last four to five years.

In the Kitchen

All types of peas are delightful when picked right from the garden. They are also perfect for a variety of dishes. Shell peas are particularly good for soups, casseroles, and stews. Snow and snap types lend themselves well to stir-fries and salads, or just lightly steam and season with sesame oil and crushed garlic. Peas are packed with vitamins, including A, B, C, and K, and have good amounts of protein, fiber, and various minerals.

Peppers
Capsicum species

Fish peppers add an exceptional kick to soups and stews.

Each time I travel, I seem to navigate toward peppers: Roasted mild peppers at a roadside stand in New Mexico, or peppers in a delightful Cambodian curry in Siem Reap, or served in a host of delightful dishes basically everywhere in South Asia. Thai peppers are special in that they're loaded with heat and also full of flavor. In Mexico I enjoyed a broad variety of peppers both sweet and hot, and in Guatemala I really fell in love with many of the sugary-sweet varieties offered.

The pepper captivates taste buds, brings

Lightning Bolt peppers were developed by our Mennonite farmer friend, James Weaver, and come in an array of colors and shapes.

back memories, and inspires appreciation of the crop's complex heritage. Christopher Columbus first discovered chili peppers in the West Indies in 1492, when he found the New World while on his quest to find a shortcut to the East Indies. He took them with him back to Spain, and it is said that within fifty years the crop was growing in dozens of countries. Peppers have become a staple ingredient for many cuisines, from Spanish, Mexican, and Middle Eastern, to Indian and Thai. In recent years, hot sauce and salsa made with peppers have eclipsed ketchup as the most popular condiments in America.

Most early peppers were thin, small, and fiery hot, but over the last five hundred years, breeders focused on developing types that are sweet, mild, and perfect for those with less daring palates. Today, mild peppers have become some of the most popular plants in the garden. This bright, flavorsome fruit has much to offer.

My first memories of growing peppers are of my Mexican grandmother, Bertha, who planted a giant bell pepper hybrid called Big Bertha, which was popular in the 1980s and grew in abundance around her garden. Ever since I was small, I've sought out unique and colorful varieties—some of my favorites are Purple Beauty, Red and Yellow Marconi, Orange Bell, Trinidad Seasoning, Chocolate Habanero, and Albino Bullnose. I love growing this easy and delicious crop each summer, remembering my grandmother and the many cultures responsible for bringing us peppers as we know them today.

Growing Tips
Peppers are easy to grow, but they take a while to germinate and like a long season of bright sun-shine. Sow seeds a quarter inch deep, indoors, eight to ten weeks before the last frost. Once temperatures are consistently above sixty-five degrees, transplant seedlings into the soil, about sixteen inches apart, and water as needed.

Raised beds are a good option for peppers, because they need warm soil, good drainage, and bright sunshine.

Pests and Disease
In most areas, home gardeners can grow peppers with no pest control. If you notice aphids or hornworms, apply an organic spray like spinosad or Safer Soap. And always make sure peppers have warm soil (throw a row cover—see sidebar on p. 60—over them if necessary)—that keeps them happy.

Seed Saving
Peppers are very easy to save seed from. Just cut open the ripe fruit, scrape out the seeds, and let them dry for a week before storing in a jar.

Peppers are a self-pollinating crop, but they will occasionally cross via bees if two varieties are planted near each other. If you want to save seeds, either plant only one variety, grow the plants in cages made of row cover, or separate varieties by at least five hundred feet.

In the Kitchen
Peppers are a joy in all their colors, flavors, and degrees of heat. You can harvest peppers at any color stage, but I prefer them when fully ripe, when they are sweetest and also highest in nutrients. When cutting into very hot varieties, wear gloves in order to prevent the fiery capsaicin oil from getting on your skin or in your eyes.

I crave peppers raw or roasted or grilled, and they're a must in any curry, soup, or stir-fry. Peppers stuffed with seasoned rice are a unique comfort food, as are peppers when they're pre- served into pickles, chutneys, and jellies. Peppers are an excellent source of vitamins A and C, and the active ingredient in hot peppers, capsaicin, is a well-documented anti-inflammatory.

Etude pepper—a sugary-sweet tangerine-orange variety.

Potatoes
Solanum tuberosum

Potatoes are yet another member of the nightshades, the same fascinating family that gives us tomatoes, peppers, tomatillos, and eggplants. This one's name means "tuberous" in Latin, and of course it's the tubers that are eaten. Potatoes were always a standard crop in our gardens, where we would grow large quantities of russet and red and some deep blue tubers that we stored in our root cellar for a year-round supply of this Gettle family staple. Many a hard Montana winter was endured with the help of our root cellar, and the one "root" that mattered most was the humble but amazing potato. I still love growing this crop, especially varieties with brightly colored flesh, which tend to have more flavor than the traditional, white-fleshed varieties.

This crop originated in Peru thousands of years ago, among the native peoples of the high mountain valleys. It has developed into thousands of varieties, including dozens of shapes, sizes, and colors. In color they range from blue, red, and pink, to purple, brown, white, yellow, and many shades of these colors, including many with brightly colored flesh, which happens to be high in antioxidants. Their high-quality protein and solid nutrition have made these starchy tubers one of the staples in diets around the globe. In the wild, there are numerous species that grow throughout the Andes, and in fact there are wild potato species even in the United States, though the tubers they yield may be inedible.

Potatoes were introduced to Europe after the Spanish conquest of Peru. They caught on there fairly quickly and were grown throughout western and southern Europe, with the exception of France, within a century of their introduction. The infamous Irish Potato Famine in the mid-nineteenth century occurred when the one or two varieties grown throughout Ireland were devastated by the potato blight. The blight destroyed the Irish potato crops, as none of those few varieties happened to be resistant to that particular strain of blight. The Irish, in turn, had come to depend upon the potato, which was and is so productive in Ireland's cool, moist climate. A million people died in this tragic example of the dangers of inadequate crop diversity.

Today potatoes are the world's fourth-largest food crop.

Growing Tips

Potatoes like a cool and moist setting, and rich soil that is high in organic matter. They do best when planted in early spring. Young potato plants can take some frost, and the seed tubers are set into the garden before the last frost date of spring. (Seed tubers are small potatoes, ideally the size of an egg, or larger tubers that have been cut to one to two "eyes," or buds, per piece. They are always planted directly in the soil and shouldn't be started indoors.)

Put them an inch or two deep in well-worked soil, or into three- to four-inch-deep trenches that are gradually filled back in, never completely covering the sprouts as they grow. Mulch potato beds with straw. As they grow, add more mulch gradually, until a foot or more has been applied. The new tubers, which eventually grow along the length of the stem, will form throughout the mulch and in the upper inches of soil.

The tops will eventually turn brown and dry; that means that the new tubers are ready. But often before this point is reached, the mulch can be pulled back here or there and a few early tubers taken out. The mulch is then carefully replaced. Don't leave any tubers bare, and if you ever spot any bare ones, cover the area with mulch as soon as they are noticed. Direct sunshine on the surface of the tubers causes sun-scald, which in the case of potatoes means that the skin turns green, and incidentally develops toxic solanine, an alkaloid poison also found in other members of this family. It is a nightshade, after all!

Once dug up, the tubers are cured in an airy location out of direct sun for about a week. They may then be brought indoors, where storage

Heirloom potatoes come in a variety of taste-tempting colors!

temperatures of sixty to seventy degrees work well for a month or two, although for long-term storage potatoes keep best in high humidity at around thirty-nine degrees. Freezing them changes some of their starch to sugar, which many people feel spoils the flavor.

Pests and Disease

Potatoes are heir to a variety of different pests, including flea beetles, aphids, and the Colorado potato beetle. The latter is a brightly colored; three-eighths-inch-long; yellow-green, orange, and black-striped bug. All of these pests can be eliminated by covering the spuds with row covers (see sidebar on p. 60). Spinosad spray is also very effective.

Some forms of Bt were created specifically to battle the potato beetle, and they work when applied to young larvae (which lay eggs on the undersides of leaves). When examining and treating your crop with any of these natural pesticides, target the larvae rather than the adults. The larvae look like fat, reddish-brown caterpillars, and they're the ones that do the real damage. If you reduce the number of larvae, you reduce the adults who lay the eggs.

Winter tillage to a depth of six to eight inches will destroy most of the beetles in your garden, which is a help, but more can always fly in, which means prevention isn't always sufficient.

Seed Saving

Saving seeds from potatoes is generally not done, at least not in the sense of saving true seed that is formed by a flower.

Potatoes do make true seed, in a berry resembling a small green tomato. But the offspring

Buy organic potatoes from your local farmer—or grow your own!—because a few of the Russet potato types these days have been genetically modified to produce an insecticide that is present throughout the potato. And many scientists and doctors believe this toxin may harm human health, after several studies showed that it caused damage to the vital organs of rats.

seldom come true to type. Instead, there will be fascinating and enormous variation among the progeny, most of which, unfortunately, will be of inferior quality. Any attempt at growing the seeds should be undertaken only as an experiment. For the record, potato flowers are self-pollinating but may be crossed by insects. And it may take two years to grow the first sizable potato tuber from seed.

Tubers are the usual way of propagating potatoes. Save tubers "the size of a hen's egg." Store them as for eating. Tubers of this size should be planted whole the following spring.

In the Kitchen

There are literally thousands of ways to prepare the potato, from baked to fried, in everything from desserts and breads, to stews, soups, and curries. Two of my favorites are Aloo Gobi, a spiced Indian dish with potato and cauliflower that my family adores, and a strudel recipe passed down in my family from my German ancestors to be enjoyed on special occasions. The potato is a terrific source of protein, fiber, carbohydrates, and many minerals and vitamins. Keeping the skins on when cooking potatoes is a great idea when possible, because they contain a lot of fiber.

Radish

Rhaphanus sativus

There are two main types of radishes: salad varieties, which are on the small side, and winter radishes, which grow up to twenty-four inches in length and half a foot in diameter. The small, colorful salad types, like French Breakfast, White Icicle, and Purple Plum, have a peppery tang and reach maturity faster than almost any other vegetable out there—only cress is faster—and many varieties are ready to harvest within three to four weeks. Even lettuce and green beans take longer, and they are pretty fast!

Larger winter radishes, such as Red Bartender and Japanese Minowase, take longer to grow and can be stored for four to six months. These varieties are great to cook with. Despite their big size, they've got fine, crisp texture and range in flavor from mild to flaming hot. They look striking, too—European varieties, such as Round Black Spanish and Long Black Spanish, have black skin and white flesh. The purple-hued Violet de Gournay is also a beauty. Like turnips, winter types take up to seventy-five days or longer to reach full maturity.

I've been attracted to this ancient root, for its diversity and color range, since I was a child. The standard red types can get almost boring when you consider the pink, purple, black, white, mauve, green, and even sunny yellow or bicolored ones. Some Chinese varieties have lime-green or berry-pink flesh that is rich in antioxidants, and all the varieties with different-colored flesh tend to taste sweeter than common radishes. In size, this root ranges from the tiny European salad

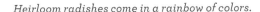

Heirloom radishes come in a rainbow of colors.

types to strains from Japan that can grow to more than fifteen pounds!

The radish is said to have originated in China, where wild varieties of it still grow today. In ancient times, it was eaten in Egypt and Greece, where artists made ritual images of radishes in lead and bronze. This crop made it to America with the very first Europeans—it's believed that Columbus brought them on his later voyages, and they were also brought over by the first English colonists.

Some radish seedpods are actually edible if you pick them really young. The Rat-tail radish is one example of a variety that is bred for its pods rather than its roots. In Southeast Asia, they cultivate the long, slender pods to pickle or toss into stir-fries.

Growing Tips

Radishes are cool-weather crops that grow best in spring and the fall, but can be grown through summer (except in the hotter regions of the country). They like rich, well-drained soil that has ample moisture. Give radishes plenty of organic matter, like compost or mulch, and they will thank you for it! Sow seeds directly in the garden in full sun, a quarter to a half inch deep.

For smaller salad varieties, like French Breakfast or Philadelphia White Box, it's a great idea to sow a new batch every two weeks if possible, starting four weeks before your last frost date and continuing through September, to ensure a continuous harvest. In hot summer areas, discontinue planting about a month before the temperatures reach their peaks (highs consistently above ninety degrees) and resume when it cools off. Salad types take thirty to forty days

to harvest. To pick them, just tug them gently out of the dirt. Make sure to harvest promptly. The roots will become fibrous and woody if left in the dirt too long.

For giant radishes, like Daikon, Spanish, and Bartender types, make sure your soil is worked very loose all the way down for a couple of feet; if you expect a root to grow fifteen inches in length, the soil needs to be loose for at least that amount of space, and probably more.

Sow winter radishes in the late summer at least two months before the first frost is expected, for a fall harvest and winter storage. Once they are growing well, thin seedlings to four to six inches apart. When thinning, be ruthless. Crowded plants will fail to bulb properly, giving you nothing but skinny, stringy roots. Always apply a layer of mulch after you thin, to keep weeds at bay.

Pests and Disease

We've never needed to do any kind of pest control on radishes, but some people get flea beetles attacking the leaves and cabbage root flies eating the roots. Both problems are easily avoidable if you put row covers (see sidebar on p. 60) over the young plants quite early.

Seed Saving

Radishes are pollinated by insects, so if you're saving seeds, leave them in the ground and they'll bloom, eventually yielding seedpods. To grow radishes for seed, allow just one type to bloom and set seed at a time, isolated from other varieties by up to one half mile. When it blooms, you'll get large purple or white flowers and then seedpods that start out soft and green and eventually darken to brown. Compared to other brassicas, these pods are pretty large, so it's best if they are picked individually. Once they are dry, you can thresh out the seeds by pounding the pods with a rubber mallet (they're cheap and readily available at any hardware store) and winnowing in front of a fan. But if you only need a few hundred seeds, just open the pods by hand.

If stored properly, radish seeds will keep for five years.

In the Kitchen

Though seldom cooked in America, radish leaves are a delicious green. In early spring, we cook them like other greens, in stir-fries, or as a side dish made by wilting the leaves in a skillet with sesame oil, garlic, and a dash of lemon juice.

As for the root, small salad types are, of course, traditionally sliced thin and add crunch to salads. Some people also carve them into "radish roses" for garnishes.

The word "radish" comes from the Latin *radix*, meaning "root." The genus name, *Rhaphanus*, comes from a Greek word meaning "easily reared," and radishes are certainly that, being one of the fastest-maturing crops there is.

I love using the big ones, like the mighty daikon, chopped into stir-fries and Asian-style soups. They're also great for pickling. Other winter radishes are also delicious if you use them like turnips, which they resemble in flavor. Boil, then peel and mash with salt and pepper. My favorite radishes are the unique Chinese winter varieties with pink or green flesh, which are more flavorful than common white-fleshed varieties. I find them superior both fresh and steamed. Radishes have loads of vitamin C, potassium, folate, and fiber. They also provide some protein, sugars, sodium, and iron, and a variety of other minerals and vitamins.

Red- and green-meated Chinese radishes are more sweet and flavorful than common varieties, and very beautiful.

Rhubarb
Rheum rhabarbarum

There are many fruits that we treat as vegetables: tomatoes, peppers, squash, and cucumbers. But rhubarb is a vegetable that we treat as a fruit, and no wonder why. The tart, sweet flavor of pink, green, and red rhubarb stems is the basis for some of the tastiest confections in American cookery: rhubarb pie, crumbles, jams, and preserves. The leafy greens of the rhubarb plant are not edible (and in fact, they are actually mildly poisonous), but the peppy taste of its sturdy, straight stems (which are also called petioles) make rhubarb a treasured early spring crop. Boiled down and concentrated with other fruits, it creates an unforgettable taste sensation.

Records of rhubarb go back to ancient times, after it was first discovered in either Siberia or the Kansu province of China, depending on whom you ask and which type you're asking about. There are actually several species of rhubarb; the one we grow for pies is *R. rhabarbarum*, while the Chinese type is *R. palmatum*. Chinese herbalists loved it and used it frequently in their homeland. The Pen Khing, a Chinese herbal guidebook that dates to 2700 B.C., mentioned use of rhubarb for both treatment of constipation and as a laxative. It has been revered over the years as a remedy for burns, jaundice, and women's complaints, and is listed in the Chinese pharmacopeia to this day. The Himalayan species is highly valued in ayurvedic medicine, as well as a digestive aid.

The rhubarb we grow in America for pies and such is believed to be of Siberian origin. But there's been a lot of crossbreeding over the cen-

turies, so there is some doubt. It may be a cross of several different species.

Some form of rhubarb was known in Europe, having made its way westward from China via Arab traders. It was primarily the medicinal varieties that were grown in Europe prior to the nineteenth century and planted in Italy in 1608. The plant gradually spread throughout Europe, to England in the late eighteenth century, and to America, some say first to Maine, by 1800. It became popular in the nineteenth century in the West, in desserts and winemaking. Rhubarb's introduction as a food in England was largely the result of marketing by a clever nurseryman named Joseph Myatt, who rhapsodized about it being indispensable to tarts, for which he distributed the recipe—coincidentally, Myatt was also a purveyor of strawberries. And it has become a staple in both English and American pies and crumbles since then.

Growing Tips

Rhubarb is a perennial that thrives in cold regions and grows year after year without replanting. But it takes two seasons before you can actually harvest it. The cool air of northern climates sweetens its delicious stems. It can also work in warm Southern areas, if it has ample afternoon shade.

To start from seed, sow in pots indoors four to eight weeks before the last frost date of spring, or directly in the garden two to three weeks before the last frost. Set transplants outdoors only after the danger of frost has passed. Be sure the soil is very rich, preferably containing a lot of organic matter, such as leaf mold and compost.

Soil should be moist. Rhubarb can tolerate considerable drought, but it doesn't thrive in consistently dry soil because those succulent leaf stems are mostly made of water! Grow rhubarb in full sun, except in hot areas, where temperatures reach more than ninety degrees, in which case they need afternoon shade. In extreme heat, they may go dormant for a few weeks in summertime, as they are, after all, cool-climate plants.

Mulch helps conserve moisture, but don't apply it directly to the top of the plant. The crown will rot if it gets buried by too much organic matter. Instead, just mulch around the plant about a foot in each direction.

Rhubarb—perfect for pies, this old-fashioned plant will grow even in the far north.

Rhubarb is hardy throughout the U.S. and northward into much of Canada. But it needs cool winters to do really well; otherwise it won't thrive—temperatures should drop below forty degrees regularly to get new growth in the spring.

During its second or third year, rhubarb will begin to send up stalks that are big enough to harvest (i.e., about as big as a large celery stalk, or bigger). To harvest, either cut with a sharp knife at ground level, leaving an inch above the crown, or twist free with a sharp tug when the petioles are still tender and succulent. They will be one to two inches in diameter, and similar in shape and firmness to celery stalks. But rhubarb, depending on the variety, is either red, pink, or light green.

Continue harvesting until the new stalks coming on start to look spindly. Allow these to grow into mature leaves to renew the plant for next spring. The plants send up flower stalks in the summer. If you are not saving seed, you should remove blossoms when they appear, so that more energy is diverted to root maintenance underground.

After two to three years, rhubarb crowns tend to become overgrown, which causes the center stems to grow spindly even in early spring. When this happens, plants should be divided. Lift the entire plant and break or cut the large fleshy root into pieces. Any piece having at least one bud or eye and some root tissue can be replanted to form a new plant. Replant a nice division where the plant has been growing, and plant the other pieces elsewhere to get even more rhubarb.

Pests and Disease

Rhubarb isn't bothered by too many pests. In some areas, though, the rhubarb curculio beetle can be bothersome. This dark gray-brown snouted beetle has an odd-looking, yellowish powdery deposit on its back and is a half inch to three-quarters of an inch long. Vigilant weed control will help deter this little bug.

Seed Saving

To save rhubarb seeds, allow the flower stalk to remain on the plant. The inconspicuous white flowers will eventually yield individual seeds, which you can pick from the stem by hand as they ripen. Allow the seeds to dry in a cool place indoors, to be planted again the following spring. Rhubarb seeds are viable for two to three years.

In the Kitchen

Strawberry-rhubarb pie is a delight in summer. But I also like rhubarb mixed with sweeter crops, like apple, pear, and grape, or to jazz up jellies, ice cream, muffins, cobblers, and applesauce (dice and sauté the stems before adding to sauce). A one-cup serving of raw rhubarb offers about half of the RDA for vitamin K and a good amount of vitamin C, calcium, potassium, and manganese. But bear in mind, the rhubarb in a slice of pie has had a lot of the water cooked out of it, and when cooked, rhubarb's nutrients are more concentrated than when it is in its raw form.

Salsify
Tragopogon porrifolius

Rarely grown in America these days, salsify is an odd-looking, curious-tasting root vegetable that is a member of the sunflower family. The black version is called scorzonera. This mysterious vegetable is native to the Mediterranean and was popular in Italy in the sixteenth century. Though Thomas Jefferson grew it at Monticello and recipes for it appeared in cookbooks such as *The Joy of Cooking* in the 1930s, it eventually stopped being produced on a large scale and largely disappeared from our tables.

It is sometimes called "goat's beard," for the wispy roots on its thin stalks, or "oyster vegetable," due to what some people consider an oysterlike taste. But to me, salsify resembles a nutty, rich-tasting parsnip with a hint of artichoke flavor.

Salsify is mainly grown for its roots, which, when peeled, are creamy white and carrot-shaped, though the tender young leaves and flower buds are also edible. If allowed to bloom, its flowers are large, purple, pointy-petaled and daisy-like—surely one of the showier flowers in the vegetable garden.

Growing Tips

Salsify is a slow-growing crop that is sown in spring and harvested in the fall. It also has very specific soil requirements when it comes to acidity.

Long Island salsify.

Salsify wants a slightly alkaline soil, with a pH of 7 or above. If yours is more acidic than that, lime the soil a couple of months before planting. Amend the soil with well-rotted compost and a sprinkling of wood ashes if you have them. Only a soil test can accurately determine the need, but in the eastern third of the country at least, most soils are going to need an application of lime prior to planting.

Following the last frost, sow seeds directly in the garden, a half inch deep, one inch apart, in rows that are one to two feet apart. Once they are growing strongly, thin the plants so they are two to four inches apart. They don't need too much room between one another. Apply a three- to four-inch-thick layer of mulch to control weeds once the plants are large enough to spread mulch without burying them.

Salsify takes up to five months to reach full size, which is usually about the size of an adult's index finger (though sometimes they can grow much larger). To harvest, use a garden fork to loosen the soil and dislodge the root from the ground. Harvest only what you will eat right away, because salsify doesn't store as well as other roots and it keeps just fine in the ground.

As winter approaches, add another layer of mulch, this time covering the plants themselves, to keep the soil from freezing solid. When you want to harvest salsify during the cold months, you can just pull the mulch back, dig up what you need, and put the mulch back into place. Any roots still present in spring will sprout asparagus-like side shoots, which may be boiled or eaten raw as a salad, but they will go to seed in their second year, and the idea is to dig and eat all of them, reserving some plants for seed production if you wish.

Pests and Disease

Not many pests bother salsify, except root maggots. If these become a problem, try putting a row cover (see sidebar on p. 60) over the plants the following year, to help keep pests away.

Seed Saving

Salsify is a biennial that blooms in its second year. To harvest seeds, let the plant bloom into pretty flowers and develop a seed head. Once mature, the seeds will turn brown and woody. Gather them by hand before they drop into the dirt or get carried away by the wind.

In the Kitchen

Though it's not well known to the general public, more and more chefs are discovering salsify's earthy flavor. It can also be used in a variety of ways in home cooking. The flesh discolors immediately upon peeling, so drop slices into water with lemon juice or vinegar to keep them white.

You can braise, roast, or sauté slices of salsify with olive oil, salt and pepper, and garlic. It adds an earthy dimension and oystery kick to soups and stews. You can also add tender greens to salads.

A one-cup serving of salsify contains about 20 percent of an adult's daily requirement of manganese, as well as appreciable vitamin C, vitamin B_6, and riboflavin, and about four grams of protein, which is approximately 8 percent of an adult's daily requirement.

Sorghum
Sorghum bicolor

Though it's a bit under the radar in North America, this wonderful crop is one of the most important grains in the world. After wheat, rice, corn, and barley, sorghum is the fifth most popular grain, feeding more than a half billion people in more than thirty different countries each year.

This towering, hardy grass resembles corn in appearance and has similar uses. It was originally developed in the warm-weathered plains of eastern and southern Africa. And it is actually known to grow even taller than many corn varieties, to between eight and twelve feet high. Unlike corn, sorghum yields bountiful harvests even in regions with excessive heat or drought.

In North America, people with wheat allergies particularly appreciate sorghum, as it is a gluten-free alternative to flour and can also be boiled and eaten whole, in place of oatmeal.

Light-grained varieties, like Tarahumara Popping sorghum, are mainly used as grain, because they don't yield much sap. But dark or red-grained varieties, like Sugar Drip, Black Amber, and Mennonite, can be made into a sweetener that's similar to maple syrup but with a lighter flavor (this is done by pressing the sap from the stems of mature plants and boiling it down). A few varieties, such as White African, are tasty as both a grain and a syrup.

Sorghum syrup was a dietary staple in the South until around the 1950s, when the tradition of using it as a sweetener dwindled as self-sufficiency farming fell out of style, or came to be seen as "old fashioned." But it's making a come-back now, and you can find it again at some rural grocery stores. I see sorghum presses at auctions in the country all the time—people buy and restore them, to make this sweet syrup again.

Crafty homesteaders and adventurous suburban gardeners will be happy to hear that making sorghum syrup is rather simple. After the juice is extracted, it must be boiled down until the desired consistency is reached. Some syrup is light and some is dark. The lighter the color, the higher the quality.

Growing Tips

Sorghum revels in heat. Sow seeds one-half to one inch deep, directly into fertilized soil, three to four weeks after the last spring frost, or when soil temperatures have reached sixty to sixty-five degrees.

Seeds should be planted about an inch apart, in rows that are two to three feet apart. After the plants are a few inches tall, thin them to four to six inches apart in the rows. Weeds can be controlled with mulch, but larger plots can be hoed, since the sorghum grows so fast that most weeds are shaded out very quickly. We typically hoe a couple of times early in the season, then hand-weed once, and that takes care of things.

RED'S RED: THE BEST SORGHUM VARIETY FOR SHORT SUMMERS

Our favorite short-summer sorghum variety is Red's Red. If you have a short growing season (fewer than ninety days of temperatures above eighty degrees), start seeds indoors and plant once the soil warms up, using row covers (see sidebar on p. 60) to keep heat in during colder nights and help things along.

Sorghum tolerates extreme drought, but do give the plants a deep watering if things get really dry. And always water if the leaves begin to curl—that's how this plant shows water stress.

Sorghum plants reach full size in eight to twelve weeks, after which point green flower heads emerge, each eventually turning into something that resembles a tassel of corn. But unlike corn's tassels, these seed heads produce pollen and seeds. The seeds are mature when they reach the "hard dough stage," meaning that when the kernels are popped open, there is no free moisture, and the interior of the seed looks and feels like a tiny ball of dough. Ripe seeds show a color change—syrup types usually change to a red-brown, grain types to white or tan. If the weather continues to be warm and dry after their initial maturity, seeds may be allowed to remain on the plants, where they will eventu-

ally dry completely. But in most of the Midwest and much of the South, you should cut off the stems and seed heads, to be dried indoors, away from moisture.

If you're interested in making syrup, the first thing to do is harvest stalks when the seed heads are mature, before a hard frost. To do this, use a sharp knife to remove the seedheads from each stalk. Then use a knife or pruning shears to cut stalks off just at ground level, remove the leaves from the stalks, and process them in the press. The juice is collected and gently boiled down until the desired consistency is reached. Stalks will keep for two to four weeks if stored in a shady, frost-free location such as a garage or a shed.

Pests and Disease

Though sorghum has pests that affect it in its native land of Africa, this vegetable isn't bothered

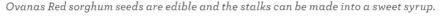

Ovanas Red sorghum seeds are edible and the stalks can be made into a sweet syrup.

by too many insects when it's planted in North America. Some bugs, like the leaf-footed plant bug, will crawl around on emerging seed heads, but they don't do much damage. Birds are actually the main problem for sorghum. Finches and other small, seed-loving birds fly into the rows and steal mature seed from the heads. Though it's possible to use row covers, sorghum grows so tall that this really isn't a viable solution. Instead, put up a scarecrow once the plants become mature, and change its location daily or the birds will become used to it. And harvest right away when the birds start raiding the seeds—they always seem to know when it's ripe!

Seed Saving

Sorghum is self-pollinating and doesn't cross with anything except other varieties of sorghum, which isn't an issue for most gardeners, who will often only be growing one variety. To gather seeds, let the grasses grow until a seed head develops and dries. A handful of seeds should be enough for home gardeners. To get larger quantities, you can thresh the seed heads in a sturdy bag by stomping on them to free the seeds from their heads.

Pull out the coarse stems and then winnow the fine chaff away from the seed. Sorghum seed is viable for three to five years.

In the Kitchen

Sorghum syrup is a delight on pancakes or waffles or on any sort of hot cereal. Sorghum flour can replace up to about half the wheat flour used in the pancakes themselves, with little impact on the taste or texture. Sorghum can be substituted for part of the flour in any recipe for unleavened bread and can also be used in traditional Indian chapatis and roti.

Spinach
Spinacea oleracea

Spinach is thought to have originated in Persia as early as the fourth century, before it migrated eastward to China—it was introduced to that country in the seventh century A.D., when the king of Nepal sent it as a gift to that country. This nutrient-packed green is also known as one of the favorite vegetables of the sixteenth-century monarch Catherine de Médicis (who was a vegetarian, and also the wife of one French king and the mother of three others). When she left her home in Florence, Italy, to marry the king of France, she brought cooks with her who could prepare her favorite dishes, including eggs on a bed of spinach "á la Florentine." These days, China and the United States are the world's largest spinach producers.

This distinctive-tasting green is the most cold-hardy of the better-known veggie crops. And it won't grow if temperatures are too warm. Consequently, the dark green, rich-tasting leaves are at their peak when comparatively little else is available in the garden. Gardeners of old, who had neither freezers nor vitamin pills, eagerly awaited the first greens of spring, calling them "tonics." Spinach, which reaches maturity between thirty and fifty days after planting, was often the earliest available cultivated spring tonic. I always feel better after eating a healthy serving of fresh spinach. It is amazing how delicious it is. And in mild and southern climates it can be harvested in the dead of winter!

Growing Tips

Spinach is one of the first crops we plant each year, between four and six weeks prior to the

Bloomsdale spinach.

last frost, because young plants can tolerate temperatures as low as fifteen degrees and the seeds germinate better in the cool spring air. They tend to just sit there if soil reaches temperatures above seventy degrees. You can also try a late summer planting, to keep the plants growing through winter—I've grown spinach through January and February when it got as cold as five degrees.

This fast-growing crop doesn't do well if transplanted, so it's best to sow seed directly into the garden. Plant a half-inch deep, three to four inches apart, in rows that are twelve to eighteen inches away from each other. Once plants have started to grow and their leaves are just touching one another, thin those baby leaves so individual plants are six to eight inches apart.

Add mulch after planting to thwart weeds and maintain soil moisture. Spinach bolts to seed easily, so succession-plant every two to three weeks until temperatures start going over seventy degrees. You can start planting again in late summer, up to a month before the last frost. If needed, these plantings can be protected with a row cover (see sidebar on p. 60) when the frost comes.

To harvest, cut individual leaves whenever they're big enough to eat, or cut the whole plant with a sharp knife, leaving about an inch above the root.

Pests and Disease

The tiny, tunneling leaf miner bug is the most common spinach pest, but it usually doesn't do too much harm. It burrows into the skin of each leaf, marking a white or translucent path that you'll notice in the rich dark green of the healthy leaf tissue. In the case of minor infestations, just discard the affected leaves. If the bugs are a bigger problem, use a row cover (see sidebar on p. 60) to keep the leaf miners at bay.

Seed Saving

Spinach is wind-pollinated, so for home gardeners it is usually best to grow only one variety if you plan on saving seed. Commercial seed growers isolate by several miles, but even a few hundred feet is far better than no isolation at all. Be sure to grow a minimum of twenty plants for seed production to protect against inbreeding depression (see sidebar on p. 71).

The main concern is to save seed, not from the earliest bolters, but rather from the later ones. The plant sends up a stalk of tiny white flowers, which turns into a seed head. When the seeds feel dry to the touch, it is time to harvest them. Pick them individually from the stalks. Gloves might be advisable for prickly-seeded spinach varieties.

In the Kitchen

One of the original superfoods, spinach is big on flavor and packed with vitamin C. The leaves also contain great supplies of other vitamins, calcium, protein, manganese, magnesium, zinc, potassium, iron, and folate. Spinach reduces dramatically when it is cooked, so double the amount if you're going to sauté it or add it to a hot dish.

Baby spinach leaves are excellent when picked fresh and eaten out of hand, added to salads, or steamed with salt and pepper. This crop is so full of minerals that seasonings are not necessary, and often they just mask this crop's true flavor.

Squash

Cucurbita maxima, C. moschata,
C. pepo, C. mixta.

*Galeux d'Eysines squash—this warty beauty
tastes incredible in pies and soups.*

Another introduction from ancient Meso-America—the regional and cultural area that extends from, roughly, central Mexico all the way down through Costa Rica—is squash. (Other important crops that are native to this region include corn, beans, tomatoes, and certain types of peppers.) The word "squash" comes from a Massachusett Native American word, *askutasquash,* meaning "eaten raw or uncooked." Squashes had already spread throughout North and South America by the time the first Europeans arrived. My parents and grandparents grew a dozen or so varieties each season. I practically grew up in a squash and pumpkin patch; as a small child, I always marveled at the diversity of shapes, sizes, and colors in the squash my family grew. When I was three, I vividly remember planting and growing Benning's Green Tint Scallop squash in my little garden in Adrien, Oregon.

So-called **summer squashes** are varieties whose fruits are harvested at a very immature and tender stage of growth, like Yellow Crookneck, Black Beauty zucchini, or Lemon squash. Such varieties have been bred to bloom prolifically, and if picked frequently, they will crank out dozens of fruits in a season when well grown. The fruits are usually eaten fresh, cooked or raw, in the summer. By contrast, the fruits of **winter squash** are allowed to mature on the plant, which takes most of the summer. These are then stored away from freezing, and used over the lean months of winter; and many varieties, such as Australian Butter, Butternut, and Blue Hubbard, will keep through an entire winter. Winter squashes tend to be starchier and often surprisingly sweet, with some, like Upper Ground Potato or Thelma Sanders, rivaling sweet potatoes in the sturdy, stick-to-your-ribs nourishment they provide in the depths of winter, when the outdoor garden is mostly asleep. Winter squashes sometimes grow to unbelievable size, like Atlantic Giant, a pumpkin that has reached more than fifteen hundred pounds. Pumpkins, incidentally, are merely a category of winter squash; many heirloom ones aren't globe-shaped, but they do have flesh that makes great pumpkin pies.

I love the diversity of squash, which ranges from tiny to gigantic, in many colors, shapes, and textures. I like to eat this fruit as much as I like to arrange and make displays of it. For several years, I've organized and arranged massive displays at the Silver Dollar City Theme Park in Branson, Missouri, as well as displays for smaller events.

Squashes are a vital part of my business, and I currently have more than 250 varieties in my collection. Ever since I planted my first squash seed, I have been addicted to this truly American crop, which has become the second most popular crop in our seed catalog (second to, what else? tomatoes).

Growing Tips

Squashes need the richest possible soil, but they also require excellent drainage. Soil should be amended with large quantities of manure or compost, dug in as deeply as possible. The soil in the row or bed should be well worked, without a lot of clods or clumps. The plants will require full sun and abundant soil moisture all summer long, though irrigation may be tapered off going into the fall.

Seeds are sown at about one to two weeks after the time of the last frost in spring. (Or set out transplants that were started indoors at about that time.) Many summer squashes and a few winter ones are of bush habit, which means they don't make long vines. Squash seeds should be sown

Gelber Englischer Custard squash is a stunning old variety that is so uniquely shaped and delicious, too.

*Yokohama squash. This Japanese heirloom was brought to
the United States in the 1860s; it has rich, nutty-tasting flesh.*

about three-quarters of an inch deep and a foot apart in rows that are six to ten feet apart—yes, the vines will really run that far; sometimes as far as 20 feet! After the seeds sprout, thin young plants to two to three feet apart. Mulch controls the weeds and helps retain soil moisture.

After six weeks or so, the flowers appear. Squashes have separate male and female flowers; usually the male flowers appear before the female ones. The males do not set fruit. The female flowers start out with a tiny fruit at the base of each flower. If pollination occurs (and the bees do love squash blossoms), the female flowers will wilt and the fruit will begin to grow. If it's a summer squash, leave the fruit in place until it looks like the size you're used to seeing in the grocery store. If you haven't seen the variety, trial and error will tell you at what size you favor the fruits.

Winter squash fruits are left on the plant until the rind is so tough that it's difficult to dent the skin with your thumbnail. If your nail pops through, the squash isn't mature and won't keep if picked, and also won't be as starchy and as sweet as a good winter squash ought to be. Squash plants and fruits will endure the mildest of frosts; anything more than that kills the leaves and may damage the skin of the fruits, rendering them unfit for long-term storage. It's safest to pick all the fruit before the first hard frost.

Pests and Disease

Squash experiences the usual *Cucurbita* pests: cucumber beetles, squash vine borers, and squash bugs. The last two are difficult to beat organically. Early or late planting is sometimes said to foil them, but in our area it hasn't helped much.

Proper garden sanitation, such as destroying spent squash vines in the fall and tilling once or twice in the winter, may reduce their numbers. But these two are very mobile pests and will usually fly in from somewhere else.

Squash bugs may be handpicked and destroyed if their numbers are few enough, in the cool early morning temperatures that slow the critters down. If there are too many to handpick, the next step is to try to destroy as many eggs as possible. The brown eggs are usually in clusters on the undersides of leaves. If the eggs hatch, you'll see dozens of tiny black nymphs, which is what the babies are called. At that point, spraying is necessary. We think that neem oil and spinosad give some control; other folks use pyrethrum-based insecticides, and still others swear by diatomaceous earth, which is a white powder mined from ancient seabeds. Some authorities recommend planting buckwheat near the squash plants. The flowers are said to draw the adults of a parasitic wasp, who then lay their eggs on the squash bugs, which are eventually killed by the parasitic larvae.

The cucumber beetle may be deterred by the same sprays as the squash bug. Left unchecked, these beetles can eat the stamens of the squash flowers and interfere with pollination and fruit setting. But even a few of them can carry wilt or blight, which kills the plants outright and has no remedy.

The borer can be somewhat controlled with Bt. Spray it at the base of the plants, and renew it after every rain for best results. If borers are a big problem in your area, grow resistant varieties, such as Butternut, Seminole Pumpkin, or Cushaw.

All the squash pests may be excluded using

Yugoslavian Finger Fruit squash looks great in fall decorations.

a row cover (see sidebar on p. 60). The material must be removed when the female blossoms appear, since the flowers need pollination to yield fruits, but the row cover may be left over the plants for their initial six weeks of life or so, at least excluding the pests until the plants are larger and better able to cope.

Seed Saving

It's vital to realize that there are four species of squash and the fact that they virtually never cross with other species, so it's possible to save seed from up to four kinds in the same season. (Reputable seed companies will usually list the species on each packet or in their catalogs.) Crossing within the same species can be prevented by isolation of varieties up to a half mile or by bagging blooms and hand-pollinating.

Seeds are collected from fully mature fruits. Whether the variety is a summer or a winter type, the fruits should be fully developed, with a very hard rind. Bring the fruits indoors and cure them for at least two weeks before extracting the seeds. This step will improve the germination of the harvested seeds, which are allowed a little extra time to finish their growth.

The seeds are simply scooped out, just as they would be when preparing the fruit to eat, and in fact, the fruit may indeed be utilized at this point. (Sometimes summer squash make a passable winter squash as well, like Zucchino Rampicante, and it's worth trying the mature fruit of any summer squash if it looks appetizing.) The pulp is placed in a bowl or bucket and just covered with water. After one to two days in room temperature conditions above seventy-five degrees, the pulp may be rinsed away in a colander, under a faucet or using a hose if available.

In the Kitchen

Squash has long been a major source of nourishment for my family, which has grown and cooked them for generations. They are very high in vitamins and other nutrients and are easy to prepare in myriad ways. Our family loves Pumpkin Curry, baked squash, roasted squash, stuffed squash, squash turnovers and pies, squash breads, and of course fried squash served with just a little salt or soy sauce. The seeds are delicious, too; any seeds not being saved for planting may be soaked overnight in salt water and then roasted in a three-hundred-degree oven. The squash blossoms are superb stuffed, battered, and deep-fried.

Squash is good for you! It's a power source of vitamin A; in fact a single serving of Butternut squash can give you five times your daily recommended minimum serving of that vitamin, along with healthy amounts of carbohydrates, iron, calcium, and potassium.

Strawberry

Fragaria vesca, F. X ananassa

A seventeenth-century English writer named Dr. William Butler once said of strawberries, "Doubtless God could have made a better berry, but doubtless God never did." These sweet, fragrant, and exceptionally delicious fruits are synonymous with the start of summer. My parents grew tons of them, and I have many fond memories of spending time in wild strawberry patches, harvesting the tiny wild berries in the Montana mountains, and then later eating strawberry pie and preserves. One of my favorite ways to eat strawberries is on pancakes.

This plant is a distant relative of the rose and grows on short little plants with sawtooth leaves and dainty white flowers. Wild types, and many of the cultivated varieties, are June bearers—they bloom at mid-spring and ripen during a short period in June. They bloom in response to how much sun they get. As days get longer, the plant blossoms, and the flowers become berries. June bearers are the kind to plant for freezing and preserving, because you can harvest all of them at once, which makes processing them a lot easier.

But there's another class, the ever-bearing and day-neutral varieties, which are the ones to grow if you're interested in fresh eating all season long. So-called Alpine strawberries, which are a nearly wild type, fall into this category. Many folks feel that Alpines possess the sweetest, most fragrant, and intensely flavorful berries of all, despite their diminutive size. The ever-bearing types bloom all season and ripen throughout the summer. They might yield the same general amount as June-bearers, but because the fruit comes over a long season, just a few at a time, it pretty much precludes making jam or doing other processing with the berries.

The strawberry is unusual in that there are different native types both in the Old World and the New. The Romans knew of strawberries, although they used them as medicine more than as food. The jumbo-size large-fruiting types did not appear until after the discovery of the Americas. It was a Frenchman who, in 1714, first crossed two American species, one from Chile and the other from the eastern United States, to produce these, and they were much in demand in Europe even before American independence.

Growing Tips

Strawberries need TLC and aren't the easiest fruits to grow, but most home gardeners feel they're worth a little extra trouble.

If you're starting Alpine types from seed, sow the seeds indoors in pots, on the surface of seed-starting mix, and keep the pots in bright light, with rather cool indoor conditions—temps of sixty-five degrees are good. Let them grow indoors until they are four to six inches high before transplanting. They won't be as large as purchased cultivated seedlings, but that's okay. Starting them indoors in early spring will result in good transplants by the time frosts are over.

Set transplants, whether home-raised or purchased, into the ground in spring, after danger of frost has passed. The soil should be rich in nutrients and organic matter, well drained, and in full sun. The plants must be set so that the crown (the area where the roots meet the leaf stems) is just level with the soil surface. If you put them too deep (with the leaf stems partially buried) or too shallow (with any part of the roots exposed above the soil's surface), the plant will die.

Plant them fifteen inches apart, in rows that are two to three feet apart. Apply a mulch immediately after planting. Straw is ideal and may possibly be the source of our common name for the berries. Occasionally a weed or two survives in spite of the mulch—pull these by hand as soon as possible. Some folks pick off any flowers that form the first year, so that they do not develop fruits, believing that this will set the plants back. For ever-bearers, a first year harvest is all right, provided that the plants were set in early spring, which gives plants time to reach a good size before blooming commences.

In the late summer, the plants will send out runners—long stems that travel across the soil surface and which have a new plant at the tip. One by one these runners will take root. For ever-bearing or day-neutral varieties, you should simply prune off the runners. This keeps new plants to a minimum and keeps existing plants free from crowding. (Alpine types rarely make runners at all.) For June-bearers, let them take root, but don't allow more than five of these new plants per square foot.

The second year, berries are harvested from the original plants. After the harvest, which may not be concluded until late summer or autumn, the original plants are removed. Yes, it's painful, but they won't yield well in future years. Dig, cut, or pull them up. Then put mulch over the soil that has been thus bared. New runner plants will soon fill the space. In future

years, last year's runner plants become this year's bearers, and the current year's bearers are removed after fruiting. This keeps the bed always productive—no older plants are permitted to remain. If all this seems too complicated, just let the bed go for two to three years, then renovate it by digging up plants in autumn or early spring, discarding the oldest ones (which will have an overgrown, woody look about them), and setting in the younger ones (which will be smaller, and more succulent-looking) as outlined previously.

Pests and Disease

Strawberries can be badly damaged by slugs, which thrive in the moist shade under the low leaves. Handpicking keeps them under control, or you can place a shallow tray of beer in the patch to draw them away from your plants. Spider mites and aphids can be a problem; control them with insecticidal soap or vegetable oil sprays. A number of other insects cause occasional damage as well; neem oil or pyrethrum usually furnishes adequate control. Remember to always practice good sanitation: Don't allow the berries to rot in the bed, and don't allow weeds to add to the already crowded conditions in a mature strawberry bed.

Seed Saving

Seeds should probably not be saved from most cultivated varieties of strawberry, because they're hybrids and can't be counted on to breed true. But seeds may be saved from the Alpine types. Simply allow the fruits to become very ripe, mash them in a bowl or bucket, and wash the pulp away by using successive rinses. Spread the washed seeds out in a thin layer and allow them to air-dry. Strawberry seeds are very tiny; even a quarter teaspoon contains hundreds of seeds.

In the Kitchen

The strawberry is at its best freshly picked and perfectly ripe, eaten right in the garden or after dinner or for breakfast in a fruit salad, in the summertime. But they also shine in jellies and preserves, pies, cobblers, muffins, tarts, or made into a delicious juice. Strawberries have a lot of vitamin C and are a good source for fiber and manganese. I particularly like the Alpine types; the fruits are smaller, but these little jewels pack a lot of flavor and sweetness. Besides red, they also grow in yellow and white. Alpines are always a hit with everyone, from four-star chefs to children in Grandmother's garden.

Alpine strawberries have bright red fruit that are quite small, but loaded with sweetness and flavor!

Tomatillo

Physalis ixocarpa

Purple tomatillo—the truest purple of any garden fruit, this variety also has fine flavor.

This gorgeous vegetable is native to Central and South America and popular in Mexico, where it was a staple of Mayan and Aztec cultures. Tomatillos are commonly found in Mexican dishes today, especially when the yellow tomatillos are still green. The tart, almost citrusy taste of the immature fruit bulks up green salsas and other cooked sauces, such as cooked chili verde stew.

Like ground cherries, the tomatillo is enclosed in a papery husk (the botanical name for which is *calyx*) and has smooth, bright green leaves. Within the calyx, ripe tomatillos will be either yellow or purple.

Growing Tips

Tomatillos are usually started indoors and transplants set out after frost, like tomatoes. They can be grown throughout most of the United States, since they are cool-weather tolerant (though they can't take frost) and fairly quick to yield, much more quickly than most tomatoes. Sow the tiny seeds a quarter inch deep in well-drained soil that is between seventy and eighty-five degrees, with access to full sun. Tomatillos grow similarly to regular tomatoes—though they should not be staked. They are also similar to ground cherries, but bigger. Because they will sprawl, you need to give them room to grow—plants should be two feet apart, in rows that are five feet apart.

When they reach full size, their husk will split. The husk will still be green at that point and will soon dry to a tan-brown. Harvest yellow-ripening varieties, like Green Tomatillo and Dr. Wyche's Yellow, when the fruits themselves are still green, for use in salsas and chilis verdes. For vibrant purple types, like Purple, Purple de Milpa, and Purple Cobán, go ahead and wait until they are actually purple before picking. The purple types are sweeter than the green ones, and some folks make preserves or jam from the fruits.

If left undisturbed within their husks, tomatillos will keep for four to five weeks in the refrigerator, and often much longer.

Pests and Disease
Tomatillos have no pests or diseases in general. Occasionally they will be afflicted by cutworms or various beetles, but only rarely will they require any insect control, as problems are usually minimal.

Seed Saving
Tomatillos are self-pollinating plants but may cross freely with other tomatillo varieties, so if you want to save seeds, grow only a single variety at a time, or isolate each variety by a minimum of five hundred feet or cage the plant (see sidebar on p. 71). A minimum population of at least five plants is suggested for seed saving. The fruits are left on the plants until after they've reached full ripeness, as indicated by their final color change, with fully ripe fruits also being soft to the touch. Fully ripe fruits generally fall from the plant, so the best ones for seed saving will be lying on the mulch under the plant. As with tomatoes, seeds may be extracted individually, or in quantity by a fermentation process.

In the Kitchen
The husks are always removed before preparing tomatillos. The tart fruits are rich in vitamin C. The fruits lend a velvety smoothness to cooked green chili sauces and are also great to blend with hot green chilis, as the tomatillo has no heat of its own and the ratio to the green chilis may be varied to tone down the chilis' degree of heat. The flavor of tomatillos blends superbly in many combinations, including with cilantro, avocado, onion, garlic, and fresh chili peppers of any degree of heat.

Tomato

Lycopersicon lycopersicum

Gold Medal tomato—at the top of its class in both looks and flavor.

Tomatoes are the most popular crop that people grow around the world, and the undisputed queen of the garden. Every summer, gardeners vie with their neighbors in good-natured competition to see who will produce the earliest ripe tomato. And when that day comes, you know summer has really arrived. Not bad for a fruit that was once believed to be poisonous!

First discovered in the Andes more than two thousand years ago, the tomato was quickly traded north, and the Aztecs enjoyed it in the sixteenth century. Eventually it reached Europe, where it was greeted with disdain, as it was a member of the nightshade family and was thought to be poisonous back then (indeed, many nightshades, such as belladonna or henbane, are poisonous). Instead of being a major food crop, the tomato was grown as an ornamental, and

often referred to as a "love apple." The Italians, of course, were the first Europeans to introduce it into their cuisine, and from there people started to realize that tomatoes weren't poisonous. Slowly they became an unstoppably popular fruit throughout Europe, and with the colonists of the New World.

The first cookbook recipe featuring tomatoes appeared in 1692. Thomas Jefferson grew them at Monticello, and French and Italian immigrants grew them from San Francisco to Poughkeepsie. There is a famous story of a Colonel Robert Gibbon Johnson eating tomatoes on the courthouse steps in Salem County, New Jersey, to prove their safety as a food crop in 1820, even after receiving warning from his doctor that if he proceeded to eat this fruit he would "foam at the mouth" and die. It is said that two thousand people watched as he consumed a full basket, the crowd believing they were about to see Johnson commit tomato suicide, which of course didn't happen. Nonetheless, some folks remained skeptical, and it took many years for tomatoes to be finally accepted in the United States, in the late nineteenth century.

Tomatoes are so important to me. My first experience in growing them inspired me to grow and save seeds for the rest of my life. When I was just three years old, I planted Yellow Pear—a miniature tomato variety that dates to the eighteenth century—and I've been hooked ever since. A year or so later, even though I still couldn't read, I gathered up all my parents' seed catalogs in the winter and pored over them, staring at the colorful, exciting varieties and pictures of tomatoes. By the time I was ten, I was ordering all the catalogs I could find to learn about every variety they listed, from the tiny little Currant tomatoes, which are only the size of a pea, to colossal varieties like the Giant Belgium, which can get up to four pounds, and every size and shape in between.

The color spectrum of tomatoes is dazzling: Besides every shade of red, there are purple, green, pink, orange, yellow, white, brown, and even multicolored varieties, like Green Zebra, which is lime-green with bright yellow stripes. Each color has its own unique taste. Some are sweet and fruity; others are rich, complex, and acidic.

Growing Tips

Tomatoes take a long time to grow. Start them indoors eight to ten weeks before the last frost. They're frost-tender, so you need to be 100 percent sure that frost is gone before you transplant them into the garden.

Sow seeds a quarter inch deep in pots, with a fine layer of soil. Keep them warm and moist until sprouts appear, which can take up to fourteen days. Once sprouted, the seedlings need good light—putting them on a sunny windowsill is best (though some gardeners grow them under fluorescents or grow lights).

Other than regular watering and a little feeding of diluted fish emulsion or other organic fertilizer, little care is necessary until it's time to transplant to the garden. Be sure to harden off your plants prior to setting them outside (see sidebar on p. 54).

Tomatoes are heavy feeders, so you should amend their soil heavily with compost or manure. Seedlings grown indoors are apt to be leggy (tall and sometimes a little stretched-looking), so bury them deeply, all the way up to where the leaves start. This allows the buried stems to strike more roots, and strengthen the

Violet Jasper tomato—this Chinese variety is among the earliest I grow; it also produces like mad and is so fine-looking.

Orange-flesh Purple Smudge tomato—
glowing tangerine-orange
orbs are splashed in true violet-purple.

plant. Apply a layer of mulch around the plants immediately to thwart any weeds. As they grow, you'll notice right away that tomatoes are big plants.

And they need something to grow on. As you put them into the ground, or if you're a city gardener, plant them in a large container, put a wire trellis or cage in at the same time. In the garden, tomatoes should be two or three feet apart, in rows that are six to seven feet apart.

Tomatoes are ripe when they have reached their final color. Another sign of ripeness is that the fruits become soft. (Too soft to ship, of course, which is why commercial tomatoes are picked and shipped while green and hard. That is why store-bought can never compare to vine-ripened, fresh-picked tomatoes. Unripe tomatoes will ripen off the vine, but they are never as sweet or rich-tasting as those vine-ripened ones.) Pick the ripe tomatoes carefully to avoid bruising them by rough handling.

Pests and Disease

Not many insects bother tomatoes, but the tomato hornworm is a spectacular exception. Really the larva of a moth, it can grow as big as a man's finger and strip even a large plant of its leaves in a matter of days. If leaves are missing on your plants, with only short stumps of their stems remaining, suspect the hornworm. Their green camouflage can make them hard to find while they're nestled in the plants, but they are usually near the base of the plants by day. The most effective way to get them off is to handpick them. Wear gloves if you are squeamish, and dispose of them in a bucket of soapy water. Usually they occur only here and there, but if you en-counter a major infestation of more than a dozen or so in a few plants, spray with Bt or spinosad right away and regularly.

Tomatoes are also susceptible to a number of diseases, most of which have no reliable organic cure. Proper crop rotation is vital—never grow tomatoes or other nightshade family crops on the same ground more than once within four years. And instead of tilling or composting spent tomato plants, dispose of them by burning or throwing them away. This keeps diseases from building up in your garden.

It's also best to avoid using sprinklers in the tomato patch, because moisture on the leaves is an invitation to the fungi and bacteria that cause most problems.

Finally, don't crowd tomato plants. They need plenty of air circulation and sunshine to keep them disease-free. Organic sprays such as fish emulsion and vegetable oil–based preparations may inhibit the growth of diseases, but they aren't really a cure, especially where blights are a problem, though a weekly spray of these products may keep diseases at bay.

Seed Saving

Tomatoes are a fine choice for beginning seed savers. They are mostly self-pollinating and inbreeding plants, which means seed can be saved from multiple varieties, so long as fifteen to fifty feet of isolation is allowed. They will seldom cross even when grown closer than that.

To harvest seeds, allow the fruit to fully ripen (the seeds are mature before that, but they'll be best when you take them from a ripe fruit). To get just a few seeds, cut open a tomato and scoop them out individually. A single fruit

CANNING WITH LOW-ACID VS. HIGH-ACID VARIETIES

In the old days, nearly every housewife canned tomatoes each year, and it's still one of the most glorious ways to preserve the summer's bounty. Once you get started, you'll find that there are countless recipes and methods for canning.

When choosing a recipe, make sure it's approved for safety by the USDA, and be careful when canning with tomato varieties that have lower acidity (the colors that have lower acid tend to be white and yellow, as well as some kinds of pink and red types).

Proper preservation methods take the level of acidity of a vegetable or fruit into account, and tomatoes with lower acidity might not be safe if they're canned with a recipe that was originally developed for high acid varieties.

If you wish to preserve the lower acid varieties, look in any modern cookbook on the topic (our canning bible is Ball's *Blue Book Guide to Preserving*) or ask the home economist at your local Extension Office.

might yield fifty to one hundred seeds, which is plenty for most home gardeners. If you want to save a larger amount, scoop out the pulp and seeds from inside a bunch of tomatoes or crush whole fruits thoroughly and set the mixture aside so that it can ferment in a large bucket for two or three days. As the seeds ferment, the contents of the bucket will develop a rather sour, unpleasant aroma—it's no accident that disappointing actors were once pelted with rotten tomatoes!—so place the bucket in the backyard out of the way (but not so far out of the way that you forget about it). And be sure to cover the mixture with an old towel or cheesecloth, whatever you have that will allow air circulation but keep flies out. The fermentation process is complete once the top of the mixture is covered with a layer of white mold.

As soon as this layer appears, pour the mixture into a larger container, stir, and wash seeds with a powerful spray from a water hose (the velocity of the water stream will jar seeds loose from the pulp).

Once that container is full, turn off the water and let the contents settle for a minute or two. During this time, seeds will sink to the bottom. Pour off the top layers of water and pulp, then repeat until the rinse water is nearly clear. Pour that mixture into a mesh strainer to drain the water but hold the seeds. Pluck any non-seed debris (leaves, stems, peels) from the seeds and spread them out in a thin layer on a sheet of newspaper to dry.

They will be pretty much dry within twenty-four to thirty-six hours, but it is helpful to point a gentle fan breeze toward the drying seeds, because prolonged exposure to moisture will cause them to sprout, which you *don't* want.

When the mass of seeds is nearly dry, they are apt to stick together in clumps resembling granola. Gently break them apart at this stage, working them by hand so that loose individual seeds do not stick together. When they are absolutely bone-dry—we leave our tomato seeds out for two to three extra days, even after they appear dry, just to be safe—store in a cool, dry place. Tomato seeds are viable for up to five years.

In the Kitchen

Home-grown heirloom tomatoes are so much juicier and sweeter than their pale, horrible-tasting

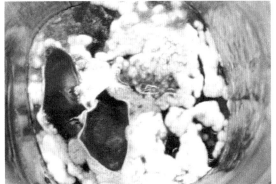

5 EASY STEPS TO SAVING TOMATO SEEDS

CLOCKWISE FROM TOP LEFT: *First, slice a tomato in half and crush its pulp and seeds into a jar. Wait for the pulp and seeds to ferment. After three days, the mixture will have a white film on top. Rinse and drain off the pulp. Seeds will sink to the bottom. Rinse seeds with water repeatedly until the seeds are clean. Spread seeds out to dry in a clean, dry place with a gentle breeze.*

TOMATO COLORS

Tomatoes come in a fascinating rainbow of colors, ranging across almost every shade imaginable—from green to orange, from pink to purple to brown and red, from black to pale yellow and almost white. They also have many other variations, as well as bicolored and striped varieties. Each color generally comes with its own unique flavor, texture, and level of acidity.

HIGH ACID: red, green, purple, brown
MEDIUM ACID: orange, yellow, pink
LOW ACID: white, larger bicolors

Red. Red tomatoes are often very acidic, and excellent for sauces and canning. They're some of the juiciest ones, and superstars when they're cooked in so many different ways.

Purple and brown. The most delicious and intensely flavorful type of tomato, these dark varieties have a more complex flavor than all other tomatoes. They're our biggest sellers. Once people try the dark tomatoes, they're hooked for life. The depth of flavor is sweet and earthy. Recommended for use in salsas and sauces, and of course eaten out of hand, standing in the garden or over the kitchen sink.

Green. Of all the other colors, these taste the most like red tomatoes: sweet, with a full, rich flavor. The first time people taste a green tomato, they often think they've tasted a really good red tomato. It reminds you of Grandma's garden, and they're good in salsas or made into a sauce.

Orange. Sunny, golden-hued varieties tend to have a citrus taste that is very sweet and mild.

Pink. Pretty pink tomatoes taste a lot like red ones but are typically sweeter and milder. Many people who don't do well with high acid prefer these over red ones.

Yellow. These tomatoes tend to have low-to-medium acid levels and a citrusy taste occasionally with a hint of lemon. They're best in salads and also good for making cheerful-looking salsas.

Striped and multicolored. These varieties are typically lower in acid, high in sugar content, and not only look like candy, but kind of taste like it, too. They tend to be large-fruited (especially pineapple and German types). They're a favorite for fresh eating, but not recommended for canning. They remind me of a piece of fresh tropical fruit.

White. Some people think white tomatoes are a bit bland, but I enjoy their mild fruitiness. They are excellent for fresh eating, but their low-acid content isn't suitable for preserving or cooking. For people who have a hard time with acid, this is a go-to tomato.

store-bought counterparts. My favorite way to eat them is right off the vine, at the peak of ripeness, while standing in the garden.

But it's also really fun to see the different colors in familiar dishes. You can make green-colored ketchup with green varieties, pale-yellow salsa, or bright orange spaghetti sauce—the possibilities are endless. The best tomatoes are perfect drizzled with olive oil and salt. But they can also be stuffed, chopped into salads, or roasted. The various colors of heirloom tomatoes contain a varied array of nutrients and flavors that are lacking in many newer hybrids. That's why top chefs and home horticulturists alike adore the heirlooms that are quickly replacing hybrids in gardens. Even the first lady, Michelle Obama, grows them.

Chile Verde tomatoes are perfect for making green ketchup and tomato sauce.

Turnip and Rutabaga

Brassica rapa var. *rapifera* and
Brassica napus var. *napobrassica*

The Golden Ball turnip has smooth, yellow flesh.

Though these two root crops are largely underappreciated in the United States these days, I wouldn't be without either of them. I adore their cabbagey-tasting "twang" (which folks either love or hate), as well as the fact that they store very well in a root cellar or cool basement throughout winter. Their pungent flavor is an important part of lunch and dinner throughout autumn at Baker Creek. I'm also especially fond of turnip greens, which are a staple in many Southern kitchens, where they are served as wilted greens (fresh with just enough hot oil poured on them to make them wilt) or steamed and served with a dash of lemon or vinegar and a slab of hot cornbread.

Turnips (*Brassica rapa* var. *rapifera*) are quick growers that are harvested at about the size of a baseball. They yield roots forty-five to sixty days after planting and are hardy in cool weather. Their fuzzy greens are popular even

with people who don't like the root taste. This ancient crop has been cultivated since prehistoric times, and Romans wrote about a number of varieties, including long, flat, and round types. Roman naturalist and historian Pliny the Elder said of the turnip, "There is no plant that is of more extensive use." Turnips were first brought to North America by French explorer Jacques Cartier, who planted them in Canada in the mid-sixteenth century. Some fifty years later, they were planted by the first colonists in Virginia.

Rutabagas (*Brassica napus* var. *napobrassica*) are said to be a rare natural cross between turnip and cabbage and were first documented in 1620 by a Swiss botanist named Caspar Bauhin. Their popularity in Swedish gardens led them to be referred to as the "Swede turnip," and Americans called them the "turnip-rooted cabbage" in the 1800s. Rutabaga leaves are smooth, like cabbage leaves, and the roots are larger and starchier than a turnip's. Despite their larger size, their flavor is much milder. I generally prefer this vegetable over its turnip cousins because of its sweeter and richer flavor.

Growing Tips

Rutabagas and turnips are both cool-weather crops that thrive in rich, well-watered and well-drained soil. Turnips are usually grown as a fall crop, except in coastal or northern climates where springs are longer and cool; they will be fine as long as temperatures seldom reach above eighty degrees.

Plant seeds a half inch deep, and once the plants are growing, thin them to between four and six inches apart, in rows that are one to two

Round Red turnip—this Asian favorite is so sweet and mild.

feet apart (bring those thinnings into the kitchen for an early mess of greens!).

Rutabagas grow more slowly than turnips, so plant them in the mid-summer for a fall harvest. Young seedlings can take quite a bit of heat, although fall planting is recommended for the hottest areas of the deep South. Thin, to six to eight inches apart, in rows that are eighteen to twenty-four inches apart.

Immediately after planting either crop or as soon as sprouts are visible, apply a layer of mulch to control weeds and retain soil moisture.

Pests and Disease

Rutabagas and turnips are afflicted by the same pests as other crops in the cabbage family. The shiny red-and-black harlequin bug often descends on turnips in the summertime and disfigures the leaves. Use a row cover (see sidebar on p. 60) or handpick the bugs to avoid a full infestation.

Seed Saving

Rutabagas only cross with other rutabagas. Turnips are bee-pollinated, and they cross easily among different varieties of turnips and also with certain types of Chinese cabbage. If you have a lot of land and want to ensure a pure strain, isolate varieties by at least a half a mile. Otherwise it's best to grow just one variety if you plan to save seed.

As biennials, both turnips and rutabagas must grow through winter before they'll throw up spikes of cheery yellow blossoms. Allow the blooms to mature, and they will eventually give way to long, pointed seedpods.

Collect seeds before the pods turn brown and dry up. Otherwise, the seed heads will shatter and seeds will scatter in the dirt. To collect the seeds, harvest individual seedpods as they ripen, or cut off the seed head and hang it upside down over a large container indoors to catch the seeds as they ripen and drop.

In the Kitchen

When picked young, turnips are mild and creamy-tasting and can be cooked in most of the same ways that potatoes are. They are delicious when mashed, as a less starchy alternative to mashed potatoes, and can be made into a slaw salad with carrots or fried in oil with diced onion until crisp. They are also sometimes grated and made into sauerkraut.

Rutabagas are a nice addition to soups and stews. They also taste great boiled and mashed and can be mixed with potatoes for that purpose—they add a complexity to the flavor of the potatoes, which, in turn, soften the rutabagas' twang. And they're just superb roasted in the oven with a little olive oil and salt.

Steamed turnip greens are especially healthy, not to mention delicious! Turnips are a great source of iron, which is sometimes lacking in modern diets, and contain cancer-fighting isothiocyanates, as well as magnesium, potassium, manganese, and various antioxidants.

Watermelon
Citrullus lanatus

One of our customers sent us the seeds for the Ancient watermelon, a sugary sweet variety that was first discovered in a cave in the later part of the twentieth century.

ers. Some had crimson-red flesh; others were pink, canary-yellow, or the deepest orange.

I know the taste of pure, fresh heirloom watermelons so well that I can barely stand to eat the store-bought ones. They usually just taste like water-soaked sponges and are sad imitations of what a watermelon should taste and smell like.

Watermelon is native to Africa's scorching hot Kalahari Desert, where it is a vital source of water during severe drought. It was eventually domesticated in central and southern Africa. Watermelons have been grown by farmers for thousands of years and were known and grown in ancient Egypt, southern Europe, the east as far as India, and even China.

Watermelon seeds were carried to the New World aboard slave ships and distributed around the Caribbean and Brazil long before reaching Massachusetts in 1629 when Native Americans recognized the watermelon's wonders right away and started cultivating it, and it was rapidly

Sasha Gettle with a big Kolb's Gem watermelon; these can grow up to 100 pounds!

My love for this refreshing crop began when I was a toddler crawling around in the tangled vines in my parents' garden. My dad planted great quantities of this luscious, fragrant fruit, and we devoured them throughout July and August and well into autumn—sometimes we ate a whole giant watermelon in one day.

Each melon was like a treasure chest of flavor and color. We grew giant Kolb's Gem, Crimson Sweet, Sugar Baby, Tendersweet, King and Queen, Orangeglo, Rattlesnake, and many oth-

An Orangeglo watermelon.
Dripping with sweet orange juice, this variety has incredible flavor.

traded from one tribe to another. Later European explorers were surprised to discover watermelon patches growing when they reached the interior portions of North America. In Russia the juice is boiled down into amber-colored syrup and drizzled over coffee cake. And the seeds are pressed for cooking oil in India and China.

Watermelons come in all sizes, from dwarf types weighing only a couple of pounds to gigantic ones tipping the scales at more than three hundred pounds. But huge and tiny watermelons are not necessarily the best for eating. I prefer the flavor of the medium-size ones, like Ali Baba, Orangeglo, and Stone Mountain.

Growing Tips

Watermelon needs hot weather and plenty of moisture to thrive. A couple of weeks after the danger of frost has passed, sow watermelon seeds one inch deep in loose, rich soil that has been amended liberally with organic matter, such as compost. Watermelons need full sun—which means more than eight hours of sunshine per day. Seeds should be twelve inches apart in rows that are eight feet apart. Once vines start growing, mulch liberally with straw. Within three weeks, the vines will start growing quickly and will then cover the soil surface themselves, which assists the mulch in shading out weeds.

Judging ripeness takes practice, though there are a few subtle indicators. Some people, including me, believe that when a watermelon is ripe, it will make a duller, hollow-seeming sound when you thump it with your knuckle. I also look closely at the tendril that is located immediately opposite the stem of each fruit. When that ten-

dril is brown and dry, it's likely that the watermelon is ripe.

Pests and Disease

Watermelons are susceptible to numerous pests and diseases, but less so than their squash relatives. They're particularly apt to demonstrate stress when they don't get enough heat. If that happens, the plants will stop growing, and be more vulnerable to pests and diseases due to their lack of vigor. So make sure not to plant them too soon after the last frost of spring, as they will just sit in the ground unless soil temperature gets above seventy degrees.

If you see cucumber beetles (yellow-green bugs about the size of ladybugs, but striped or spotted in glossy black), spray the leaves with spinosad. Row covers (see sidebar on p. 60) are also very effective but should be removed when the flowers begin to open, so that bees can pollinate.

The squash bug is another potential problem, if it is still hungry after it has attacked the squash. Thwart it with pyrethrum. Spider mites may be an issue in climates that are hot and dry, but they will leave when the rain comes, or they can be handled with with Safer Soap, neem oil, or vegetable oil–based insecticides.

Seed Saving

Watermelons can be crossed only by other varieties of watermelons—never by cucumbers, squash, or any other species of melon. Bees can carry the pollen for up to a half mile. Caging is workable only if bees can be kept inside of the cages, or if hand-pollination can be employed. Once isolation is assured, seed production is exactly the same as fruit production, because if you have a ripe fruit, you have ripe seeds.

To save seeds from watermelon, simply slice in and select them from the flesh. Allow the seeds to dry in a cool, dry place and then store them in a jar. Watermelon seeds store well for three to five years.

In the Kitchen

Of course, nothing can beat the taste of a juicy, refreshing watermelon eaten fresh at the height of ripeness, in the middle of a sweltering summer day. But watermelon can also be made into jellies, syrups, or even a delightful salsa. Citron watermelon is grown only for preserving, in which it is candied for use in fruitcakes and other desserts.

In Asia, they often roast large seeds and serve them as a snack (similar to how we eat pumpkin seeds in America). An old-fashioned Southern treat is pickled watermelon rinds, which you can make by peeling the rind from a watermelon and mixing it with water, vinegar, sugar, whole cloves, and spices such as cinnamon, mustard seed, cloves, lemon, or even cherries, for a pop of color.

Watermelons are also, of course, a favorite for making a juice that is so refreshing and healthy, perfect served chilled in a glass by itself or mixed with other juices. Watermelon is a great source of vitamins A and C. It also contains modest amounts of many other nutrients, including a decent amount of the possible cancer fighter lycopene.

Jere, Emilee, and Sasha with some of the watermelon harvest.

Appendix

Roadside Produce Stands

In some communities throughout America, it seems like every driveway ends with a little lean-to that is sheltering an assortment of homegrown produce—baskets of tomatoes, cucumbers, zucchini, corn, beans, and other vegetables—up for sale, waiting for a traveler to happen by and snatch them up. Oftentimes, someone is hanging around nearby to help facilitate payment for the produce. And sometimes it's more of an honor system, where you'll find a tin can or a mason jar holding the day's earnings.

These little roadside produce stands are a great resource for farmers to augment their normal income (especially when they're situated near a busy road) and a convenient place to get wholesome, fresh vegetables at little expense.

In the South, hand-painted signs start popping up in April and May, announcing the season's produce, making your mouth water with every mile that ticks by. These three-sided sheds protect the treasure trove of jams, jellies, and local fare from the weather, and vegetables and fruits in weathered crates are offered for sale. If you pull your car over and check out the goods, watermelons still damp from the morning's dew are sliced open to reveal juicy flesh, with free samples offered on an enamelware plate. Locals and visitors alike can be seen swapping stories and buying produce. If you're on a road trip, all you need to do is stop and take a look-see, and you'll experience a collage of the community and find local staples.

U-Pick Farms

U-pick farms are another great way to participate in the local harvest. Visitors pay a nominal fee to "pick" their own harvest from the farm. And since you become the "picker," you'll save serious money while gaining wonderful memories and experiencing the relaxing feeling of escaping the rat race and enjoying the peaceful serenity that comes with spending time on a farm. Visiting a u-pick farm is like having your own garden for an afternoon—without having to worry about responsibilities like watering, pests, and weeds.

Some u-pick farms offer vegetables and fruits; others offer u-pick flower bouquets. Often there is a produce stand of prepicked produce and flowers for sale at the entrance, while other farms operate on the honor system, with a scale and tin can cash register. Some larger farms offer classes and events, depending on the season and what's growing. Each u-pick farm is just as unique as the family who runs it, so visiting several in a season is an excellent way to see a diversity of gardening methods in practice.

Farmer's Markets

I've visited farmer's markets around the country and in other countries. They're the highlight of the frequent road trips that I take with my family. Brimming with fresh vegetables, flowers, local crafts, music, and locally minded people, each market is unique and reflects the local flavors and produce of the region. They're like an edible snapshot of a community.

Farmer's markets have been around for centuries. Asian street markets and Mexican produce stands surrounding the mission courtyards have marked the passage of time. For generation after generation, the same families grow and sell produce to their community, all the while sharing good conversation and great food.

In America in the mid-twentieth century, the novelty and supposed "convenience" of grocery stores and packaged foods was introduced to our growing country, and the curtain was temporarily drawn on farmer's markets. But in the past decade, people have rediscovered the desire to connect with where their food comes from. More and more, people want to eliminate the middleman between themselves and their local farmer. Markets help them do just that, and have grown significantly in popularity since the mid-1990s. In 1994 there were about 1,700 markets in the country. In 2009, that number had grown to over 5,000. And there are more markets popping up each month.

The reason for the surge in popularity of markets is not only because they offer an eclectic atmosphere that can be enjoyed by young and old alike. It's also because finally we are awakening from the delusion that "big box" stores and things that are billed as "convenient" are good for us. By choosing locally sourced produce, we are demonstrating our passion for fresh, nutrient-rich food that is produced in our own community by farmers, instead of chemists.

Supporting local markets also supports the community and the economy around us. It's easy to see why farmers have been popping up their little white-and-blue tents all over the United States in rural and metropolitan areas alike—there's a viable, thriving market out there to be tapped into, and they're doing their fellow men a real service.

If you can't grow your own garden, farmer's markets are the perfect solution! You can get fresh produce without a commitment while supporting local growers as well as your community and economy.

If you don't have a farmer's market in your area but you do have a garden, consider rounding up some of your gardening friends, pooling your resources, and starting your own market. Check out www.localharvest.org for more detailed information and resources about farmer's markets near you.

CSA

Community Support Agriculture, or CSA, is another great resource for those who do not have their own garden, or for those who do and want to supplement their own gardens and support a local farm. A CSA is simply a group of individuals who support a farm by becoming shareholders. Each shareholder pays a set fee per growing season. In exchange, they get a weekly "share" from the farm, which will include whatever is growing that week. This ripe produce is either delivered to their door or available at the farm for pick-up, depending on where they live.

Some CSAs also offer a subscription option that can be started or stopped at any time according to each individual's needs, and some CSA farms have a rotating schedule where shareholders work in the gardens helping to pick produce, weed, or pack boxes for delivery.

The produce boxes might also include optional add-ons, such as herbs, seasonal fruit, preserves, and/or dairy products. If you are new to gardening, joining a CSA is a great way to learn the ropes and participate in the growing process.

Produce Auctions

Auction barns dot the rural Amish and Mennonite communities throughout the United States. We have a few nearby in Missouri, and frequent them as a cost-effective, pure way of getting vegetables. Each week from spring through fall, we purchase produce for our restaurant to support our local farmers, as well as to supplement our own garden. You can often score amazing deals on an abundance of produce that can be prepared that same day and then you can preserve or store the rest for winter.

And the auctions are so fun to watch. During the bidding, a procession of horses or tractors pulls large wagons filled with boxes of vegetables and flowers in front of an audience of excited buyers. The bounty is then auctioned off by a fast-talking gentleman with a microphone who guides the proceedings.

As each wagon approaches, Amish or Mennonite men stand nearby and showcase the merchandise—which can range from onions, root vegetables, and flowers, to rows of pumpkins that weigh hundreds of pounds, to boxes of an Amish family's heirloom tomatoes—so that bidders can take their pick and place their bid. In between bids, the men talk about their crops and the weather, and women compare notes on what they'll be canning or freezing later in the day. Produce auctions are a wonderful peek into a community, and a great place to take children. There's such a community atmosphere about the place, not to mention a bit of bidding competition, which makes the experience all the more enjoyable.

Family-run grocery stores and produce stands, as well as the general public, pick up their "local" produce at these auctions. When we travel throughout the United States, we try to plan our trips around the local produce auctions because it's one of our favorite ways to see a new community and meet the locals.

Resources

BAKER CREEK RESOURCES

Baker Creek Heirloom Seed Company
This is our original seed store and order fulfillment center.
2278 Baker Creek Road
Mansfield, MO 65704
417-924-8917
seeds@rareseeds.com
www.rareseeds.com

The Petaluma Seed Bank
This seed store is a branch of the Baker Creek Heirloom Seed Company that is housed in an old bank building in downtown Petaluma, in Northern California.
199 Petaluma Boulevard North
Petaluma, CA 94952
(707) 509-5171
paul@rareseeds.com
www.rareseeds.com/petaluma-seed-bank

The Heirloom Gardener Magazine
Our magazine is devoted to growing, documenting, and preserving heirloom varieties.
2278 Baker Creek Road
Mansfield, MO 65704
417-924-8917
mary@theheirloomgardener.com
www.theheirloomgardener.com

Comstock, Ferre & Company, LLC
Our sister company, which is located in a historic town just outside of Hartford, has been selling seeds for over 200 years.
263 Main Street
Wethersfield, CT 06109
860-571-6590
sales@comstockferre.com
www.comstockferre.com

The National Heirloom Exposition
The first annual exhibition to celebrate heirloom varieties was held in September 2011 in Santa Rosa, California, and featured a long list of world-class speakers, natural food vendors, and experts on local farming and gardening.
199 Petaluma Boulevard North
Petaluma, CA 94952
(707) 509-5171
info@theheirloomexpo.com
www.theheirloomexpo.com

www.idigmygarden.com
Our online forum for gardeners, seed savers and natural foodies

HERE IS A LIST OF SOME OF OUR OTHER FAVORITE RESOURCES:

Abundant Acres
Growing and shipping strictly heirloom veggie plants since 2004
PO Box 256
Hartville, MO 65667
(417) 462-1019
abundantacres@yahoo.com
http://www.abundantacres.net

Bountiful Gardens
This gardening center sells a wide range of garden products. It is sponsored by Ecology Action, which is a non-profit organization that is dedicated to helping end world hunger by teaching sustainable agriculture.
18001 Shafer Ranch Road
Willits, CA 95490
(707) 459-6410
bountiful@sonic.net
http://www.bountifulgardens.org
http://www.growbiointensive.org

Fedco Seeds
Since 1978, this co-operative has been offering cold-hardy varieties that are specifically selected for Northeast gardeners.
PO Box 520
Waterville, ME 04903
(207) 873-7333
questions@fedcoseeds.com
http://www.fedcoseeds.com

Gardener's Supply Company
A wide variety of products for home and market gardeners
Gardener's Supply Company
128 Intervale Road
Burlington, VT 05401
info@gardeners.com
http://www.gardeners.com

Grit Magazine
Celebrating rural America since 1882
1503 Southwest 42nd Street
Topeka, KS 66609
(866) 803-7096
editor@grit.com
http://www.grit.com

Hobby Farms Magazine
Covering a wide range of topics of interest to small farmers, homesteaders, and gardeners
PO Box 8237
Lexington, KY 40533
800-627-6157
hobbyfarms@bowtieinc.com
http://www.hobbyfarms.com

Marianna's Heirloom Seeds
Wide selection of heirlooms including a superb collection of Italian varieties
1955 CCC Road
Dickson TN, 37055
(615) 446-9191
mj@mariseeds.com
http://www.mariseeds.com

Mother Earth News
The original guide to living wisely
1503 Southwest 42nd Street
Topeka, KS 66609
(800) 234-3368
letters@motherearthnews.com
https://www.motherearthnews.com

Native Seeds/SEARCH
A not-for-profit devoted to preserving locally adapted Southwestern and northern Mexican varieties
3584 E. River Road
Tucson, AZ 85718
(520) 622-5561
info@nativeseeds.org
http://www.nativeseeds.org

Organic Gardening
The original magazine devoted to all phases of organic gardening
400 South Tenth Street
Emmaus, PA 18098-0099
(800) 666-2206
ogdcustserv@rodale.com
http://www.organicgardening.com

Peaceful Valley Farm & Garden Supply
Supplying everything needed for the organic garden since 1976
PO Box 2209 | 125 Clydesdale Court
Grass Valley, CA 95945
(530) 272-4769
(888) 784-1722
www.groworganic.com
helpdesk@groworganic.com

Sand Hill Preservation Center
This organization is a pioneer in preserving heirloom breeds of vegetables and poultry.
1878 230th St.
Calamus, IA 52729
(563) 246-2299
www.sandhillpreservation.com
sandhill@fbcom.net

Seeds of Diversity Canada
This Canada-based non-profit organization promotes biodiversity and traditional knowledge of food crops and garden plants.
PO Box 36
Stn Q
Toronto ON M4T 2L7
CANADA
(866)-509-7333
www.seeds.ca
mail@seeds.ca

Seed Savers Exchange
Since 1975, this not-for-profit organization has been dedicated to the preservation of heirloom seeds.
3094 North Winn Road
Decorah, IA 52101
(563) 382-5990
http://www.seedsavers.org
customerservice@seedsavers.org

Southern Exposure Seed Exchange
Established in 1982, offering heirloom and organic seeds, garlic and perennial onions, garden supplies, and seed-saving equipment
PO Box 460
Mineral, VA 23117
(540) 894-9480
gardens@southernexposure.com
http://www.southernexposure.com

Victory Seed Company
Quality heirloom seeds and superb documentation on the history of various heirloom varieties
PO Box 192
Molalla, OR 97038
(503) 829-3126
info@victoryseed.com
http://www.victoryseeds.com

Index